ESSAYS ON DAVIDSON

Essays on Davidson

ACTIONS AND EVENTS

EDITED BY

BRUCE VERMAZEN

AND

MERRILL B. HINTIKKA

CLARENDON PRESS · OXFORD

Oxford University Press, Walton Street, Oxford OX2 6DP

Oxford New York Toronto
Delhi Bombay Calcutta Madras Karachi
Petaling Jaya Singapore Hong Kong Tokyo
Nairobi Dar es Salaam Cape Town
Melbourne Auckland

and associated companies in
Beirut Berlin Ibadan Nicosia

Oxford is a trade mark of Oxford University Press

Published in the United States
by Oxford University Press, New York

First published 1985
Reprinted (new as paperback) 1986

British Library Cataloguing in Publication Data

Essays on Davidson: actions and events.
1. Davidson, Donald, 1917–
I. Vermazen, Bruce II. Hintikka, Merrill B.
128'.4'0924 B945.D3
ISBN 0–19–824749–4
ISBN 0–19–824963–2 (Pbk.)

Library of Congress Cataloging in Publication Data
Main entry under title:
Essays on Davidson.
Includes index.
1. Davidson, Donald, 1917–. Essays on actions
and events—Addresses, essays, lectures.
2. Act (Philosophy)—Addresses, essays, lectures.
3. Events (Philosophy)—Addresses, essays, lectures.
I. Vermazen, Bruce. II. Hintikka, Merrill B., 1939–
B105.A35D3734 1985 128'4 84–18923
ISBN 0–19–824749–4
ISBN 0–19–824963–2 (Pbk.)

Set by DMB (Typesetting), Oxford
Printed in Great Britain
at the University Printing House, Oxford
by David Stanford
Printer to the University

ACKNOWLEDGEMENTS

The editors wish to thank Donald Davidson for his help and encouragement in bringing this book into being. For their editorial efforts, we wish to thank the staff of the Oxford University Press. Savannah Ross, Julie Martinson, and Yulia Motofuji have our gratitude for photocopying manuscripts, and Professor Vermazen is grateful to the University of California, Berkeley, for granting him a sabbatical leave to complete the project and to the Humanities Research Fellowship Committee of the university for partial support during the leave.

Permission to quote from H. E. Kiefer and M. K. Munitz (eds.), *Language, Belief, and Metaphysics* (Albany, NY, 1970), was granted by the State University of New York Press. Permission to quote from Julius Kovesi, *Moral Notions* (London, 1967), was granted by Routledge and Kegan Paul and Humanities Press, Inc.

CONTENTS

Donald Davidson Responds

NOTES ON THE CONTRIBUTORS

Judith Baker is a former member of the Philosophy Department at the University of Washington and currently Visiting Assistant Professor of Philosophy at Glendon College, York University.

Michael Bratman is Associate Professor of Philosophy at Stanford University.

Dan Bennett is a former member of the Philosophy Departments at Stanford University, Brown University, Brandeis University, Swarthmore College, and the University of Nebraska.

Roderick M. Chisholm is Andrew W. Mellon Professor of the Humanities at Brown University.

Paul Grice is Professor Emeritus of Philosophy at the University of California, Berkeley.

Donald Davidson is Professor of Philosophy at the University of California, Berkeley.

Harry A. Lewis is Lecturer in Philosophy at the University of Leeds.

Christopher Peacocke is Fellow and Tutor in Philosophy at New College, Oxford, and CUF Lecturer at the University of Oxford.

D. F. Pears is Reader in Philosophy at Christ Church, Oxford.

J. J. C. Smart is Professor of Philosophy at the Research School of Social Sciences at The Australian National University.

P. F. Strawson is Waynflete Professor of Metaphysical Philosophy at the University of Oxford.

Patrick Suppes is the Lucie Stern Professor of Philosophy at Stanford University.

Irving Thalberg is Professor of Philosophy at the University of Illinois, Chicago.

Bruce Vermazen is Associate Professor of Philosophy at the University of California, Berkeley.

INTRODUCTION

BRUCE VERMAZEN

The topics addressed and texts discussed in this collection are for the most part the topics and texts of Donald Davidson's *Essays on Actions and Events* (hereafter referred to as *EAE*),[1] and the three main sections of this book correspond to those of the *Essays*. Davidson's views on intention and action, event and cause, and the philosophy of psychology are of course tightly connected with each other and with his views on language, truth, and interpretation. This is reflected in his essays, which thus approach the condition of material objects in the Anaxagorean scheme: each one contains bits of all the others. The present essays, however, generally concentrate on one or a group of Davidson's views in isolation from the rest, so that assignment to a section indicates more about the essay's content than it does in the case of Davidson's own work.[2]

Eight of the twelve essays directly discuss and criticize Davidson's published views on various topics in metaphysics, the philosophy of action, and the philosophy of psychology. The papers by P. F. Strawson, Roderick Chisholm, and Dan Bennett are instead independent discussions of topics Davidson has written about, with only brief reference to Davidson's views, and my own contribution is an attempt to extend Davidson's analysis of action to the case of intentional not doing.

The contributors are friends of Davidson's who have variously been his students, colleagues, collaborators, and adversaries in print. Roderick Chisholm and Davidson were graduate students together in the Harvard Philosophy Department, and in 1967-71 opposed each other in a series of papers on the relative merits of

---

[1] Oxford, 1980. All the essays by Davidson referred to in this introduction, unless otherwise footnoted, are from this collection.

[2] The present essays were written for a 1979 deadline, except for those of Vermazen (1980) and Bratman (1982), so they agree also with *EAE* in not reflecting what Davidson has written on these topics since 1979.

events and states of affairs as basic ontological items.[3] Patrick
Suppes arrived at Stanford only a few months before Davidson,
and early in their seventeen years as colleagues (1950-67) they col-
laborated on two articles and a book.[4] During the Stanford years,
Davidson was in charge of inviting speakers to the Department,
and it was in that capacity that he first met Paul Grice, David
Pears, J. J. C. Smart, and P. F. Strawson. Grice and Davidson
have written (and differed) much on the same topics, particularly in
the philosophy of mind and theory of action. Davidson discusses
Grice's views on the relation between intending to do something
and believing that one will do it in 'Intending' (pp. 83-102), and
Grice responded to an early version of that paper at the Chapel Hill
Colloquium in Philosophy in October 1974. Pears and Davidson
have worked on the topic of rationality in recent years, exchanging
views in a variety of forums, and Pears has commented extensively
on Davidson's theory of *akrasia* in 'How Easy Is *Akrasia*?'.[5] Smart
often comments on Davidson's ideas in his published work,[6] and
Davidson credits Smart's writings on mind and body with stimulating his own thought on the subject.[7] Strawson has criticized
Davidson's views on logical form in 'On Understanding the Structure of One's Language'.[8] Davidson discusses some passages from
Individuals (London, 1959) in 'The Individuation of Events' (pp.
163-180), and in 'Mental Events' (pp. 207-225) notes a similarity
between anomalous monism and Strawson's position on mind and
body in a paper in *Freedom and the Will*.[9]

  Dan Bennett, Irving Thalberg, Harry Lewis, and I were all dis-

---

[3] The relevant Davidson essays are 'The Logical Form of Action Sentences' (*EAE*,
pp. 105-22), 'Facts and Events', also known as 'On Events and Event-Descriptions'
(in J. Margolis (ed.), *Fact and Existence* (Oxford, 1969), pp. 74-84); 'Events as
Particulars' (*EAE*, pp. 181-88), and 'Eternal vs. Ephemeral Events' (*EAE*,
pp. 189-204). The Chisholm essays are 'Events and Propositions', *Noûs* 4 (1970),
15-24; and 'States of Affairs Again', *Noûs* 5 (1971), 179-90.

[4] 'Outlines of a Formal Theory of Value' (with J. C. C. McKinsey), *Philosophy of
Science*, 22 (1955), 140-60; 'A Finitistic Axiomatization of Subjective Probability
and Utility', *Econometrica* 24 (1956), 264-75; and *Decision-Making: An Experimental Approach* (Stanford, 1957).

[5] *Philosophia* (Israel) 11 (1982), 33-50.

[6] See e.g. 'Prior and the Basis of Ethics', *Synthèse* 53 (1982), 3-17, and 'Sellars on
Process', *Monist* 65 (1982), 302-14.

[7] *EAE*, p. xvi.

[8] *Freedom and Resentment and Other Essays* (London, 1974); reprinted in Gareth
Evans and John McDowell (eds.), *Truth and Meaning: Essays in Semantics*
(Oxford, 1976).

[9] Ed. D. F. Pears (London, 1963).

sertation students of Davidson's at Stanford, and have continued to work on lines related to his. Bennett wrote his dissertation while at Oxford, where he attended lectures on action theory by G. E. M. Anscombe and Stuart Hampshire, and his conversations with Davidson upon his return to Stanford were a major force in getting Davidson seriously interested in the topic. For a year Bennett taught at Stanford, collaborating with Davidson on a seminar in action theory. Thalberg's book, *Perception, Emotion and Action* (Yale, 1977), contains extensive discussions of Davidson's writings on action and reasons. Lewis has published a very sensitive and informed review of *Truth and Meaning*,[10] placing the essays in the context of Davidson's work. I have written a number of pieces discussing Davidson's work, most recently 'General Beliefs and the Principle of Charity' and 'The Intelligibility of Massive Error'.[11]

Christopher Peacocke was a second-year undergraduate at Oxford when he attended Davidson's John Locke Lectures (1970). Much of his work has been on topics central to Davidson's work, most notably 'Truth Definitions and Actual Languages' in *Truth and Meaning* and his book *Holistic Explanation* (Oxford, 1979). Michael Bratman studied with Davidson at The Rockefeller University from 1971 to 1974, accompanying him to Oxford in 1973-4, where Davidson was a Guggenheim Fellow and Bratman wrote his dissertation. His paper 'Practical Reasoning and Weakness of the Will'[12] is concerned with Davidson's understanding of weakness of the will.

INTENTION AND ACTION: BRATMAN, GRICE AND BAKER, PEACOCKE, PEARS, BENNETT, VERMAZEN

All six papers in this section raise objections to various of Davidson's published views on action, but some are less purely critical than others. I have arranged them so that the papers that are more centrally concerned with raising objections come first, and those that offer the author's own view on a subject discussed by Davidson come later.

Bratman summarizes the main body of Davidson's thinking on the subjects of doing something intentionally, future intention, and their relationship, and expounds two problems in the account,

[10] *Philosophy* 53 (1978), 404-7.
[11] In *Philosophical Studies* 42 (1982), 111-18, and *Philosophical Quarterly* 33 (1983), 69-74.
[12] *Noûs* 13 (1979), 153-71.

diagnosing both 'as rooted in an overly limited conception of the role of intentions and plans in practical reasoning'. His texts are 'Actions, Reasons, and Causes', 'How is Weakness of the Will Possible?', 'Agency', and 'Intending' (pp. 3-20, 21-42, 43-62, and 83-102). Both objections hinge on the idea that future intentions must be 'agglomerative', that is, that someone who intends to do *A* and intends to do *B* also intends to do *A* and *B*. The second of the objections hinges also on the nature of the belief one must have about one's future act if one is to intend to do it. Bratman explores three candidates for the belief, but does not settle on any one of them. Peacocke's paper briefly discusses the topic of the required belief, and it is the central topic of Pears's paper.

Grice and Baker examine Davidson's account of weakness of the will in 'How is Weakness of the Will Possible?' That account proposes that we think of some of an agent's judgements about his actions as prima-facie comparative judgements about pairs of alternative acts, and of his final judgement on his action—his intention in acting—as an unconditional comparative judgement. Grice and Baker suggest that Davidson needs to make three substantial alterations in the account in order to capture the elements of *akrasia*: the conditional judgements that constitute deliberation must not be all comparative, for there must be conditional judgements that some course of action is best; the relation between courses of action expressed by 'prima facie' should be interpreted as something other than a sentential connective; and the role played in the theory by the judgement that some act is best, all things considered, might better be played by the judgement that the act is best unconditionally, but by such a judgement that is 'not fully present' to the agent. The essay is largely critical, but at the end some suggestions are made as to how one might pursue a theory of weakness of the will not subject to their objections.

Peacocke presents the core of a theory of *akrasia*, starting from Davidson's work on the subject. His main concern is to develop a theory of intentions that will allow him to say how it can be that a person can do something intentionally despite the fact that he has a set of reasons, wider than the one on which he acts, in the light of which he finds his act irrational. Like Grice and Baker, Peacocke rejects the idea that the judgements involved in practical deliberation are prima-facie judgements of the comparative goodness of prospective acts. Like Bratman and Pears, he examines candidates for the belief that intention requires one to have about one's future act, at one point directly discussing the candidate favoured by Pears and producing objections to it. Peacocke claims that the view of intention finally developed—that it is a disposition, with a specific kind of causal history, to try to do a certain act given the ability to try and the belief that the time to do it has arrived—'allows an agent to be irrational simply in what he does without being irrational in thought'.

Pears primarily discusses a passage in 'Intending' in which Davidson claims that it is an implicature, in Grice's sense, that holds between one's statement that one intends to perform an act of a certain kind and the statement that one believes that one will perform such an act. Pears argues that the implicature view is not a 'rival' of the traditional view that the first statement *implies* the second; rather, the implicature is founded on the implication. The problem with the implication is to settle on a belief about one's future act that is of the right strength, since it is clear that one does not always believe with full confidence that one will succeed in one's intentions, and sometimes it appears that one has hardly any confidence at all. Pears's candidate for the implied belief is 'that my intention confers some probability on my performance'. As noted earlier, Peacocke disputes this conclusion in his paper.

Bennett briefly explores David Hume's account of pride, which Davidson also explored in 'Hume's Cognitive Theory of Pride', and suggests several difficulties in it: whether the object of pride is oneself or an idea of oneself, whether, since self is an illusion, pride is also, and whether Hume has not got the causal relation between one's pride and one's pleasing qualities backward. Davidson does not address the first two difficulties, partly because he limits his examination to the case of 'propositional pride', being proud that something is the case; but on the third question, he sides with Hume. Bennett finds a parallel to the third difficulty in Davidson's view, in 'Actions, Reasons, and Causes', of the relation an act bears to the beliefs and desires that rationalize it. It is not, says Bennett, that the beliefs and desires cause the act, but that 'the therefores, musts, and becauses of practical reasoning are actually predicates of the action, to which there is nothing causally prior'. The view is developed in greater detail in Bennett's 'Actions, Reason, and Purpose.'[13]

[13] *Journal of Philosophy* 62 (1965), 85-96.

My own paper contains very little criticism of Davidson's views. I attempt to start from the account of action in 'Actions, Reasons, and Causes', 'Agency', 'Freedom to Act' (pp. 63-82), and 'Intending' (but without the notion of intention developed in the last of these, which I find obscure) in order to suggest a way to analyse what have been called 'negative acts', cases in which an agent intentionally does not do something. I distinguish four kinds of negative act—resisting, simple refraining, displacement refraining, and disobedient refraining—and present a view on which they may be understood in terms of Davidson's explanatory concepts. The view requires giving up (for some cases) the requirement that an act be an event, if we want negative acts to be acts; the claim is a consequence not of a metaphysical thesis in conflict with Davidson's, but of a search for the proper metaphysical location of negative acts. The trick is turned, if it is, by an explication of what it is for an event to cause another not to occur. The non-occurring event is of course not one of Davidson's dated particulars, but an event-type.

EVENT AND CAUSE: CHISHOLM, STRAWSON, THALBERG

The three papers on events and causation bear different relation to Davidson's work. Thalberg's paper is a defence of Davidson's position that events form a basic ontological category. He summarizes and tries to meet the objections of Bruce Aune, Russell Trenholme, Terence Horgan, Roderick Chisholm, N. L. Wilson, and Jaegwon Kim. Most of the argumentation is in Davidson's spirit, except for one strategy used several times, which consists in disarming criticism based on difficulties with what Davidson says is the logical form of a certain description of a situation by finding an alternative description of the situation, to which the criticisms do not apply.

Chisholm's paper is a follow-up to the 1967-71 controversy mentioned earlier, concerning the ontological status of events and states of affairs. Davidson had challenged Chisholm to develop a full theory of states of affairs that could do for semantics what Davidson thinks an ontology of events can. Chisholm takes a first step toward meeting the challenge by attempting to state the nature of states of affairs. He uses five primitive notions—accepting, obtaining, conceiving, exemplifying, and *de re* possibility—to define an array of further pertinent notions, including that of state of affairs itself and the problematic notions of conjunctions, disjunctions, and negations of states of affairs. Then he answers objections and allays suspicions that may occur to the careful reader. There is no explicit attempt to take the next step and show that these notions are semantically useful in the ways required by the issues left open in the earlier controversy. But there is a distinct echo of that controversy when he says that Davidson 'might do well to consider it [the present account] when he completes his theory of recurrence and possibility'. For Chisholm earlier claimed[14] that Davidson's view could not, as Chisholm's could, provide a semantic basis for theoretically innocent talk about merely possible events and about events happening more than once, since, for Davidson, events are dated particulars.

Strawson's paper resembles Chisholm's in forgoing discussion of Davidson's view to present instead a position of his own that contradicts Davidson, though the position presented is much richer than it needs to be for that purpose. The pertinent text of Davidson's in 'Causal Relations' (pp. 149-62). There Davidson presents an account of the logical form of singular causal sentences that makes clear semantic sense of central cases of some sentences containing 'cause', but not of some others, for example 'The slowness with which the controls were applied caused the rapidity with which the inflation developed' (p. 161). This leads him to the claim that sentences of the latter sort are not singular causal sentences, but instead are sentences that present 'rudimentary causal explanations' (p. 161). Earlier in the article, Davidson had made use of the Hempelian view that (one form of) causal explanation takes the form of deduction of a singular causal statement from a causal law and a statement of the circumstances, and suggested that all singular causal statements involve the backing of causal laws in the following way: 'if "*a* caused *b*" is true, then there are descriptions of *a* and *b* such that the result of substituting them for "*a*" and "*b*" in "*a* caused *b*" is entailed by true premises', one of which is a causal law of a particular form and the other a sentence asserting the occurrence of a unique event of a type to which *a* belongs which is a sufficient condition of the occurrence of an event of a type to which *b* belongs (pp. 159-60). This in turn carries the Hempelian suggestion, not made explicit by Davidson, that all causal explanation somehow depends on this sort of 'backing' by laws.

[14] In 'States of Affairs Again', *Noûs* 5 (1971), 180.

Against these views, Strawson advances a different picture of the relation between causation and explanation. He suggests 'that at the level of ordinary causal explanation of particular events and circumstances, the level at which we employ the common vocabulary of description rather than the technical vocabularies of physical theories, there is no reason to think that our explanations presuppose or rest upon belief in the existence of general, exceptionless and discoverable laws frameable in terms of that common vocabulary; and that, further, there is no reason to think that our explanations are, for this reason, in any way deficient'. The qualification 'frameable in terms of that common vocabulary' lets him out of any direct contradiction of Davidson's view, but a hint lingers that he thinks that common-vocabulary explanations also do not need the backing of general laws framed in some other vocabulary, and that of course does contradict Davidson.

PHILOSOPHY OF PSYCHOLOGY: LEWIS, SMART, SUPPES

None of the three papers in this section is in complete sympathy with Davidson, but the degree of dissent increases from Smart to Lewis to Suppes. Smart thinks that Davidson argues 'ingeniously' for a material mind in 'Mental Events', 'The Material Mind' (pp. 245-60), and 'Psychology as Philosophy' (pp. 229-39), and finds the argument 'congenial', though not such as to convince someone who is not already a materialist; he further stresses the independent importance of one premiss of the argument, the claim that there are no psychophysical laws and no laws connecting mental events as mentally described. He objects to Davidson's criterion of the mental and to some other details of the argument, but is concerned for the most part to explicate rather than to object.

Lewis also concentrates on Davidson's denial of psychophysical law, but his reservations about it result from his doubts about Davidson's prior claim that mental properties supervene on physical properties, and most of his paper is concerned to examine this latter claim. His main text is 'Mental Events'. He stresses the differences between the supervenience alleged by Davidson and the more familiar (though no less difficult) cases of the supervenience of moral properties on 'natural' properties of persons or acts and that of aesthetic properties on the observable and measurable properties of aesthetic objects. Much of his discussion supports Davidson, for example in his claim that supervenience does not imply that there are laws linking instances of supervening properties with the properties upon which they supervene, but in the end he urges us to remain sceptical about the supervenience claim itself.

Although Suppes says he agrees 'with much of what Davidson says' about psychology, he finds Davidson's arguments wanting in fairly drastic ways. He argues for five theses that 'more or less contradict views that Davidson has advanced' in 'The Material Mind', 'Thought and Talk',[15] and 'Psychology as Philosophy'. Suppes proposes that the differences between psychology and physics, and between higher animals and human infants, are not as great as required by Davidson's arguments, and that decision theory can be tested without interpretation of the experimental subject's language. Thus Davidson's standards for 'fundamental scientific theory' are too high, and some of his key premises are false. But Suppes' main concern is to urge Davidson to provide more detail in his arguments, since the issues with which they deal are so centrally important to any psychology that is to have 'a proper scientific foundation'.

One sort of understanding of a thesis, and perhaps the only sort, consists in becoming conscious of its relationships to other theses, placing it in various possible networks of thought. What does the thesis entail, what would entail it, and what would give it a weaker kind of support? What contradicts it altogether or casts a less dark shadow on it? This collection offers anyone interested in Davidson's thought a splendid opportunity for such understanding, for placing his thought among the objections urged against it, the refinements and alternatives advanced, the defences mounted, and the extensions proposed. Perhaps most directly productive of understanding are Davidson's comments on the essays, printed at the end, for there the objections, refinements, alternatives, and so on are placed in a network; a pattern is produced from which the reader may begin in seeking his own patterns. It is a bonus that the pattern is itself a newly clarified part of the desired object of understanding.

[15] D. Davidson, *Inquiries into Truth and Interpretation* (Oxford, 1984), 155-70.

INTENTION AND ACTION

I

DAVIDSON'S THEORY OF INTENTION

MICHAEL BRATMAN

In an important and fascinating series of papers, spanning a decade and a half, Donald Davidson has sketched a general theory of intention, a theory that tries to explain what it is to do something intentionally, what it is to intend to do something later, and how these two phenomena are related.[1] In this paper I say what this theory is, argue that it faces a pair of serious difficulties, and diagnose these difficulties as rooted in an overly limited conception of the role of intentions and plans in practical reasoning.

I. DAVIDSON'S THEORY: MAIN IDEAS

Davidson begins with intentional action. In his classic paper 'Actions, Reasons and Causes',[2] he sketches the following general view. Intentional action is action that is explainable, in the appropriate way, by appeal to the agent's reasons for action. The reasons that explain intentional actions are appropriate pairs of the agent's desires (and other 'pro-attitudes') and beliefs. When one acts *for* a certain reason an appropriate desire-belief pair *causes* one's action. Suppose, for example, that I intentionally go to Davies Hall because I want to hear Pavarotti sing and believe going to Davies Hall would be a way of doing this. Since I act *for* this reason, the pro-attitude and belief *cause* my action.

This conception of intentional action makes no essential appeal to any distinct state or event of *intending* to go to Davies Hall that intervenes between my desire-belief pair and my action. The intentionality of my action lies, rather, in its relation to my desire-belief pair.

---

[1] These papers are all reprinted in *EAE*. The crucial papers for my purposes here are 'Actions, Reasons and Causes', 'How is Weakness of the Will Possible?', and 'Intending'.

[2] In *EAE*, pp. 3-19.

This is a compromise position. On the one hand it insists that in explaining actions in terms of their reasons we are citing *causes* of those actions. So it rejects radical suggestions to the contrary— typically rooted in strong behaviouristic assumptions—offered by Anscombe, Melden, and others.[3] On the other hand, in seeing the intentionality of action as solely a matter of its relation to the agent's desires and beliefs, Davidson rejects the *volitional* concep-tion that frequently accompanies causal theories. On a volitional conception of, for example, an intentional arm-raising, a volition in favour of so acting is, as Davidson says, 'an event that is com-mon and peculiar to all cases where a man intentionally raises his arm' ('Actions, Reasons and Causes', p. 13). Further, on such a conception this volitional event plays a crucial causal role in the arm-raising. While embracing a causal theory of the relation between reason and action, Davidson explicitly denies that there is any such volitional event involved in the causation of intentional arm-raisings.

Now, even granting that when I act for a reason my reason is a cause of my action, there will also be some sort of *logical* relation between my reason and my action. In 'How is Weakness of the Will Possible?'[4] Davidson tries to characterize this logical relation in terms of a general conception of practical reasoning.[5] The guiding idea is that the reason for which I act provides me with premisses from which I could have reasoned to a conclusion which corresponds to my action.

Consider again my intentionally going to Davies Hall because I want to listen to Pavarotti. This pro-attitude provides one premiss for my potential reasoning, and my belief that going to Davies Hall is a way of doing this provides another. The premiss provided by my belief is just *what* I believe: the proposition that going to Davies Hall is a way of listening to Pavarotti. The premiss provided by my pro-attitude is not, however, so easily arrived at. What I want is *to listen to Pavarotti* or, perhaps, *that I listen to Pavarotti*. But, on Davidson's view, the relevant premiss is neither of these, but rather the prima-facie *evaluative proposition* that any act of mine would be desirable in so far as it is an act of listening to Pavarotti. David-son supposes that such an evaluative proposition is the 'natural

---

[3] For references, see Davidson's initial footnote in 'Actions, Reasons and Causes'.

[4] In *EAE*, pp. 21-42.

[5] The main ideas of this conception are also usefully discussed in 'Intending'. In what follows I draw on that discussion as well.

expression' of my pro-attitude.[6] Finally, my intentional action corresponds, on the theory, to an 'unconditional' (or, as he later says
in 'Intending', 'all-out')—rather than a merely prima-facie— evaluative proposition that my action is desirable. This unconditional
evaluative proposition can, on the theory, be represented as a non-
deductive conclusion of an argument whose premises are provided
by my pro-attitude and belief. In intentionally going to Davies Hall
I accept this all-out evaluative conclusion.

This signals a modest retreat from the rejection of a volitional
conception. On this later version of Davidson's theory, there *is* an
element 'common and peculiar to all cases' of intentional concert-
going, namely the acceptance of an all-out evaluation that the
concert-going being performed is desirable.[7] But this retreat is not
a capitulation, for Davidson supposes that when I intentionally go
to the concert my acceptance of this all-out evaluative proposition
in favour of my action need not be distinct from my very act of going. This is why he says that on his theory 'Aristotle's remark that
the conclusion (of a piece of practical reasoning) is an action
remains cogent'.[8] And, of course, if my acceptance of this all-out
conclusion is not distinct from my action, it cannot be a cause of
my action.[9]

---

[6] Davidson's explanation of this prima-facie evaluative proposition leans on
a supposed parallel with inductive-statistical explanations, as they are understood
by Hempel in *Aspects of Scientific Explanation* (New York, 1965), pp. 376-403.
While I am convinced by Davidson that there is some important parallel here, I am
unsure about the details of his treatment of this parallel. As Hempel emphasizes,
inductive-statistical explanations involve two distinct concepts of probability:
statistical probability, and inductive probability. The former is used in the major
premiss of such explanations, the latter characterizes the *relation* between premisses
and conclusion of the explanation. Davidson's main idea is to treat 'prima facie' as
relating premisses and conclusion of practical syllogisms. In this respect, 'prima
facie' is seen as analogous to inductive probability. But Davidson also understands
the major premisses of such practical syllogisms as using the concept of prima facie.
Given the analogy with probability, this suggests that there is a notion of prima facie
analogous to that of statistical probability. But the problem is that we seem to have
only a *single* notion of prima facie, in contrast with the probabilistic case. This
disanalogy between the two cases does not emerge clearly in Davidson's discussion,
because the distinction between two concepts of probability is lost in his formalism.
(See 'How is Weakness of the Will Possible?', p. 38.)

[7] 'Evaluation' is ambiguous between the evaluative proposition accepted, and the
acceptance of that proposition. So I will only use this term when the context clearly
disambiguates.

[8] 'How is Weakness of the Will Possible?', p. 39.

[9] Given Davidson's metaphysics of action as presented in 'Agency' (*EAE*,
pp. 43-61), however, my acceptance of this conclusion *could* cause the upshot in
terms of which the action is described. Thus, my acceptance of an all-out conclusion

My all-out evaluative conclusion has two further features it is important to note. First, it is at least implicitly comparative. It assesses my action favourably in comparison with the other options I actually considered (which in some cases may only include the option of refraining from so acting).[10]

Second, my all-out evaluation is about the *particular* act of concert-going I am now performing. In this respect it differs from my initial pro-attitude, which was in favour of actions in so far as they were of a certain *type* (for example, concert-going). Davidson's view seems to be that desirability is, strictly speaking, always a property of particular actions, rather than of types of actions.[11] Different instances of a given type of action may well vary in their desirability. Some ways of going to the concert (for example, by hijacking a cab) will be quite undesirable. Only when we are given a particular action are we given something which is either desirable or not (relative to the agent's values).

We have so far seen the main outlines of Davidson's theory of intentional action. A theory of intentional action cannot, however,

---

in favour of raising my arm may cause my arm's rising. This suggests that Davidson's theory *is* compatible with a volitional theory in the spirit of Prichard's 'Acting, Willing, and Desiring' (In A. R. White (ed.), *The Philosophy of Action* (Oxford, 1968)).

[10] As I urged in 'Practical Reasoning and Weakness of the Will', *Noûs* 13 (1979), 153-70, I think that at this point the theory encounters serious difficulties with weak-willed intentional conduct. But here I am interested in other matters.

The implicitly comparative nature of these all-out evaluations is clearer in Davidson's earlier discussion in 'How is Weakness of the Will Possible?' than in his later discussion in 'Intending', where he typically uses the apparently non-comparative predicate 'is desirable'. Suffice it to say here, in defence of my interpretation of these all-out evaluations as implicitly comparative, that if they really were non-comparative the problem of agglomerativity, discussed below, would arise even more immediately. It would be immediately clear that one could have future-directed all-out evaluations both in favour of going to the concert and in favour of not going.

[11] Davidson's main discussion of this feature of all-out evaluations is in 'Intending', pp. 96-7. In this discussion he seems to me not to separate two different issues. First, there is the issue of when there can be *demonstrative reference* to a particular action. Here Davidson supposes that there can be no demonstrative reference to an event in the future. Second, there is the issue of what the property of desirability is a property *of*. Here Davidson's view is, I take it, that it is always a property of *particular* acts. As I see it, it is this second view that is critical to his discussion of future intention.

What about an all-out *comparison* that my action is better than certain alternatives? what does such a comparison compare my particular act *to*? The answer, I take it, is that it compares my particular act to other particular acts *of different types*, where the relevant types are determined by the alternatives I have considered.

stand alone. It needs to be related to a plausible conception of future intention—intending (or, having an intention) now to do something later. After all, both phenomena in some sense involve *intent*; our theory needs to say in what sense.

I may now have various reasons—appropriate desire-belief pairs —in favour of going to the concert tomorrow. But such desires and beliefs do not suffice for an intention to go. What is the nature of the new state I am in when I come to intend to go?

Davidson's strategy here is to *extend* his account of the role of all-out evaluations in intentional action to the future-directed case. In just having reasons for acting in a certain way I only accept certain prima-facie evaluative propositions. When I actually act for those reasons—and so act intentionally—I accept an appropriate all-out 'evaluative proposition. Similarly, on Davidson's theory, when I come to intend to go to the concert tomorrow I come to accept a future-directed all-out evaluative proposition in favour of going to the concert then: my future intention is this all-out evaluation. By extending his theory of intentional action in this way Davidson can ensure that future intention, like intentional action, can be a conclusion of practical reasoning. And he can exhibit a common feature in the two cases of intent.

However, Davidson sees a problem with this strategy. As we have seen, in the case of intentional action the involved judgement of all-out desirability is about a particular action; desirability is a property of particular acts, not of types of acts. But when I intend to go to the concert tomorrow I have in mind no single, particular act of concert-going. And there may well never be in the world an actual, particular concert-going to judge desirable. So, how could my intention be an all-out evaluation?

Granted, I could judge that *any* particular act of concert-going would be desirable; for such a judgement would still only ascribe desirability to particular acts.[12] But this would normally be an insane judgement. Some concert-goings—for example, those that involve hijacking a cab—will surely be undesirable. Future intention should not require insanity.

Davidson's solution to this problem is couched in terms of a different example—that of intending to eat a sweet in a moment. Here is what he says:

[12] As John Perry has emphasized to me in conversation.

It would be mad to hold that any action of mine in the immediate future that is the eating of something sweet would be desirable. But there is nothing absurd in my judging that any action of mine in the immediate future that is the eating of something sweet would be desirable *given the rest of what I believe about the immediate future*. I do not believe I will eat a poisonous candy, and so that is not one of the actions of eating something sweet that my all-out judgement includes. ('Intending', p. 99, emphasis in the original).

Returning to our example, when I intend to go to the concert I judge that any act of mine that is both a concert-going and *whose other features are all consistent with my beliefs* would be desirable. I believe that I would not go to the concert by hijacking a cab. So the undesirability of going that way does not stop me from holding that any concert-going of mine that *is* consistent with my beliefs would be desirable. And that is just what I hold when I intend to go.

II. DAVIDSON'S THEORY: BELIEF CONDITIONS ON INTENTION

We have now seen the main features of Davidson's theory of intentional action and future intention. On the latter theory, my beliefs provide a critical background for the all-out evaluations which are my future intentions. As Davidson puts it, my future intentions are 'conditioned by my beliefs' ('Intending, p. 100). But having said this it remains unclear just what these beliefs must be. So let us ask just what I must believe for me to intend to go to the concert tonight.

Consider three candidates for necessary conditions for such a future intention:

(1) My going to the concert is consistent with my beliefs.
(2) I believe I will be able to go.
(3) I believe I will go.

Davidson sees his theory as imposing (1) as a requirement on my intention. He says that 'wishes for things that are not consistent with what one believes' cannot be intentions, for that is 'ruled out by our conception of an intention' ('Intending', p. 101). His reasoning seems to be that if, in our example, my going to the concert is inconsistent with my beliefs, then there 'can be no judgement that such an action consistent with [my] beliefs is desirable. There can be no such intention' ('Intending', p. 101).[13]

What about (2)? Note that (2) is not entailed by (1). It *is* necessary for (1) that I do not believe I will not be able to go. But my going may be consistent with my beliefs even though I do not actually believe I will be able to go. So we need to ask whether, on the theory, (2) is also required for intention.

I find Davidson's remarks on this issue unclear. At times he seems to think that (2) is indeed required.[14] But this cannot be his considered view. Let me note three reasons why.

The first concerns Davidson's discussion of (3). Grice[15] and Harman[16] have both argued that (3) is necessary for my intention. In Grice's example I think I may well be in jail by tonight, and for that reason do not believe I will go to the concert. Grice claims that I then do not intend to go, but only, perhaps, hope to go or intend to go if I can.

Davidson disagrees. He claims that in such a case I still may intend to go, though it might be misleading for me simply to report this intention without mentioning my worries about jail. Now in such a case I surely will not satisfy (2). The whole point of the example is that I believe I may well be in jail, and for that reason do not actually believe I will be able to go to the concert. At most, I will not believe I will not be able to go, and so be in a position to satisfy (1). Since Davidson insists that in such a case I may still intend to go, he must not see (2) as necessary for my intention.

Second, in his discussion of Grice's paper Davidson seems to commit himself to the view that future intention cannot be subject to a stronger belief requirement than is intentional action.[17] So, for

[13] I am puzzled by this, for it seems that in such a case there *can* be a judgement that any concert-going act consistent with my beliefs would be desirable. Indeed, if this is ordinary universal quantification, it seems that the theory is in danger of saying that, once I believe I will not go, I get an intention to go by default. This suggests that Davidson is *adding* to his account of my future-directed all-out evaluation in favour of *A*-ing, the further condition that my *A*-ing be consistent with my beliefs. In any case, in what follows I will assume Davidson's interpretation of my future-directed all-out evaluation in favour of *A*-ing as requiring that my *A*-ing be consistent with my beliefs.

[14] For example, at one point he describes a future intention as a judgement in favour of 'something I think I can do' ('Intending', p. 101).

[15] In 'Intention and Uncertainty', *Proceedings of the British Academy* 57 (1971), 263-79.

[16] In 'Practical Reasoning', *Review of Metaphysics* 29 (1976), 431-63.

[17] See his remarks at 'Intending', p. 92. Let me note that in my view this assumption is not obvious. It seems to me likely that I need a stronger belief about my

Davidson to accept (2) as a condition on my future intention he would also have to suppose that to *A* intentionally I must believe, while I am *A*-ing, that I can *A*. But Davidson himself has an example that shows that this latter view is not plausible. I might try to make ten carbon copies of a paper on my typewriter while doubting that I can. Nevertheless, if I actually do make ten copies, if my success is due to my relevant skills, and if making ten copies is also my goal in acting[18] then I *intentionally* make ten copies. This shows that intentional action does not require a belief that one can so act. So, given his assumption about the relation between belief requirements on intentional action and future intention, Davidson cannot accept (2) as a condition on my future intention.

There is, finally, a third reason why Davidson must reject (2) as necessary for my intention. To explain this I need to touch on Davidson's approach to the distinction between simple and conditional intentions.

III. DAVIDSON'S THEORY: SIMPLE AND CONDITIONAL INTENTION

Suppose my going to the concert is consistent with my beliefs, but I do not actually believe I will be able to go. Perhaps I just do not know whether there will be any tickets left. I ask myself: would any concert-going act, consistent with my beliefs, be desirable?

There is an initial problem in answering this question. Let us call a condition whose presence I believe to be required for my being able to *A* an *enabling condition for* A-*ing*. In our example, the availability of tickets is an enabling condition of my going to the concert. This condition is consistent with my beliefs, but not guaranteed by them. So among those future situations which are consistent with my beliefs there will be some in which this enabling condition will hold, and some in which it will not. When I try to answer my question, do I consider all of these future situations, or only those in which the appropriate enabling conditions obtain?

I think Davidson must suppose that I need consider only those future situations in which I *can* go to the concert. After all, there

ability to *A* to intend now to *A* later, than I do just to give *A* a try when the time comes.

[18] These last two qualifications are mine, not Davidson's, but I think they are needed to make the example convincing. I was convinced of the need for the second qualification by Harman's discussion in 'Willing and Intending' (in R. Grandy and R. Warner (eds), *Philosophical Grounds of Rationality* (Oxford, forthcoming)).

will be no *un*desirable concert-goings in those other situations, consistent with my beliefs. In answering my question, then, I limit my attention to futures consistent with my beliefs *and* in which obtain all enabling conditions for going to the concert. I limit my attention, for example, to those cases in which there are tickets left and ask whether, in such cases, my going would be desirable. I do this even if some enabling conditions, though consistent with my beliefs, are not guaranteed by my beliefs.

Suppose I conclude that any such concert-going act, consistent with my beliefs, would be desirable. And suppose I reach this conclusion even though some enabling conditions for my going—for example, the availability of tickets—are not guaranteed by my beliefs. Do I *simply* intend to go; or do I have only the *conditional* intention to go if I can?

I think it is clear that Davidson's answer is that I simply intend to go; for consider his remarks about 'genuine conditional intentions':

Genuine conditional intentions are appropriate when we explicitly consider what to do in various contingencies; for example, someone may intend to go home early from a party if the music is too loud. If we ask for the difference between conditions that really do make the statement of an intention more accurate and bogus conditions like 'if I can' . . . it seems to me clear that the difference is this: bona-fide conditions are ones that are reasons for acting that are contemporary with the intention. Someone may not like loud music now, and that may be why he now intends to go home early from the party if the music is too loud. His not being able to go home early is not a reason for or against his going home early, and so it is not a relevant condition for an intention . . . ('Intending', pp. 94-5).

On Davidson's view, then, mere enabling conditions are not 'bona-fide' conditions for 'genuine conditional intentions', for they are not 'reasons for acting that are contemporary with the intention'. The availability of tickets is, by itself, no reason for my going to the concert, though it is an enabling condition for my going. Of course, to intend to go I cannot believe such enabling conditions will *not* be present; for then I would not satisfy (1). But even if I do not actually believe they will all be present I may still have a simple intention to go.

In our example, then, I simply intend to go to the concert, despite my lack of belief in the availability of tickets. But then (2) cannot be necessary for my future intention.

I now want to consider two interrelated problems for Davidson's theory. The first problem is an analogue of the old problem of Buridan's Ass. Buridan wondered how an ass, midway between two piles of hay judged equally desirable, could intentionally go to one.[19] Our problem concerns the possibility of *future* intention in the face of equally desirable future options.

Suppose I know I can stop at one of two bookstores after work, Kepler's or Printer's Inc., but not both. And suppose I find both options equally attractive. I judge all-out that any act of my stopping at Kepler's would be just as desirable as any act of stopping at Printer's Inc., given my beliefs. Does it follow from Davidson's theory that I have both intentions? Neither intention?

These questions highlight an unclarity in Davidson's discussion. An all-out desirability judgement in favour of A-ing is implicitly comparative. But there are weak and strong comparisons. A *weak* comparison would see A-ing as at least as desirable as its alternatives; a *strong* comparison sees A-ing as strictly more desirable than its alternatives. Which sort of comparison does Davidson's theory require for future intention?

There is a dilemma here. If all that is required is a weak comparison, then in the present case I both intend to go to Kepler's and intend to go to Printer's Inc. But this seems wrong. Recall that I know I cannot go to both stores. So I cannot, on Davidson's view, intend to go to both. But then, if I were to have each intention, I would be in a position in which I (rationally, we may suppose) intend to A and intend to B, but cannot intend to do both.

This violates a natural constraint on intention. Rational intentions should be *agglomerative*. If at one and the same time I rationally intend to A and rationally intend to B then it should be both possible and rational for me, at the same time, to intend to A *and B*. But if all that is required for future intention is a weak comparison, then intentions will not be agglomerative in this way.

Granted, many practical attitudes are not agglomerative. I might rationally desire to drink a milk shake for lunch and rationally desire to run four miles after lunch, and yet find the prospect of doing both appalling. But this is one way in which intentions differ

---

[19] For a useful discussion of such cases see E. Ullmann-Margalit and S. Morgenbesser, 'Picking and Choosing', *Social Research* 44 (1977), 757-85. I was first led to consider the relevance of such cases to Davidson's theory by a remark of Saul Kripke's.

from ordinary desires. Rational intentions are agglomerative, and this fact should be captured and explained by our theory.

This suggests that Davidson should insist that to intend to *A* I must hold a strong comparative evaluation in favour of *A*. Thus I neither intend to go to Kepler's, nor intend to go to Printer's Inc. So, in the present case, agglomerativity is not threatened.

But now we have our Buridan problem. It seems that I can just decide on which bookstore to go to, while continuing to see each option as equally desirable. Such a decision provides me with an intention which does not correspond to a strong comparative evaluation. I might just decide to go to Kepler's even though I do not judge all-out that so acting would be strictly more desirable than going to Printer's Inc. But the intention I thereby reach does not satisfy the demands of Davidson's theory as we are now interpreting it. In trying to avoid the horn of agglomerativity, Davidson's theory is threatened by the horn of a Buridan problem.

V. A FURTHER PROBLEM WITH AGGLOMERATIVITY

The second problem is that even if future intention requires a strong comparative evaluation, Davidson's theory still will not ensure that rational intentions are agglomerative. This results from the weak belief condition on intention.

An example will make my point. I have for a long time wanted to buy copies of *The White Hotel* and *The Fixer*, and know I will be at a bookstore this afternoon. Further, I know the bookstore will have one or other of these novels in stock, but not both. Unfortunately, I do not know which one will be in stock.

I ask: would any act of my buying *The Fixer* be desirable, given my beliefs? In answering this I limit my attention to possible futures consistent with my beliefs and in which all enabling conditions—including the condition that *The Fixer* is in stock—obtain. And, let us suppose, I reasonably judge that any such act of buying *The Fixer* would be strictly better than its alternatives, and so, in the relevant sense, desirable. Note that the relevant alternatives here will include buying no novel, but will not include buying *The White Hotel*. This is because the latter is not open to me in any future which is both consistent with my beliefs and in which I can buy *The Fixer*. In this way I reach a simple intention to buy *The Fixer* this afternoon.

By an analogous route I might also reasonably judge that any act of my buying *The White Hotel* that is consistent with my beliefs would be desirable, thereby reaching an intention to buy *The White Hotel.*

Of course, in each case I do not believe all the required enabling conditions will obtain. But on Davidson's account that does not turn my intentions into mere conditional intentions to buy *The Fixer* / *The White Hotel* if I can. Rather, I both intend to buy *The Fixer* and intend to buy *The White Hotel.* And on Davidson's account both intentions might be perfectly reasonable.

But recall that I believe I cannot buy both novels. So it is not possible for me to intend to buy both. We are led to the result that though I rationally intend to buy *The Fixer*, and rationally intend to buy *The White Hotel*, it is not even possible for me to intend both to buy *The Fixer* and to buy *The White Hotel.* On Davidson's theory rational intentions may fail to be agglomerative. And that seems wrong.

VI. INTENTION AND PRACTICAL REASONING

I now want to try to diagnose the source of this pair of difficulties. My conjecture is that both difficulties are in large part rooted in Davidson's conception of just what facts a theory of future intention must account for. In particular, I think Davidson's theory is constrained by an overly weak conception of the role of future intentions in further practical thinking.

To my knowledge, Davidson says almost nothing about this role. His picture seems to be that the basic inputs for practical reasoning about what to do—either now or later—will just be the agent's desires and beliefs. Such reasoning, when concerned with the future, can issue in future intentions. And these intentions are fundamentally different sorts of states from the desires and beliefs on which they are based. But there is no significant further role for these intentions to play as inputs into one's further practical thinking. Future intentions are, rather, mere spin-offs of practical reasoning concerning the future.

This is an attenuated conception of the role of intention in practical reasoning. It receives support from Davidson's *strategy of extension*: the attempt to extend the materials present in his account of intentional action to an account of future intention. In intentional action, there is no temporal interval between all-out evaluation and action. So there is no room for further practical reasoning in which that all-out evaluation can play a significant role as an input. When we extend the notion of an all-out evaluation to the future-directed case, it will then be easy to overlook the possibility that *future* intentions *will*, at least typically, play such a role.

I believe that this limited conception of the role of future intentions in practical reasoning fails to accommodate the facts; for such intentions typically play an important role in our practical thinking. Moreover, I suspect that Davidson's acceptance of this limited conception may well account for his failure to be concerned with the pair of problems I have emphasized.

Let us begin with my first point. A theory of future intentions needs to explain why we ever *bother* to form them. Why do we not just cross our bridges when we come to them? One answer is that we want to avoid the need for deliberation at the time of action. But, more importantly, we form future intentions as parts of larger plans whose role is to aid *co-ordination* of our activities over time. Further, we do not adopt these plans, in all their detail, all at once. Rather, as time goes on we add to and adjust our plans. As elements in these plans, future intentions force the formation of yet further intentions and constrain the formation of other intentions and plans. For example, they force the formation of intentions concerning means, and constrain later plans to be consistent with prior plans.[20] This means that they play a significant role in our further practical thinking, in the on-going creation and adjustment of our plans—a role Davidson neglects.

My second point is that Davidson's neglect of this role may well account for his neglect of the pair of problems I have emphasized. This is because this neglected role is a major source of the facts about future intentions that generate these problems.

Let us call the role my future intentions play in constraining and influencing the further construction and adjustment of my plans in pursuit of co-ordination, their *co-ordinating role*. Rational intentions will be capable of playing this role well. To do this they must be capable of being part of an overall plan that can successfully co-ordinate the agent's activities. So rational intentions are to be agglomerative.

[20] I discuss these and related ideas further in 'Taking Plans Seriously', *Social Theory and Practice* 9 (1983), and in 'Two Faces of Intention', *Philosophical Review* 93 (1984).

Further, the search for co-ordination of my activities over time may sometimes require me to settle in advance on one of several options judged equally desirable. Perhaps in order to get on with my plans for the day I must settle now on one of the bookstores, despite their equal attractiveness. Or, having settled on a bookstore I must settle on a means to getting there, even if there are several equally desirable routes.

So, the co-ordinating role of future intentions underlies the further facts about future intentions that have been the basis of my pair of criticisms. This co-ordinating role both imposes a demand for agglomerativity and creates a need for the ability to settle in advance on one of several options judged equally desirable. If one's conception of the facts to be explained about future intention does not include this co-ordinating role, it may be easy for it also not to include these further facts.

My conjecture is that this is what happens to Davidson's theory. He begins with an attenuated conception of the role of intention in practical reasoning, a conception partly supported by his strategy of extension. This attenuated conception blocks from view the facts about agglomerativity and Buridan cases which I have emphasized, and allows Davidson to accept a theory that does not accommodate these facts. If this is right, Davidson's difficulties with agglomerativity and the Buridan problem are symptoms of a deeper problem. They are symptoms of an overly limited conception of the role of intentions and plans in rational motivation and practical reasoning.[21]

[21] I want to thank Robert Audi, Myles Brand, John Dupré, Dagfinn Follesdal, John Perry, Howard Wettstein, and members of a spring 1982 Stanford seminar, given jointly by John Perry and me, for their helpful comments and criticisms.

II

DAVIDSON ON
'WEAKNESS OF THE WILL'

PAUL GRICE AND JUDITH BAKER

I

We shall approach the topic of incontinence via consideration of Donald Davidson's recent admirable paper, 'How is Weakness of the Will Possible?' (*EAE*, pp. 21-42), and we begin by rather baldly summarizing what are for our purposes the salient points of that paper. An incontinent act is, in effect, initially defined as an act done intentionally, an alternative to which is both open to the agent and judged by the agent to be, all things considered, better than the act in question. A primary conceptual difficulty about incontinence is seen as being the inconsistency of a triad consisting of the statement (P3) that there are incontinent acts together with two further principles which state, in effect, (P1) given that a man does either *x* or *y* intentionally, preference in wanting (wanting *x* more than *y*) is always reflected in preference in intention (intentionally doing *x* rather than *y*) and (P2) that preference in wanting always follows preference in evaluative judgement (judging *x* to be better than *y*) if such preference in evaluative judgement obtains. We have a suspicion that, though he does not say so, Davidson is committed by what seems to be the rationale for accepting these principles, as he does, to accepting also the converses at least of P1, and possibly also of P2; that is to say, to holding not only that if there is preference in wanting there is also preference in intention (if either act is done intentionally) but also that if *x* is preferred in intention to *y* then *x* is also preferred in wanting to *y*. And similarly, perhaps, not only if there is preference in evaluative judgement there is preference in wanting, but if there is preference in wanting there is preference in evaluative judgement. This suspicion however obviously will need further elaboration and substantiation.

Davidson's solution to this paradox utilizes a suggested analogy between evaluative statements and probability statements to reach and deploy a distinction between conditional and unconditional judgements which, it is contended, makes possible an interpretation of the members of the apparently inconsistent triad on which they are no longer inconsistent; suitably interpreted, all three principles can and should be accepted. More specifically, the man who incontinently does y rather than x does indeed judge that x is better than y, but the judgement is the *conditional* judgement that all things considered, x is better than y; but only an *unconditional* judgement that x is better than y would require to be reflected first in preference in wanting and second in preference in intention. The incontinent man does not judge unconditionally that x is better than y; indeed, if we interpret Davidson aright, the incontinent man combines the conditional judgement that, all things considered, x is better than y, with the unconditional judgement in line with his preference in intention, namely that y is better than x.

The attachment to the idea of preserving both P1 and P2 is, it seems, rooted in a view about the analysis of the notion of intentional action. The proper analysis of this notion is seen as requiring, in a way to be more fully discussed in a moment, that there should be some interpretation of the expression 'judges x to be better than y' such that such a preferential evaluative judgement should be reflected in an intention formed with respect to doing x or doing y. Davidson's view of action seems to lead him to maintaining also, though the basis of this contention is less obvious, that if an action is done intentionally then it is done for a reason.

It emerges from Davidson's survey of previous discussion of the subject of incontinence that he considers there to be two themes which are liable to be confused, both of which, if we interpret him aright, are at least to some degree mistaken. To quote him: 'One is, that desire distracts us from the good, or forces us to the bad; the other is that incontinent action always favours the beastly, selfish passion over the call of duty and morality.'[1] As presented, an exemplification of the second theme would entail an exemplification of the first theme. This logical connection seems to us inessential; the statement of the themes can be recast in such a way as to make them logically distinct. The first theme would be that in incontinence it is always the case that desire or passion makes us act against our better judgement: desire or passion is always the *victor* over better

[1] 'How is Weakness of the Will Possible?', p. 29.

judgement. The second theme would be that in incontinence what our better judgement calls for is always action in line with duty or morality; it is always duty or morality which is the *loser*. Davidson's example of the man who allegedly acts incontinently by getting out of his comfortable bed in order to remedy his forgetful failure to brush his teeth may be envisaged as a counter to these themes in certainly two, and possibly three, ways.

(1) It is not always the passion which wins, if we can take the reluctance to get out of bed as falling under the heading of desire or passion, because this is the element which loses in this case, thereby invalidating theme one. (2) If duty or morality is involved at all, that is, if we think brushing one's teeth to be a duty, duty or morality is involved not as a loser but as victor. This example may also be used to make the even stronger point that since the call upon me to brush my teeth is not a call of duty or morality but only the call of self-interest, in this case as in Davidson's reference to the man who acts incontinently when concerned to maximize his own pleasure (the allusion to Mill) duty or morality is not involved at all, on either side. And we might say he might have produced (though he does not), as his example suggests, some cases in which desire or passion are not involved at all. We can imagine a case in which a man is diverted from what he knows to be his duty by what he judges to be in his self-interest. While someone who wished to distinguish wickedness from incontinence might wish to classify such cases as wickedness rather than as incontinence, it is clear that they would fall within the characterization of incontinence given by Davidson himself.

II

The conditional/unconditional distinction stems, as we have already remarked, from an attempt to provide for the logical possibility of incontinence while retaining the two principles P1 and P2, and to do so via a distinction of content between those evaluative judgements which carry with them intention or decision and those which do not. Crucial to this distinction is the analogy which Davidson finds between, on the one hand, probability judgements and those non-practical arguments within which they figure, and, on the other hand, evaluative judgements and the practical arguments in which they figure. The relevant type of probability judgement, for example, 'given that the skies are red this evening, it will probably rain tomorrow', is seen by Davidson as exemplifying the canonical form $pr(m_1, p)$ where 'pr' represents a sentential connective, 'm_1' represents a sentence specifying an evidentially relevant considera-tion, and 'p' represents a sentence specifying a state of affairs to which m_1 is claimed to be relevant.[2] While a procedure is needed to enable us sometimes to infer by detachment from such a probability judgement, together with the premiss that m_1, to the conclusion that p, unrestricted detachment cannot be allowed since (1) $pr(m_1, p)$ and (2) $pr(m_1$ and $m_2, -p)$ may both be true. As Hempel and others have noted, inferences of this type have, therefore, to be subject to a 'principle of total evidence', the proper formulation of which we do not at this point have to discuss, but which would prevent an inference by detachment from (1) when (2) is available. Analog-ously, some evaluative judgements are considered by Davidson as representable by the structure $pf(m_1, a$ better than $b)$ where 'pf' (pronounced '*prima facie*') is a sentential connective which parallels 'pr', and 'a' and 'b' represent possible actions. Inferences from such conditional value judgements to the corresponding unconditional value judgement that a is better than b are, like their counterparts in the area of probability, and for the same reasons, subject to a principle of total evidence. A special case of a condi-tional value judgement is, according to Davidson, a judgement of the type 'all things considered, a is better than b', representable by the structure $pf(e, a$ better than $b)$ where e represents the total available evidence. Davidson's solution to the problem of incontin-ence consists in the thesis that the typical incontinent man combines the conditional judgement that $pf(e, a$ better than $b)$ with the unconditional judgement that b is better than a. The latter judge-ment is the one on which the incontinent man acts, and since the type of evaluative judgement which supposedly is in line both with preference in wanting and with intention to act is taken to be the unconditional value judgement, the phenomenon of incontinence is compatible with the principles P1 and P2. We may note here for future reference that on Davidson's account the unconditional judgement, which in the case of the incontinent man is in quasi-

---

[2] Our notation for probability judgements reverses the standard form utilized by Davidson, in that we make the representation of the evidential base precede rather than follow the representation of that to which probability is ostensibly assigned. We make this change in order to hint at, though not to affirm, the idea that prob-ability and its practical analogue might be treated as attributes of conditional propo-sitions (statements), on some suitable analysis of non-material conditionals.

conflict with the 'all things considered' judgement, stems from a consideration which is an element in the set of considerations covered by the phrase 'all things considered', for example, from the thought that to do b would be more pleasant than to do a. Such a consideration is treated as being the incontinent man's reason for doing b and as being the cause of, though not his reason for, the unconditional judgement from which his act proceeds (*EAE*, p. 41).

While we agree with Davidson about the existence and importance of the analogy between probabilistic and evaluative statements and arguments, we are dubious about certain aspects of Davidson's characterization of it. A discussion of this question however, will not be undertaken on this occasion.[3] This issue apart, two modifications of the Davidsonian scheme seem to us to be initially demanded if it is to be advanced as a model for practical reasoning. The first of these does not seem in any way damaging to the essence of Davidson's treatment of the problem of incontinence, but the second leads us on to some serious objections. There seem to us to be cogent grounds for providing room for evaluative judgements to the effect not just that (1) relative to certain considerations a is better than b, but that (2) relative to certain considerations, a is best. Given Davidson's conditional/unconditional distinction it looks as if for many, if not all, cases the final conditional evaluative judgement in practical argument should be thought of as being of form (2) rather than form (1), and the same may be true of some of the non-final evaluative judgements contained in such an argument. It is true that in some cases the judgement that a is best is tantamount to the judgement that a is better than b, where b is the most promising alternative to a: but this is not always so. Sometimes we seem to decide that relative to certain evidence a is better than any of a range of alternatives without deciding on any evaluative ordering of the remainder of the range and sometimes even without identifying any of the elements in that remainder. If we are right in supposing that an 'all things considered' judgement would characteristically be of form (2), then clearly the incontinent man must be supposed to reach this type of judgement. It is tempting, but we suspect wrong, to suggest that a judgement to the effect that, relative to m_1, a is best is to be represented as a special case of form (1), namely, that given by the schema recognized by Davidson, $pf(m_1, a$ is better than

---

[3] Discussed in Paul Grice, 'Probability, Desirability, and Modal Operators' (unpublished).

$-a$) (for example, *EAE*, p. 38). The latter schema unfortunately can be read in either of two ways; as a way of saying that, relative to m_1, a is good, and as a way of saying that relative to m_1, a is better than any alternative. These readings are clearly distinct and examples of each of them may occur in practical argument.

Our second modification may have more awkward consequences for Davidson's account. Davidson wishes 'pf', like 'pr', to be treated as a special sentential connective. While this proposal may be adequate for dealing with many examples of conditional judgement, there are some important candidates which raise difficulties. If judgements expressed by the sentence forms 'all things considered, a is better than b' or 'relative to the available evidence, a is better than b' are to be regarded as instances of conditional judgement, as Davidson seems to demand, the proposal will have to be modified. For in the expression of these judgements the relevant considerations are not sententially specified but are referred to by a noun phrase, and in such cases characterization of 'pf', and for that matter of 'pr', as sentential connectives would seemingly flout syntax.

It would be no more legitimate to treat the phrases 'the available evidence' or 'all things considered' (or 'all things') as substituends for a sentential place marker (as 'e' should be to parallel 'm_1') in one of Davidson's canonical forms than it would be to treat 'the premisses of your argument' (as distinct from 'The premisses of your argument are true') as a substituend for 'p' in the form 'if p then q'. So if the account of conditional judgement is to be both uniform and capable of accommodating 'all things considered' judgements (interpreted in the manner just suggested), 'pr' and 'pf' will have to be thought of as representing not connectives but relational expressions signifying relations between such entities as sentences, statements, propositions, or judgements, according to philosophical predilection.

These reflections, however, raise a doubt whether we have, after all, correctly interpreted Davidson's notion of an 'all things considered' judgement. Such a judgement might, as we have suggested, be a judgement expressible in a sentence of the form 'Prima facie, relative to the available evidence, a is better than b', but, alternatively, it might be thought of as a judgement expressible in a sentence of the form 'Prima facie, given that p_1 and p_2 ... and p_n, a is better than b', where the conjunctive schema 'p_2 ... and p_n, represents a specification of what is, *in fact*, the available evidence. If this alternative interpretation should prove sufficient for a Davidsonian solution to the problem of incontinence, its adoption would enable us to preserve the characterization of 'pr' and 'pf' as representing connectives. But is it sufficient for this purpose? The question whether, to discharge its role in Davidson's scheme, an 'all things considered' judgement can be regarded as specifying a set of propositions which *in fact* constitute the body of evidence, or whether it has to be regarded as referring to such a set of propositions *as* constituting the body of evidence, is, to our minds, bound up with the further question about the meaning of the expressions 'all things considered' and 'available evidence'. 'All things considered' might mean either 'relative to everything which has so far been considered' or 'relative to everything which should be considered'. Similarly 'the available evidence' might mean 'the evidence of which I have so far availed myself' or 'all the evidence of which I should avail myself'. In each case the natural interpretation seems to us to be the second, but there is some indication (albeit in passages not altogether unambiguous) that Davidson intends the first.

It might be helpful, before we examine possible interpretations of 'all things considered' judgements, to consider what might be the maximal set of stages through which a man might pass in practical deliberation. We offer an expanded sequence of stages which we hope Davidson would not individually reject, although he might wish to claim that not all of them are distinct. As we note below, Davidson might himself argue that stage (7) is not distinct from stage (6), and we will later present as our first interpretation of an 'all things considered' judgement one that corresponds to stage (3) (hence, on this interpretation stages (3), (4), and (5) would not be distinct) and as our second interpretation one that corresponds to stage (4) (hence on this interpretation stages (4) and (5) would not be distinct). These stages can be seen as occurring in non-practical deliberation as well, and we have included the non-practical analogues of the evaluative judgements. We may note that the labels are those of philosophical reflection and not the agent's and, most important, that the schema is of a provisional nature and, we think, will be seriously affected by criticisms offered later in this paper.

(1) Single specificatory prima-facie (pf) (conditional) judgements:
   [pf(A,z better than *not-z*)]
   [prob(A,z)]

(2) Non-final compound specificatory pf (conditional) judgements:
   [pf((A,B), z better than *not-z*)]
   [prob((A,B), z)]

(3) Final compound specificatory pf (conditional) judgement:
   [pf((A,B,C,D), z better than *not-z*)]
   [prob($(A,B,C,D),z$)]
      when (A,B,C,D) = set of relevant factors before me

(4) Summative non-specificatory pf (conditional) judgement:
   [pf((all things before me), z better than *not-z*)]
   [prob((all things before me), z)]

(5) Final non-specificatory pf (conditional) judgement:
   [pf(all things considered), z better than *not-z*)]
   [prob(all things considered), z)]

(6) Unconditional judgement:
   [z better than *not-z*]
   [z]

(7) Intention to do z
   Belief that z

(Note that Davidson might say that (7) is not distinct from (6).)

III

Let us now revert to the actual text of Davidson's paper. There seem to be four interpretations, or varieties of interpretation, of one or other of the phrases 'all things considered' and 'relative to the available evidence' which, in one way or another, need to be considered in connection with Davidson's account of incontinence. We shall argue that the first three both give unnatural accounts of an 'all things considered' judgement and, when incorporated into Davidson's framework, yield unsatisfactory accounts of incontinence; while the fourth, though it seems to represent correctly the nature of an 'all things considered' judgement, cannot be fitted into Davidson's framework without modification to that framework which, we suspect, he would find unwelcome.

1. One possible interpretation, which has already been mentioned, is to take the 'all things considered' judgement as being of the form 'pf, given $p_1 \ldots p_n$, a is better than b', where $p_1 \ldots p_n$ are in fact the totality of the propositions which the agent believes to be both true and relevant. While this interpretation preserves Davidson's stipulation that 'pf' be treated as a connective, it fails to represent the incontinent man as thinking of his judgement in favour of a as being relativized to the totality of available evidence. For all that has been said, he might think this only a partial survey of the pieces of evidence which, severally, he has considered, in which case he would not have achieved the kind of judgement that a is better than b which, intuitively, we want to attribute to him.

2. To avoid this difficulty, we might abandon the idea that 'pf' is a connective rather than a relational expression and, in line with what Davidson seems to suggest himself, interpret the 'all things considered' judgement as being of the form 'pf, relative to the totality of propositions, each of which is believed by me to be true and relevant, a is better than b', or, to put it more succinctly, 'pf, relative to all that is now before me, a is better than b'. This seems to give one legitimate reading of the expression 'available evidence' (= 'everything I have at present under consideration') but ignores what seems to be a genuine distinction between 'relative to the available evidence' (so understood) and 'all things considered'. It ignores, that is, the possibility that a man, in his deliberation, might regard the evidence at present available to him as inadequate, in which case it would seem inappropriate to suppose him to be ready to make the judgement that 'all things considered, a is better than b' (as 'all things considered' is normally understood). Surely a general account of incontinence should provide for the possibility of this measure of scrupulousness in the deliberations of the man who subsequently acts incontinently.

3. Our third candidate for the interpretation of an 'all things considered' judgement is one which it is pretty evident that Davidson would, quite rightly, reject, but it is worth mentioning in order that it should be clear just why it should be rejected. In pursuit of the proper goal of accommodating a distinction between an 'all things considered' judgement and a conditional probability judgement or

evaluative judgement which is relativized to the totality of the evidence present before the judger (an 'all things before me' judgement), one might seek to understand the idea of an 'all things considered' judgement as being the idea of a judgement to the effect that something is probable, or prima facie better than something else, relative to some totality of supporting facts, many of which would in a normal case be unavailable to the judger, at least at the time of judging, and possibly at any time. On this view, a standard piece of fully explicit practical reasoning might be supposed to contain two distinct steps: (*a*) a step from a (conditional) 'all things before me' judgement (together with the reflective judgement that certain qualificatory conditions obtain which license this step) to a (conditional) 'all things considered' judgement, which is relativized to an ideal totality of evidence; and (*b*) a step from a (conditional) 'all things considered' judgement, so interpreted, to an unconditional judgement that *a* is better than *b*.

Such a view would be open to two grave objections. First, as Davidson himself points out, if we stock this ideal totality of evidence too generously it will not merely support but will entail the content of the unconditional judgement. If I am investigating probabilistically the possibility that it is now raining in Timbuctoo, the relevant ideal totality of evidence should not include either the fact that it is raining in Timbuctoo or the fact that the residents of Timbuctoo can now see that it is raining. Such a totality of evidence would have to occupy an intermediate position between the evidence before the judger and the totality of all relevant facts of any sort, and it is far from clear that there is any satisfactory characterization of such an intermediate totality. Second, even if the idea of such a totality could be defined, it seems plausible to suppose that at any given stage in the reasoning, a reasoner's best estimate at that stage of what conclusion such an ideal totality of evidence would support would have to coincide with the conclusion supported by the evidence, so far as it goes, which is before him at that stage. In so far as the evidence before me supports *p*, I am naturally at this point inclined to believe rather than disbelieve that the totality of evidence will support *p*. On the view considered, the crucial stage in probabilistic or practical reasoning will not be that at which we become entitled to attach *some degree or other* of credence to the content of some 'all things considered' judgement, as so interpreted (if we have any evidence at all we are always in that position); it would rather be the stage at which we are entitled, in the light of the judgement that the qualificatory conditions obtain, actually to *judge*, as opposed to, say, merely conjecture, that an ideal totality would support a certain conclusion. But now it is not clear what useful function the 'all things considered' judgement, so understood, can be supposed to fulfill. For if, as seems to be the case, a rational man will automatically make the second of our two steps once he has made the first, would it not be more economical, and therefore better, to suppose that the combination of an 'all things before me' judgement, together with a judgement that the qualificatory conditions obtain, *directly* entitles a reasoner to make the appropriate unconditional judgement rather than to suppose it to entitle him to make an 'all things considered' judgement from which he is to be supposed, if rational, to make a further move to an unconditional judgement?

4. The argument of the last paragraph has led us directly to the final possibility to be here considered, namely, that for *x* to make an 'all things considered' judgement that *a* is better than *b* is for *x* to judge that, since he has a certain body of evidence, *e*, in favour of the supposition that *a* is better than *b*, and since certain qualificatory conditions are satisfied, it is best for *x* to (*x* should, *x* ought to) make the unconditional judgement that *a* is better than *b*. Whether or not this interpretation will succeed in preserving the idea than an 'all things considered' judgement is a special sort of conditional, or prima-facie, judgement is a question which we will discuss in a moment.

The only remaining alternative interpretation, so far as we can see, is one which although it might perhaps be thought to give a better representation of the meaning of the phrase 'all things considered', would certainly not preserve the conditional, or prima-facie, character of the 'all things considered' judgement. One might treat the statement that, all things considered, *a* is better than *b*, as expressing the judgement that *a* is better than *b*, with the gloss that this judgement is justified in the light of one's possession of a favourable body of evidence with respect to which the qualificatory conditions obtain; but since on this interpretation an 'all things considered' judgement would plainly involve the unconditional judgement that *a* is better than *b*, just as part of what would be expressed by saying 'Demonstrably, *p*' would be the judgement that *p*, no room would be left for the idea that an 'all things considered' judgement is a *conditional* judgement.

The crucial question to be considered is whether, if we interpret an 'all things considered' judgement in what seems to us the most plausible way which does not represent it as patently involving a commitment to an unconditional evaluative judgement, we are still entitled to classify it as a conditional, or prima-facie, judgement. Let us assume that we can facilitate exposition without introducing any relevant change in substance if we express a standard prima-facie evaluative judgement by the sentence form 'given that p, x should (ought to) do A'; the shift from 'a is better than b' to 'x should do A' seems for present purposes immaterial, and it is to be understood that the form we propose is not to be taken as entailing that p. To incorporate a commitment to the truth of p, the pattern might be varied to 'given the fact that p, x should do A'. In an attempt to assimilate an 'all things considered' judgement as closely as possible to this standard pattern, we might suppose its expansion to be of the general form 'given the fact that p, certain things are the case such that, given that they are the case, x should do A, and given the fact that certain qualificatory conditions are met, x should judge that x should do A'. The qualificatory conditions in question need not here be accurately specified; their effect would be to stipulate that 'the principle of total evidence' was satisfied, that, for example, x's judgement that, given certain facts, x should do A, had taken into account all the relevant facts in x's possession and that x had fulfilled whatever call there was upon him at the time in question to maximize his possession of relevant facts. Let us summarily express the idea that these qualificatory conditions are fulfilled by using the form 'x's judgement that, given the facts in question, x should do A, is *optimal* for x at the time in question'. Our question, then, is whether a judgement on the part of x expressible in the form, 'given the fact that

(a) given certain facts, x should do A, and
(b) x's judgement that (*a*) is optimal for x,
　　then x should judge that x should do A'

is properly classifiable as a conditional or prima-facie judgement. To put the matter more shortly, but less precisely, the kind of judgement whose status is in question is one such as 'given the fact that on my evidence I should do A, and that my judgement that this is so is optimal, I should judge that I should do A'. (Let us call a specially interpreted 'all things considered' judgement of this form ATC*.)

The question we have to ask, then, is whether ATC* is properly classified as a conditional, rather than an unconditional, judgement. On one possible interpretation of conditional judgement it clearly has strong claims, inasmuch as it would be possible to replace, in its standard expression, the opening phrase 'given the fact that' by the word 'if' without any violence to the normal usage of 'if',[4] and the resulting conditional sentence would express one part of the sense of the ATC* judgement, the other part being what would be expressed by the antecedent of this conditional sentence. The ATC* judgement would then seem to be conditional in very much the same way as one might regard a judgement of the form 'since p, q' our conditional, on the grounds that its sense includes the sense of 'if p, q'. This sense of 'conditional' is plainly not that which we need in the present context. The sense which we need is one which carries with it the idea of being prima-facie in character, of being connected in some way with *defeasibility*. In an attempt to show that ATC* is not conditional in this further sense, let us characterize the sense more precisely.

Let 'p_1' abbreviate 'x has told y that x will consider lending y \$100 towards the purchase of a new car';

Let 'p_2' abbreviate 'y is hard up and needs a car for work';

Let 'p_3' abbreviate 'y's spouse only too often gets hold of y's money';

Let 'q' abbreviate 'x should lend y \$100'; and

Let 'q'' abbreviate 'x should not lend y \$100'.

The judgement that 'given p_1 & p_2, q' is clearly prima facie in that the related argument form

$$\text{Given } p_1 \& p_2, q$$
$$p_1 \& p_2$$
$$\overline{\qquad\qquad}$$
$$q$$

is plainly defeasible, insofar as the addition of the premises that p_3 and that, given p_1, p_2 & p_3, q' to the premises above gives us, without falsifying thereby p_1 or p_2, a set of premises from which it would be illegitimate to conclude that q. All of this is, of course, familiar. For purposes of comparison with ATC*, it is important to note that the argument just characterized as defeasible could have been expressed in a telescoped form, viz.

---

[4] The relevant interpretation of 'if' may, of course, not be any of those standardly selected by logicians or philosophers of logic.

Given the fact that p_1 & p_2, q

$$q$$

Here too the inferential step will be upset without falsification of its premiss if we suppose x also to have judged that, given the fact that p_1, p_2, & p_3, q. Let us as a first stage in examining the status of ATC* make use of the notion of a specification of an ATC* judgement, that is, a judgement which differs from ATC* in that the relevant considerations are identified and not merely alluded to (Spec (ATC*)). The Spec (ATC*) appropriate for the present example will be X's judgement at t that given the fact that

(a) given the fact that p_1 & p_2, q; and that
(b) at t, x's judgement that (a) is optimal for x;
     then x should judge at t that q.

That a step by x from this judgement to the detached conclusion that q would not be a step which is defeasible in the required sense is shown by the fact that if, at t, x had made the additional judgement 'given the fact that p_1 & p_2 & p_3, q '', his making this judgement would have entailed that his judgement 'given the fact that p_1 & p_2, q' was not optimal for x at t. In this case he would not have been in a position to make the step from Spec (ATC*) to q, but this would be because a judgement by him in favour of Spec (ATC*) would, given the supposed additional judgement, be falsified. We do not, then, have the characteristic case of a defeasible inference in which the inference may be upset without falsification of any of its premisses. Since the truth or falsity of the claim that x's judgement about a certain body of evidence is optimal cannot depend on whether, in the claim in question, the body of evidence is itemized or merely referred to, if the step from Spec (ATC*) to q is not of the defeasible kind, then the step from ATC* to q is not of the defeasible kind either. It in fact seems to us that, though there is an important difference between the two cases residing in the fact that in the first case, but not in the second, the legitimacy of the inference is relative to a particular subject at a particular time, the irrationality of refusing to move from the appropriate ATC* judgement to q will be the same in kind as the irrationality involved in refusing to move (as, perhaps, Lewis Carroll's tortoise did) from 'given the fact that p and that if p, q' to 'q'; and furthermore, that the irrationality in question is not of a kind that either we or Davidson would wish to attribute to the typical incontinent man.[5]

If the above argument is correct, to preserve as much as possible of Davidson's theses we should have to suppose that the typical incontinent man judges (unconditionally) that he should judge that he should do A, but does not actually judge that he should do A. If we try to take this position, we are at once faced with the following awkward questions: the position, like what we may call the 'naïve' view of incontinence, involves the supposition that for a certain substituend for ϕ it is true of a typical incontinent man that he judges that he should ϕ but does not ϕ; it differs from the 'naïve' view in taking as the favoured substituend for ϕ 'x judges that x should do a', rather than 'x does a'. Why should this departure from the 'naïve' view be thought to give a better account of incontinence? On the face of it, the 'naïve' view seems superior. It seems easier to attribute to people a failure to act as they fully believe they ought to act than to attribute to them a failure to believe what they fully believe they ought to believe. What is there to prevent a man from judging that he should do a, when he judges that he should judge that he should do a, except his disinclination to do a, and would it not be more natural to suppose that this disinclination prevents his judgement that he should do a from being followed by his doing a than to suppose that it prevents his judgement that he should judge that he should do a from being followed by his judgement that he should do a?

So far as we can see, the only motivation for disallowing the possibility of incontinence with respect to action, as most straightforwardly conceived, while allowing the possibility of the realization of a similarly straightforward conception of incontinence of belief or judgement, lies in the supposed theoretical attractiveness of the equation of a decision or intention on the part of x to do a with a judgement on the part of x that x should do a or that it is best for x to do a. To examine the case for this theoretical idea would take us beyond the limits of the paper. But before concluding our discussion we shall mention one or two considerations which seem to tell against the account of incontinence which has just been formulated.

---

[5] The actual logical situation is even more complex than we have represented it as being; but present complexities are perhaps sufficient for present purposes.

IV

For the purposes of this discussion, we should think of the incontinent man as being just a special case of someone who

(1) is faced with a practical problem about what to do;
(2) envisages himself as settling the problem by settling what it is best for him to do (what he should do); and
(3) envisages himself as settling what it is best for him to do by deliberation.

He is a special case in that his deliberation is defective in one or other of a number of special ways. There may be occasions in which one decides, or forms the intention, to do something without reference to the question what it is best to do, though some philosophers, who may include Davidson, have been disposed to deny this possibility. There may also be occasions in which one settles on something being the best thing to do, without any recourse to deliberation, by an immediate or snap judgement. Both of these possible routes to the resolution of a practical problem may, perhaps, in certain circumstances involve incontinence, but it would not be the variety with which we and Davidson are primarily concerned. Any one who, in consequence of satisfying the three conditions specified, has recourse to deliberation in the settlement of a practical problem, whether or not he ends up by exhibiting incontinence, engages in an undertaking which is generically similar to other kinds of undertaking in that there is a specifiable outcome or completion towards which the undertaking is directed. One who is engaged in fixing the supper, whether or not as a result of prior decision, completes his operations when he reaches his objective of having the supper ready, and if he breaks off his operations before completing it, some explanation is required. Similarly, one who deliberates in the face of a practical problem completes his operations when he reaches the objective of having settled what is *unconditionally* the best thing for him to do, and again, if he fails to complete the operation some explanation is required.

We must first distinguish a failure to complete deliberation from a miscompletion; for the present discussion a failure to complete due to interruption seems irrelevant. What we need to consider are the various ways in which a man may miscomplete deliberation; and here, it seems, attraction or revulsion, rather than external sources which interrupt deliberation, are in play. Now there are forms of miscompletion which will present us with cases of incontinence which are not of the type with which we, and Davidson, are concerned; a man may see a number of initial considerations, all or some of which are favourable to *a*, and because of the attractions of *a* or his reluctance to deliberate, seize on one of these considerations and jump to the unconditional conclusion that he ought to *a*. This is not Davidson's case. Again, a man might deliberate and reach an 'all things before me' judgement which represents the totality of his evidence at that stage, though it is inadequate since more considerations are demanded. He jumps to a judgement that he ought to *a*, in line with the latest 'all things before me' judgement; this is not Davidson's case either, since here the relevant conditional judgement and the unconditional judgement are both favourable to doing *a*. This leaves us with the possibility of a man jumping to an unconditional judgement in favour of *a* at a point at which the relevant 'all things before him' judgement is in favour of something other than *a*. We shall discuss this possibility with some care since, in spite of the fact that if taken as a characterization of typical incontinence it is open to an objection which we briefly advanced earlier (pp. 34-5), we are not absolutely certain that it does not represent Davidson's view of the incontinent man.

Obviously, there is in general no conceptual difficulty attaching to the idea of someone who is in the midst of some undertaking and who, as a result of revulsion, tedium, or the appeal of some alternative, breaks off what he is doing and instead embarks on some other undertaking or action. The miscompletion of deliberation which concerns us will, however, constitute a special case of this kind of phenomenon, in that the substituted performance has to be regarded as one with the same objective as the original undertaking, namely, finding the best thing to do. Again, there is no lack of examples which satisfy this more restrictive condition; one may break off one's own efforts to get one's car running and, instead, send for a mechanic to get the job done. But even this restriction is not restrictive enough in view of the special character of the objective involved in deliberation. While there are alternative routes to realizing the objective of getting one's car going besides working on it oneself, it is not clear that there are alternative routes to settling what is the best thing to do besides deliberating; or that if there are (for example, asking some one else's advice), they are at all germane to the phenomenon of incontinence. One who arrives at a holiday resort and embarks on the undertaking of finding the best hotel to stay in may tire of his search and decide to register at the next presentable hotel that he encounters, but in doing so he can hardly regard himself as having adopted an alternative method of finding the best hotel to stay in. In fact, to provide a full parallel for cases of incontinence, if these are conceived of as cases of making an unconditional evaluation in a direction opposed to that of a current 'all things before me' judgement, the examples would have to be even more bizarre than that just offered. One would rather have to imagine someone who, with a view to winning a prize at a party later in the day, sets out to find and to buy the largest pumpkin on sale in any store in his neighbourhood. After inspecting the pumpkins at three of the local stores, he tires of his enterprise and decides to buy the largest pumpkin in the fourth store, which he is now investigating, even though he knows that the evidence so far before him gives preference to the largest pumpkin at store number two, which is, of course, larger than the one he proposes to buy. It is obvious that such a man cannot regard himself as having adopted an alternative way to finding the largest pumpkin on sale. This elaboration is required since, on the scheme presently being considered, the incontinent man may typically substitute, for the continuation of deliberation, the formation of an intention to do b, to which he is prompted by its prospective pleasantness, in spite of the fact, of which he is aware, that the considerations so far taken into account (which include the prospective pleasantness of b) so far as they go favour a. The outcome of these attempts to find parallels suggests forcibly that it is logically impossible that one should without extreme logical incoherence make an unconditional judgement favouring b when one is fully conscious of the thought that the totality of evidence so far considered favours a, unless one thinks (reasonably or unreasonably) that the addition of further evidence, so far unidentified, would tilt the balance in favour of b. This last possibility must be regarded as irrelevant to our discussion of incontinence, since it is not a feature of the kind of incontinence with which we are concerned, if indeed of any kind of incontinence, that the incontinent man should think that further investigation and reflection would, or would have, justified the action which the incontinent man performs. We are then left with the conclusion that to suppose someone to make an unconditional judgement in a direction opposed to an 'all things before me' judgement, we must also suppose the latter jugdement not to be 'fully present' to the judger, on some suitable interpretation of that phrase. We can support this point directly without having to rely on analogies with other forms of undertaking. Mr and Mrs John Q. Citizen have decided they want a dog and are engaged in trying to settle what would be the best breed of dog for them to acquire. This enterprise involves them in such activities as perusing books about dogs, consulting friends, and reminding themselves of pertinent aspects of their own experience of dogs. At a certain point, not one at which they regard their delib-erations as concluded, it looks to them as if the data they have so far collected favour the selection of a short-haired terrier, though there is something also to be said for a spaniel or a dachshund. At this point, Mrs Citizen says, 'My aunt's spaniel, Rusty, was such a lovely dog. Let's get a spaniel', and her husband says, 'All right.' This story arouses no conceptual stir. But suppose that (1) Mrs Citizen, instead of saying 'Let's get a spaniel' had said 'A spaniel's the best dog to get', and that (2) previously in their deliberation they had noted the endearing qualities of Rusty, but in spite of that had come to lean towards a short-haired terrier. The story, thus altered, will conform to the alleged course of the incontinent man's reflections; at a certain point it appears to him that the claims of prospective pleasure are, or are being, outweighed, but nevertheless he judges that the pleasant thing is the best thing for him to do and acts on the judgement. But in the altered story the judgement of Mr and Mrs Citizen that a spaniel is the best dog for them to buy, to which they are prompted by a consideration which has already been discounted in their deliberations, seems to us quite incredible, unless we suppose that they have somehow lost sight of the previous course of their deliberations. (The further possibility that they suddenly and irrationally changed their assessment of the evidence so far before them, even if allowable, will not exemplify the idea that there is *some* sense in which the incontinent man thinks that what he is doing is something which he should not be doing.)

The conceptual difficulty is hardly lessened if we suppose the example of Rusty to be a new consideration instead of one already discounted. The couple could not move from it to the judgement that a spaniel is best without weighing it in the balance together with the body of data which, so far as it goes, they have deemed to point towards a short-haired terrier in preference to a spaniel, unless again they had somehow lost sight of the course of their deliberation.

If, as we have been arguing, an unconditional judgement against *a* can be combined with an 'all things before me' judgement in favour of *a* only if the latter judgement is not fully present to the judger, a precisely parallel conclusion will hold with respect to an 'all things considered' judgement (ATC*), since an ATC* judgement consists of an 'all things before me' judgement together with an 'optimality' judgement about it. Unless it should turn out to be otherwise logically indefensible, it would be preferable, as being more in accord with common sence, to attribute to the typical incontinent man (as we have been supposing Davidson to do) not merely an 'all things before me' judgement in favour of *a* but also an ATC* judgement in favour of *a*, with the additional proviso that the ATC* judgement is not fully present. On the face of it, this would not involve the attribution to the incontinent man of an unconditional judgement in favour of *a*, and so we leave room for an unconditional judgement, and so for an intention, against *a*.

Unfortunately, as has been partially foreshadowed by our discussion of the question whether an ATC* judgement is a conditional judgement, the position just outlined is, in our view, logically indefensible, as we shall now attempt to show.

We attach different numerical subscripts to particular occurences of the word 'justify' in order to leave open the possibility, without committing ourselves to its realization, that the sense of 'justify' varies in these occurrences; and we attach subscripts to the word 'optimality' in order to refer to some formulation (or reformulation) of the optimality condition previously sketched by us on page 38 which would be appropriate to whatever sense of 'justified' is distinguished by the subscript.

Let us suppose that:

(I) *x* judges at *t* that
  (1) *x* has at *t* some body of evidence (*e*) which, in conformity with the requirements for optimality$_1$, justifies$_1$ *x*'s doing *a*.

Unless we attribute to *x* extreme logical confusion or blindness, the supposition (I) seems tantamount to the supposition that:

(II) *x* judges at *t* that
  (2) *x* should do *a*.

It seems, however, that we are merely reformulating the supposition already expressed by (I) if we suppose that:

(III) x judges at t that
  (3) x has at t some body of evidence (e) which, in conformity with the requirements for optimality$_2$, justifies$_2$ x's judging at t that x should do a.

Again, as in the case of supposition (II), supposition (III) seems tantamount to supposition (IV):

(IV) x judges at t
  (4) x should judge at t that x should do a.

This argument seems to us to establish the conclusion that, extreme logical confusion apart, one judges on what seems to one an adequate basis that one should judge that one should do a if and only if one judges on the same basis that one should do a. That is to say, any case of believing, on what seems to one an adequate basis, that one should do a is, logical confusion apart, to be regarded as also a case of believing that one's belief that one should do a is a belief which one should hold: and any case of believing, on what seems to one an adequate basis, that one should believe that one should do a is, logical confusion apart, to be regarded as a case of believing that one should do a. If this conclusion is correct it seems that we have excluded the possibility of finding a reasonable interpretation of an 'all things considered' judgement that one should do a which would be distinct from, and would not involve, an unconditional judgement that one should do a.

V

We are left then with the conclusion that to attribute to the incontinent man an ATC* judgement in favour of a is, in effect, to attribute to him an unconditional judgement in favour of a; and so, presumably, to attribute to him a not fully present ATC* judgement in favour of a is to attribute to him a not fully present unconditional judgement in favour of a. If this is so, then there seem to be initially the following options:

1. To hold that an incontinent act, though voluntary, is not intentional: on this assumption we are free to hold, if we wish, both (i) that forming an intention to do a is identifiable with making a *fully*

present unconditional judgement in favour of *a*, and (ii) that a not fully present judgement in favour of *a* is incompatible with a fully present unconditional judgement against *a* (more generally, patently conflicting unconditional judgements are not compossible, even if one or both are not fully present to the judger). To adopt this option would seem heroic.

2. To allow that the incontinent man, at least sometimes, acts with an intention; in which case it must be allowed either that (i) patently conflicting unconditional value judgements are compossible, provided that at least one of them is not fully present to the judger; or that (ii) an intention to do *a* is not identifiable with a fully present unconditional judgement in favour of *a*; the most that could be maintained would be that making a fully present unconditional judgement in favour of *a* entails forming an intention to do *a* or, altenatively and less strongly, is incompatible with having an intention to do *b*, where *b* patently conflicts with *a*.

The upshot of these considerations with respect to the search for an adequate theory of incontinence seems to be that the following contending theses remain in the field, though some of them, particularly the first, may not appear very strong contenders:

1. The typical incontinent man (who does not do *a* though in some sense he thinks that he should) reaches only a not fully present 'all things before me' judgement in favour of *a*, which he combines with a fully present unconditional judgement against *a*, and (consequentially) with an intention against *a*. Together with this thesis go the theses that intention is identifiable with fully present unconditional judgement and that patently conflicting unconditional judgements are not compossible in any circumstances.

2. The typical incontinent man reaches a not fully present unconditional judgement in favour of *a*, which he combines with a fully present unconditional judgement, and an intention, against *a*. Together with this thesis go the theses that an intention is identifiable with a fully present unconditional judgement and that patently conflicting unconditional judgements *are* compossible provided that at least one of them is not fully present.

3. The typical incontinent man reaches a fully present unconditional judgement in favour of *a* which he combines with an intention against *a*, but not with a fully present unconditional judgement

against *a*. Together with this thesis go the theses that patently conflicting unconditional judgements are not compossible in any circumstances and that an intention is not identifiable with a fully present unconditional judgement, though it is perhaps true that a fully present unconditional judgement entails the presence of an intention (or at least excludes the presence of a contrary intention).

4. The 'naïve' view: the incontinent man reaches a fully present unconditional judgement in favour of *a* which he combines with an intention against *a*. Together with this thesis go the theses that the existence of a fully present unconditional judgement in favour of *a* carries no implications with regard to the presence or absence of an intention to do *a* or, again, to do something which patently conflicts with *a*. The 'naïve' view is uncommitted at this point with respect to the compossibility of patently conflicting unconditional value judgements.

A proper decision between these contending theses will clearly depend on the provision of a proper interpretation of the expression 'fully present', used by us a dummy, an undertaking which in turn will require a detailed examination of the phenomena of incontinence. These are matters which lie beyond the scope of this paper.

III

INTENTION AND *AKRASIA*[1]

CHRISTOPHER PEACOCKE

I

The *akrates* acts intentionally. So we will not have a good theory of *akrasia* until we have a good theory of intention; and conversely the requirement that it leave room for the possibility of *akrasia* is a condition of adequacy on an account of intention. My aim is to provide an account of intention and *akrasia* in the light of Davidson's important work on these subjects.

In recent writing on the philosophy of action several important distinctions have been made between various kinds of desires. Distinctions have been drawn between first- and second-order desires, reason-providing and reason-following desires, between desires one desires to be acting on and those which one does not desire to be acting upon, and so forth. But I would claim that almost all these distinctions are irrelevant or only obliquely relevant to the problem of *akrasia*. No intrinsic distinction *within* the class of desires can provide a full understanding of *akrasia*. For to have a desire is not yet to have an intention, and it is an intention that the *akrates* has. It can even be that two people have identical patterns of appetitive, underived desires to do something while one of them forms the intention to do it and the other does not form the intention. To say that their desires cannot then have the same motivational strength is to agree that we cannot omit intention: for a motivationally strongest desire is presumably one which causes the formation of an intention to act. We need to know what it is about intention that permits this possibility, and how intention *is* related to desire.

These remarks favour a duality in our account of action explanation. The duality is one of desire and intention, or more generally desire and motivational strength of desire. But actually we need a

[1] I have been helped by comments on earlier drafts of this paper from Allan Gibbard, Derek Parfit, David Pears, Stephen Schiffer, and David Wiggins.

trinity. We need further the agent's own view of the rationality of an action relative to a given set of reasons he has for or against the action. The *akrates* is irrational because although he intentionally does something for which he has some reason, there is a wider set of reasons he has relative to which he does not judge what he does to be rational.[2]

The need for the third component of this trinity may seem obvious enough, but in fact it is implicitly denied by any theory of *akrasia* which attempts to describe the phenomenon using only the notions of desire and motivational strength of desire. Let us call such theories *dualistic*. Dualistic theories include the decision-theoretic models of action explanation which I have encountered. The question to be raised for such theories is this: how do they characterize the irrationality of the *akrates*? Naturally such theories will have to deny that rational action is action on a motivationally strongest desire; but beyond this common rejection theories may differ in their positive suggestions about rationality. I suggest that one cannot give a satisfactory description of the irrationality of the *akrates* without the third element of the trinity and that the various distinctions between higher- and lower-order desires do not help in giving the required description as long as they occur in the context of a theory which makes use only of the motivational notion of strength.[3] I cannot hope to survey all possible types of dualistic theory to substantiate this suggestion, but I do aim to raise enough difficulties in a few paragraphs to motivate the construction of an alternative trinitarian theory of intention and *akrasia*. Davidson himself would not dispute the need for a trini-

---

[2] Strictly speaking, we could recover the first component of a trinitarian theory (desires) from a careful statement of the third component (the agent's relativized prima-facie reasons for action).

[3] My claim here could be established by examples like the following. There might be two people with identical patterns of desires, with identical motivational strengths. Suppose they will both choose alcohol rather than tobacco, given that they cannot have both. Is it not consistent with the description of the case so far that, since they differ in their beliefs about the effects of these substances, for one of them this is an akratic, irrational preference while for the other it is not? If this is indeed possible then the rationality of an action is not only not definable in terms of the resources employed in a dualistic theory, but it is not even supervenient upon truths stated using those resources. It is however unclear to me whether the underlying motivations of the holder of a dualistic theory would permit him to regard this example as a genuine possibility.

Of course there are other questions to be raised about dualistic theories: in particular those consequential upon the fact that motivational strength need not at all correspond to the strength of desires the agent weighs in his deliberations.

tarian theory: it is worth arguing for the general desirability of such a theory because if we want to revise Davidson's theory, we will have a constraint to which any revision should conform.

One response a dualistic theorist might make to account for the *akrates'* irrationality is to say that the *akrates* is irrational not in terms of his desires at the time of action, but in terms of the pattern of his desires over the whole of his later life. The *akrates* knows that the pattern of his desires, and particularly his strongest desire at the moment of akratic action, is temporary: it is irrational of him to act in a way which will not best satisfy the desires he knows he will have over a longer period. But this condition is certainly not sufficient for akratic action: the agent is akratic only if he *believes* it is rational for him to satisfy as best he can his desires over his later life. The problem of how to express this requirement within a dualistic theory remains. In any case the suggestion also does not avoid the original problem: for even in the case of someone who has the belief required for such action to be akratic, we must be presupposing some principle for weighting future desires other than by their motivational strength. The question of what this principle might be is just the future analogue of the problem we have already raised for dualistic theories applied to an agent at a given time.

A more sophisticated dualistic theory has been put forward by Stephen Schiffer. Suppose we represent the desire to ϕ by '$D(\phi)$' and the relation between desires 'is of greater motivational strength than' by '$>$'. Schiffer's theory is that a man has this pattern of desires when he ϕs akratically:

$$D(\phi) > D(\sim \phi)$$

and also

$$D(\text{not act on } D(\phi)) > D(\text{act on } D(\phi)).[4]$$

So for example if you eat chocolate akratically, your desire to eat it is stronger than your desire not to eat it: what makes you akratic is that your desire not to act on your desire to eat chocolate is stronger than your desire to act on that desire. Since of course intentional action is always action on the strongest desire (in the motivational sense of strength) then we can conclude from Schiffer's description that $D(\phi)$ is at least as strong as $D(\text{not act on } D(\phi))$: for if the second-order desire were stronger the agent could have acted on it

---

[4] 'A Paradox of Desire', *American Philosophical Quarterly* 13 (1976), 195-203.

by not ϕing. So far this just confirms our earlier point that a dualistic theory cannot identify rational action with action on a motivationally strongest desire. The question in which we are interested is: what alternative account of rationality could be given in this framework?

One proposal might be that rational action is action on the motivationally strongest desire provided that this desire is one the agent would have reason to have even if he did not in fact have it.[5] Certain desires resulting from bodily appetites are sometimes said not to be such desires. But this proposal would make the range of possible akratic actions much too narrow. There can be akratic choice between a pair of desires each of which one would have reason to have even if one did not have it: an agent may akratically decide to listen to a lecture a little longer rather than to leave and take the pills without which he has a rather higher chance of a heart attack.

A second proposal might be that rational action is always action on the desire upon which one has the strongest second-order desire to act. Here one must remember that 'strongest' for a dualistic theorist means motivationally strongest, and for that reason this second suggestion is also wrong. Because of the lingering effects of his puritan upbringing, an agent might find his desire not to act on his desire for sensuous pleasures motivationally stronger than his desire to act on such desires: this could be shown by his intentional cultivation of women he finds unattractive and consumption of food he does not like. But he may still regard these actions as irrational and consider that it would be better for him to shake off his inhibitions and to enjoy the life he sees his friends enjoying. So an agent can be akratic in having a second-order desire as his motivationally strongest second-order desire: and this problem could be reproduced at any level. This lends additional support to the view that a dualistic theory does not have sufficient resources to characterize the irrationality of the *akrates*.[6]

---

[5] A 'reason-following' (r-f) desire in Schiffer's terminology.

[6] Questions similar to those raised in the text about Schiffer's theory might be asked about Richard Jeffrey's stimulating 'Preference Among Preferences' (*Journal of Philosophy* 71 (1974), 377-91). There seem to be some cases of akratic smoking in which preferring abstaining to smoking (~ S pref S) really is a recognized option in some sense ranked above all the recognized options with which it is incompatible; this is what makes such smoking very irrational. As Jeffrey is well aware, we cannot hold that there really are such examples unless either optimality or ranking above is not explained in terms of decision theory of the current kinds; otherwise such examples of *akrasia* would receive contradictory descriptions.

Before suggesting an account of intention of my own in the context of a trinitarian theory, I will look at various theories of intention to see how well they accommodate *akrasia*. I shall also operate under the following self-denying ordinance: until the point at which I explicitly discuss the issue, I will not assume that there are any examples in which someone intends to do something but does not believe that he will do it. I will follow this policy in order to show that the arguments of the earlier parts of this paper can be accepted by one who holds that intention does imply such a belief.

II

(i) *A theory of better judgement*

Davidson says that the person who does *A* rather than *B* and does so intentionally makes an outright judgement that *A* is better than *B*.[7] On Davidson's theory this is to be distinguished from the judgement that *A* is better than *B* all things considered. So what judgement is it? Clearly it need not be true that in doing *A* intentionally the agent judges that *A* will best satisfy all of his desires and values over his whole life; many who smoke intentionally do not believe that of their smoking. Nor can 'better' in Davidson's claim mean morally or aesthetically better. Nor need the intended action be judged to be better given only the agent's present desires and values. On the basis of his present desires a man may come to the conclusion that it would be better to have a drink than to play tennis. But if at the last minute there comes to him a vivid image of last week's enjoyable game, he may nevertheless intentionally play tennis. Very often in the case of irrational action there is some imaginative or perceptual asymmetry of this kind between the courses of action in question, and its presence makes the irrational action more intel-

---

[7] This theory is implicit in 'How is Weakness of the Will Possible?' in *EAE*, pp. 21-42—see principles P1 and P2 (p. 23) and also p. 39: 'Intentional action . . . is geared directly to unconditional judgments like "It would be better to do *a* than to do *b*" . . . Practical reasoning does however often arrive at unconditional judgments that one action is better than another—otherwise there would be no such thing as acting on a reason.' The theory is explicit in 'Intending', in *EAE*, pp. 83-102.

On my notation: '*A*', '*B*', and '*E*' are always schematic for complete sentences, and are never variables over particular token events. '*φ*' is schematic for predicates with or without time specification as the context requires. For brevity's sake I have been careless with the English surrounding '*A*', '*B*', and '*φ*', which often needs alteration to produce sense when particular expressions are substituted for these letters. There are large issues here that I avoid in this paper.

ligible to us. But it seems wrong to insist that such a difference in vividness must always produce a change of belief in the agent about which course will best satisfy his present desires. This interpretation of 'better' in terms of best satisfaction of present desires would also have the consequence that for someone who thinks it rational to satisfy as best he can his present desires it is impossible to act akratically. Yet such akratic action does always seem possible provided the course of action chosen has some attractive feature that the alternatives do not.

Suppose however that we did come up with an interpretation of 'judge better' common to all cases of intentional action. There would still be a difficulty: for to make such a judgement is not yet to have settled the question of what one will try to *do*. This is shown clearly when we make a revision in the account in order to accommodate Buridan's ass examples. An ambidextrous and hungry man faced with qualitatively identical bowls of fruit to his right and his left will form the intention to go to a particular one of the two; to the left-hand one, say. One cannot say that he judges going to the left to be better. At most one can say that he judges it at least as good as the alternative. But *that* is something he judges with respect to both the chosen and the rejected courses of action—and he judges it before he formed any intentions about which way to go.

Is there an argument from the connection of practical reasoning with intention to a weaker conclusion, that intending always involves making a certain kind of evaluative judgement? Perhaps we can accept the view that we can always reconstruct some practical reasoning in any case of intentional action, provided we take the view that there always has to be some feature of a course of action which the agent finds attractive (it is not intelligible that he should just want something, without it appearing to him to have some specific attractive aspect). For in that case, even if there is no means–end reasoning, there will be the belief that the action has the feature found attractive and the pro-attitude to the feature. Now if there is always such reconstructible practical reasoning in any case of intentional action, we will always be able to write out a sketch of an action-explanation in a form that looks like a practical argument. Any sentence we write down as a conclusion of this argument must, given the nature of the enterprise, be something systematically related to the agent's intention in such a way that we can recover the content of his intention from the conclusion. But it does not follow that to have the intention is to judge the conclusion, nor even that this conclusion is actually something the agent judges.

It may be felt that the explanatory power of the relativization apparatus that Davidson uses itself lends support to the view that to have an intention is to make a judgement. For isn't the prima-facie relativization precisely a relativization of a judgement of comparative goodness? And do we not want to say that when certain reasons are operative in an agent's coming to a decision that he then detaches a non-relative judgement from some particular prima-facie judgement? The answer to these questions is that it would be an error to suppose that no separation of these points is possible. We can have the relativization without it being a relativization to a judgement of comparative goodness. Suppose what is in question is my ϕ-ing in two minutes. If I hold that there is something in favour of my ϕ-ing in two minutes in that it would have property ____, we can express what I hold thus:

fav(I ϕ in two minutes, ____ my ϕ-ing in two minutes ____).

This is just an abbreviation for 'there is something in favour of ϕ-ing in two minutes in that it would have property ____': so it expresses the content of the agent's thought, rather than being a statement about the agent's thought. The content is weak, apparently weaker than the thought that ϕ-ing then would be desirable or attractive. A course of action that it seems strained to call 'desirable' or 'attractive' in any respect may still on this weak notion have something to be said for it: it may, for instance, not involve making an effort or taking decisions.

If we use this locution, a statement of a prima-facie reason against ϕ-ing in two minutes would take the form

fav($\sim$ I ϕ in two minutes, ____ my ϕ-ing in two minutes ____);

and this is of course to be distinguished from the negation of the statement that its having property ____ is something in favour of my ϕ-ing in two minutes, a negation which is expressed

$\sim$ fav(I ϕ in two minutes, ____ my ϕ-ing in two minutes ____).

So in this framework an expression of neutrality towards ϕ-ing in respect of property ____ is

$\sim$ fav(I ϕ, ____ϕ____) & $\sim$ fav($\sim$ I ϕ, ____ϕ____).

Now if we remove the sentence which fills the first argument place of

fav(I ϕ in two minutes, ____ϕ____)

we obtain

I ϕ in two minutes.

This last sentence certainly determines the content of an intention, and can be regarded as obtained from the relativized judgement by detachment. But it is not a statement about goodness or betterness.

The use of 'fav' does not involve commitment to the view that some rather unspecific notion of goodness must play a central role in practical reasoning (moral or otherwise). On the contrary, specific evaluative concepts may be employed in the sentence filling the second argument place of 'fav'. Indeed the apparatus could be employed by one who holds a cognitivist theory of the application of specific evaluative concepts.

When we replace Davidson's 'pf' and 'better' with our 'fav' and corresponding notations, we actually restore a parallelism suggested in one insight of Davidson's, a parallelism that seems hard to defend on the remainder of his own theory. This is the parallelism he suggests between reasons for action and evidence for statements. (The parallel I am endorsing is one between 'fav' and a relational concept of epistemic probability: this is not an endorsement of Hempel's theory of probabilistic explanation.)[8] Davidson suggests that the probabilistic analogue of the move from

pf(A is better than B, E) and E is the totality of the agent's reasons

to

A is better than B

is the move from

pr(it will rain tomorrow, E) and E is the total available evidence

to

it will rain tomorrow.[9]

---

[8] Indeed, I would not agree with that theory, essentially for the reasons given in Peter Railton's 'A Deductive-Nomological Model of Probabilistic Explanation', *Philosophy of Science* 45 (1978), 206-26.

[9] Strictly the parallel ought to be stated with a notion of probability that is comparative as well as relative, for such is the notion of goodness here. But for simplicity I have followed Davidson himself at this point.

I suggest that the correct analogue is rather the move from the same starting point

pr(it will rain tomorrow, E) & E is the total available evidence

to

probably it will rain tomorrow.

Now Davidson's analogue may look reasonable given his notation; do we not in both cases detach a conclusion that has a certain property relative to the total available evidence or reasons? Is there not a simply analogy between 'pf' and 'pr'?

The reply is that Davidson's notation itself is not reasonable. His 'pf' functions simply as a formal relativization device: it would be analogous to an expression 'rel' if we chose to regiment 'Cain is brother of Abel' not as 'Brother(Cain, Abel)' but as 'rel(Cain, Abel, $\lambda x \lambda y$(Brother(x, y)))'. 'pr' on the other hand is more than such a relativization device: it incorporates the notion of probability. If we are going to assess the claim to parallelism properly, it is essential that we do not distort the case by employing asymmetrical notations.

In setting up parallel notations, we have a choice: we can follow either the 'pf' prototype or the 'pr' prototype. In the text here I will follow the 'pr' model: for our purposes, it is not a substantial question which is to be followed, provided that we stick to one model consistently. Suppose, then, we introduce a ternary operator 'btr(A, B, E)' for 'A is better than B relative to reasons E' and a ternary operator 'morepr(A, B, E)' for 'A is more probable than B relative to evidence E'. It is then clear that the analogue of the move from

btr(A, B, E) and E is total

to

A is better than B

is the move from

morepr(A, B, E) and E is total

to

A is more probable than B.

Christopher Peacocke

So Davidson's parallelism does not hold with a fair notation.[10]

We do of course also know that Davidson himself holds that to judge that A is best is to intend that A. The analogue of judging that A is best is judging that A is most probable outright. This restores the parallelism only under two special conditions. The first is that we already accept Davidson's theory of intention (so the parallelism could not be used as independent evidence for that theory). The second is that we hold that there is no difference between judging that A is most probable, and judging that A is true.

On the formulation in terms of 'fav', a parallelism is present without either of those problematic assumptions. The analogue of the move which corresponds to the formation of an intention, namely

>   fav(I ϕ, E) and E is total
>   I will ϕ,

is indeed

>   pr(A, E) and E is total
> A.

More generally we have the following structural correspondences:

fav(I ϕ, E) and E is total	pr(A, E) and E is total
morefav(I ϕ, I ψ, E) and E is total	morepr(A, B, E) and E is total
there is most to be said in favour of my ϕ-ing	it is probable that A
I will ϕ	A.

This allows an answer to a second objection to the parallelism. It is sometimes said that to judge that A is probable relative to E and to hold that E is true is not to judge that A is, in some respect, true, while it is the case that to judge that it is good that A relative to reasons E and to hold those reasons E *is* to hold that A is, in some respect, good. If we state the parallelism in the way I have been suggesting, then what corresponds to A being in some respect good is A's being in some respect probable, which seems acceptable; on the

---

[10] On the 'pf' model, the probabilistic analogue of the first move would be the step from 'pf(A is more probable than B, E) and E is total' to 'A is more probable than B', and not to A itself. So again the parallelism fails.

other hand what corresponds to the unintelligible '*A* is, in some respect, true' is the equally unintelligible 'In some respect, I ϕ'.

Suppose however that we accepted Davidson's account of intention. Does his theory then show how *akrasia* is possible? Even this may be questioned. Davidson says, with great plausibility, that the *akrates* does not necessarily hold 'logically contradictory beliefs' (*EAE*, p. 41). Certainly one must agree too that 'pf(*A* is better than *B*, *E*) and *E* is the set of total available reasons' does not entail '*A* is better than *B*'. But we should raise the question of whether this is just because the first is consistent with the existence of reasons not (at present) available (to us), such that relative to a set including those reasons it is not the case that *A* is better than *B*.[11] So suppose we now consider someone who judges that both

> pf(*A* is better than *B*, *E*) and *E* is the total set of available reasons

and

> $\sim \exists P(P$ is true and pf $(A$ is not better than B, E and $P))$.

As Davidson says, 'We do not want to explain incontinence as a simple logical blunder' (*EAE*, p. 40). So it would be an objection to Davidson's view if these two displayed conditions do imply that *A* is better than *B*. Now Davidson does say that ' "*a* is better than *b*, all things (viz. all truths, moral and otherwise) considered" surely does entail "*a* is better than *b*" ' (*EAE*, p. 40). But our imagined person, in judging the conjunction of the displayed conditions, is judging something that implies that *A* is better than *B*, all truths, moral and otherwise, considered; so he judges something that according to Davidson entails something that the *akrates* does not, on Davidson's theory, judge.

This argument does not of course need to be formulated in terms of Davidson's passing claim about the entailments of '*A* is better than *B*, all truths considered'. The essential question is whether there can really be a rational difference between the judgement that *A* is better than *E tout court* and the judgement that *A* is better than *B* relative to known applicable reasons and also relative to all true extensions of that set of reasons.[12]

---

[11] Recall that in the application of Davidson's apparatus, the reasons *E* will include indisputably factual information.

[12] Excluding, of course, the trivial case in which one of the truths is that *A* is better than *B*. It is not clear from Davidson's discussion whether failure to make this

It seems to me that Davidson's discussion of an imagined objector takes a wrong turning when he writes: 'When we say that *r* contains all that seems relevant to the agent, don't we just mean that nothing has been omitted that influences his judgement that *a* is better than *b*?' (*EAE*, p. 40). The objector should answer 'no' to this question that is put in his mouth: he should say that we don't mean anything about what influences his judgement but rather something about its content, and that in some cases the judgement may be as strong in content as the conjunction of our two displayed conditions.

Davidson might say that this argument is too clever by half. He might agree that anyone rational who judges our conjunction must judge that *A* is better than *B* outright; and then he might say that since to judge that *A* is better than *B* outright requires that the agent does *A* intentionally if he does either *A* or *B* intentionally, the person who judges the conjunction of the displayed conditions cannot be akratic. Hence, Davidson might conclude, the case does not present a difficulty for his theory. But to make such a reply would leave the relation between the relativized and the outright judgements of comparative goodness quite obscure. The relativized judgements, of which according to Davidson the all-things-considered judgement is a special case, is a purely intellectual judgement in the sense that one can make it without forming any particular intentions. How then can making a judgement that is the negation of an existential quantification of the relation in the relativized conditions require the formation of an intention?

One of the reasons why Davidson's account of *akrasia* is valuable is that the *way* the existence of akratic actions is reconciled with his principles P1 and P2 is independent of his theory of intention. The distinction between a relativized all-things-considered claim and an outright claim can be retained without retaining the theory that to intend something is to judge it best (and without retaining the somewhat notorious P2). In effect I shall do just that.

(ii) The belief theory

Can we say that to have an intention to do something is to have a non-inferential belief that one will do it, a belief with a certain causal ancestry? Davidson himself has also rejected such an identi-

---

extension is the reason he says that entailment 'surely' holds. In any case the entailment, which states a kind of supervenience, is plausible even with the exclusion.

fication (*EAE*, p. 95): so I will be very brief. Here are two arguments against the identification.[13] (1) There are great difficulties in giving a correct account of the right causal ancestry of the non-inferential belief that one will ϕ. We cannot say that an intention to ϕ is a non-inferential belief that one will ϕ that is caused by one's desire to ϕ: for some electrochemical set-up may be present in me (perhaps put there by a doctor) such that for some particular ϕ, whenever I desire to ϕ this causes—and perhaps even differentially explains[14] my having a belief that I will ϕ. Should then my belief be specified as the belief that I will ϕ intentionally? That would be closer but also apparently circular. (2) Intuitively, the cause of my having the belief that I will ϕ in a case in which I in fact intend to ϕ, is my having the intention to ϕ: such a causal relation is incompatible with the intention being the very same state as the belief.

These criticisms are neutral on the question of whether intention implies belief; they imply only that the intention is distinct from the belief.

(iii)· *A dispositional theory*

If an organism in the world has beliefs and desires and sometimes succeeds in acting upon them, the organism must have an executive ability; it must sometimes get into the state of being such that when it believes the moment for action has arrived, it acts. This is a disposition it has. I will outline here very tentatively a dispositional theory of intention which can be regarded as starting from such reflections. It is a consequence of this dispositional theory that there is no propositional attitude ψ (other of course than intending and trivial variants thereof) such that intending to ϕ is ψ-ing (perhaps in some special way) that ____ϕ____. Propositional attitude expressions may be embedded in such a no-content account, but the main operator in the definition of intending offered is not a propositional attitude verb.[15]

If an intention to ϕ is a disposition caused (perhaps differentially explained by) the desire to ϕ, what disposition is it? Perhaps

---

[13] The argument of section III below that someone can intend to do something without believing that he will do it also tells against this identification.

[14] In the sense of my *Holistic Explanation* (Oxford, 1979), Ch. II.

[15] In fact the account of intention I shall develop might be used to explain (but not to justify) Aristotle's view that the conclusion of a practical syllogism is an action.

D1:   the disposition to do what one believes to be a ϕ-ing if one is able when one believes the time for action has arrived.

(Henceforth 'doing what one believes to be a ϕ-ing' will be contracted to 'ϕ-ing'.) The first problem with this is over even the weakest indisputable belief implication of intention. D1 leaves open the possibility that the agent firmly believes that it is absolutely impossible for him to ϕ at any time: and this would be inconsistent with his having the intention to ϕ.

The other complication is that 'able' seems to mean roughly 'if the agent intends to and believes the moment for action has arrived, then he acts'. If it does, then to cite the above disposition will not be shown conclusively to advance theoretical understanding until we have some further positive account of ability: for the presence of that disposition follows immediately from the fact that the agent intends to ϕ together with the expansion of the ability condition. Dispositions analogous to the one cited will be truly statable for any other concept, psychological or not, dispositional or not, if we construct for them something standing to them as ability stands to intention. But our aim was to point out something special to intention.

I have no room in this paper to develop a less vacuous characterization of ability, and I will just have to hope that the rest of what I say makes it plausible that we ought to seek such a characterization. But I will remark that this problem over ability has analogues in other psychological notions. It is an essential part of the definition of at least certain kinds of memory trace that when the subject is prompted or stimulated in certain ways, the trace produces representations of past events. But some memory traces may be inaccessible, and so one wants to add the qualification 'if they are accessible' to this condition: and then we have the same problem once again—for it is natural to give a conditional characterization of accessibility. Even more clearly, there are analogous problems in the philosophy of perception. It would be good to give a uniform style of solution to these problems: one lead that seems promising is to exploit the thought that genuine intentions, memory traces, and perceptions are sources not just of belief but of knowledge.

Let us then bracket the problem of ability. Consider the suggestion that to intend to ϕ at t is to have the disposition (D2) to ϕ when one believes t has arrived, this disposition being caused by the desire to ϕ at t. Is this definition adequate, failures of ability aside?

A man's intentions can alter; and so can the dispositional properties of a given object. But the way in which variation with time is accommodated is not quite the same in each case. If we suppose that the properties of being strong, or agile, or immune from malaria are dispositional, they are properties a person x can have at one time t_0 and lose by t_1 because a counterfactual (or some family of them) of the form $A(x, t_0) \square \!\!\rightarrow B(x, t_0)$ may be true while $A(x, t_1) \square \!\!\rightarrow B(x, t_1)$ is false.[16] But if D2 states the disposition involved in intending to ϕ, how can a man at one time have the intention to ϕ and later lose it? For D2 contains no free time variables that can be evaluated with respect to different times. And we certainly must not say that if someone has at t_0 the intention to ϕ at t_2 it is true that if at t_0 he believes that t_2 has arrived, he will then ϕ. For that is not true: the agent may for instance know of t_0 that ϕ-ing then will not have the consequences he wants it to have.

Instead we need to say rather that to intend at t_0 to ϕ at t_2 is to be at t_0 in some state such that for any time at which one is in that state and believes that t_2 has then arrived, one ϕs then; that is, if our agent is x,

$$\exists S(S(x, t_0) \ \& \ \forall t((S(x, t) \ \& \ x \text{ believes at } t \text{ that } t_2 \text{ has arrived}) \ \square \!\!\rightarrow \phi(x, t))).$$

To lose this intention by time t_1 is for there to be no such state S one is in at t_1: one may, for example, stop being in such a state S from forgetfulness, or because one changes one's view of the likely circumstances at the time of the intended action. There are other properties that vary with time in the way intentions do. A bomb may have the property of being set to explode at 5 p.m. at one time and later lose the property: the police have experts whose job it is to turn a bomb from being in one state analogous to our S above to being in no such state.[17] So, with this much by way of clarification

---

[16] Following David Lewis, I abbreviate 'If it were the case that p, then it would be the case that q' by '$p \ \square \!\!\rightarrow q$'.

[17] D2 specifies the disposition involved in having an intention with respect to a particular time: what of general intentions, like the intention to complete one's income tax return some time within the next year? These can be explained in terms of definite intentions roughly along the following lines. To intend at t_1 to ϕ some time in the next year is to be at t_1 in some state S such that if one is in S throughout any interval one believes to be next year, then there is some time in that interval such that one's being in S is part of the cause of one's forming the intention to ϕ at that time. Of course we should also add clauses that the presence of the state is caused by

behind us, let us ask again whether such a modified dispositional account is correct, failures of ability aside.

The first difficulty is that any belief implications of intending have been omitted, even the belief that one will ϕ at t_2 if one can. Here there may seem to be a dilemma. If we do not write any belief implication of intending into the account of intending, then the account is wrong. But if we do write in the belief condition, then we will not be able to say, as we wished to, that intention *causes* belief.

But that last sentence commits a familiar fallacy. It is part of an appropriate definition of a stimulant that taking it improves physical performance. It does not follow that having taken a stimulant is not part of the causal explanation of someone's performing well in a race. Perhaps it does indeed follow that the stimulant must have some other explanatorily relevant description. But then of course so can the intention. This suggests that we add to the account of intention that the state that is the ground of the disposition we cited also cause the agent's non-inferential belief that he will ϕ at t, or that he will ϕ if he can at t.[18]

We also need to consider the relations between our earlier remarks about the structure of practical reasoning and our later suggestions about what it is to have an intention. We discussed earlier the 'detaching' of a conclusion of the form 'I will ϕ at t' from a relativized judgement. What goes on according to our account of intention when such detachment moves are made? There are reasons for thinking that what we have so far said is too crude to capture all the distinctions we want to make here.

Suppose someone has to choose between working and relaxing. Each course has some considerations in its favour; but, let us suppose, the agent judges that all things considered it would be best for him to relax. Now suppose too that he does indeed relax, and intentionally, but that his all-things-considered judgement is quite inoperative in his pursuing this course of action. What influences him in deciding to relax are just those considerations that prima facie favour relaxation, and not his all-things-considered judgement: he detaches the conclusion that he will relax from a rela-

a certain desire and causes a belief, clauses of a form that will become apparent from the rest of the text. We can write analogous conditions for other quantifiers replacing 'some' in 'intending to ϕ at some time in the next year'.

[18] Note too that the account so far (as well as each of its refinements below) allows but does not require that coming to have an intention is itself intentional.

tivized judgement the second term of which does not include all his reasons.

The account so far given is too crude to capture the distinction between the case in which he acts on his all-things-considered judgement and that in which he acts intentionally in the same way, but not on his all-things-considered judgement. That the underlying state *S* is caused by the desire to relax does not discriminate the cases. In both examples we can say that the desire to relax causes the agent to be in the underlying state *S*, and in neither case could we possibly say that that was the complete cause (since non-psychological factors will also be causes). I suggest that we refine the account, and make the necessary link with the earlier description of the structure of practical reasons, by requiring of the state *S* that there be some reasons the agent has which favour his relaxing at *t*, and the fact that they favour it is a cause of his being in state *S*. So in our example the agent's being in the relevant state *S* is caused by his holding that fav(relaxing, his reasons for relaxing); it is not caused by the fact that he holds that fav(relaxing, all his reasons).

I have said nothing so far about events of trying. This is not from any acceptance of Ryle's criticisms of volitional theories:[19] on the contrary, Ryle's objections are not hard to answer.[20] It may indeed be tempting to hold that to be trying to do something is simply to intend to do it and believe the moment for action has arrived. I shall argue shortly that this equation is false: but even if it were true, it would not show that we do not need to refer to events of trying, since they may be needed in a good theory of intention. A strong argument for such a view would be provided by examples suggesting that the conditions for intention I have given are not sufficient.

Here then is such an example. Suppose that (unknown to them) human beings happened to be wired up in such a way that if they want for some particular reason to have a distinguished face suddenly at fifty, this desire causes them to be in some state *S* which, if they remain in it, makes them suddenly look distinguished when they believe themselves to be turning fifty. We could suppose too that this state causes a belief that the subject will look distinguished

---

[19] *The Concept of Mind* (London, 1949), Ch. III (2): 'The Myth of Volitions'.
[20] For some attempts at answers, see A. Goldman, 'The Volitional Theory Revisited', in *Action Theory* (Dordrecht, 1976), ed. M. Brand and D. Walton, pp. 67-84; and for some more, see D. Pears, 'The Appropriate Causation of Intentional Basic Actions', *Critica* 7 (1975), 39-69.

at fifty: this belief could even be knowledge. Yet such a person would not intend to look distinguished at fifty.

There is no such intention because the person's suddenly looking distinguished is not caused by his trying to look distinguished. It seems to me that other ways of accounting for the example without reference to trying are unsatisfactory. It would prima facie be circular to require that the disposition involved in having the intention to ϕ at t is to ϕ intentionally under given conditions. It would be incorrect too to say that there is no intention in the example because the physical state underlying the disposition is not of the same kind as other genuine intentions: for there is no reason why, particularly after surgery, some particular kind of intention should not be physically realized in a way quite different from other intentions. All this then suggests that the disposition involved in intending to ϕ at t is one to try to ϕ if one is able when one believes t to have arrived.[21]

It would be a mistake to think that the move to a disposition to try means that the ability complication no longer arises. The ability complication can arise with respect to trying itself. Someone can intend to do something and—perhaps because it is so terrible— when the time arrives be unable to try to do it. He cannot bring himself to make the attempt, even though his connecting nerves and muscles are not defective. We are not concerned here with someone who thinks he has an intention but does not: what distinguishes our man is that if he were able to try to ϕ, he would try, and all else being well, he would ϕ. The point also shows that intending to do something and believing the moment for action has arrived are not together sufficient for trying.

Let us summarize the main features of the account of intention which we have assembled to date. We will use 'A( )' schematically for the unspecified predicate of conditions which holds of a condition iff were that condition to hold, it would be sufficient in the circumstances for an agent's being able to try to ϕ. Then so far we have said that:

> an agent intends at t_0 to ϕ at t_1 iff
> he is at t_0 in some state S such that
> (i) there are some reasons R such that he is caused to be in S at
> t_0 by his holding that fav(he ϕs at t_1, R).

[21] The truth of this claim does not imply that trying can be understood prior to the notion of intention. It may be that they have to be introduced simultaneously and functionally relative to other psychological notions.

(ii) there is some condition C such that $A(C)$, and if he is in state S when he believes t_1 to have arrived and C holds then, he tries to ϕ at that time.

(iii) his being in S at t_0 causes him to have the non-inferential belief that he will ϕ at t_1.[22]

III

We cannot any longer postpone discussion of the question of whether if an agent intends to do something, he believes he will do it. This is not an issue irrelevant to the concerns of this paper, for it affects one's conception of practical reasoning. If we reject the belief implication, we cannot say (as I did earlier) that when I form the intention to ϕ, my holding that relative to certain reasons there is something in favour of ϕ-ing causes a non-inferential belief that I will ϕ.

There are many examples in which an agent plans to act, knowing his chance of success to be very low: in such cases he does not have the belief that he will succeed. It is clear that writers differ in their judgements about whether it is correct in such cases to say that the agent intends to produce the effect. My own intuition is that it is correct: one can intend to hit a croquet ball through a distant hoop while believing one's chances of success are tiny. (Any misleadingness involved in saying that one intends to hit the ball through the hoop can be explained in other ways.) But this disagreement about such examples does not matter for our purposes. For what is undisputed is that if the agent does succeed in getting the ball through the hoop, then he does so intentionally. In so far as our interest is in providing a general theory of what it is for an event to be intentional under a description, our concern must be with some notion of aiming to do something, a notion which, whether or not it can be identified with intending, does not have the belief implication. It is such a weaker notion that is common to a wider class if not to all

[22] There is one minor qualification. Someone may intend to make a cheese soufflé and to make a chocolate soufflé, but in fact have only enough eggs for one. He is able to make each but not both. A similar problem arises for trying: someone who forms both the intention to say one thing on the phone and the intention simultaneously to write exactly the opposite may find himself unable to try to do both, though perfectly able to try to do each by itself. Here is one way out: we could define the disposition corresponding to all the intentions an agent has with respect to a given time, and require that the ability condition be fulfilled with respect to all, and not just *in sensu diviso*.

cases of intentional action. I will henceforth write as if the weaker notion were intention, but these remarks suggest that those who disagree with this label should still be interested in what it labels.

If intention does not imply belief, does it perhaps imply something weaker? Does it perhaps imply that the subjective probability of what is intended's coming to pass is greater than it would be if the agent did not have the intention?[23] Even this claim seems to me too strong. A twenty-first-century child's top might be as follows. It moves randomly in a circumscribed area, so that the probability of its being in the northern quadrant of the given area at noon is one quarter. It may also contain a device sensitive to the heat of a human hand, a device which makes the top move away from the hand and move away too from the northern quadrant. The top may be so difficult to grasp that the agent's chance of placing the top in the northern quadrant at noon is one fifth. So the chances of his succeeding are less than the chances of the top's being there if he had not intervened; and the agent may know all this. Nevertheless if the agent succeeds, his placing the top in the area is intentional. The unusual features of this example do not necessarily make it pointless for the agent to intervene: it may be a game of skill to place the top there intentionally.

Not all examples of this kind can be dismissed as cases in which only the *effects* of the agent's action are less subjectively probable than they would otherwise have been. It might be that if I am not trying to do anything with my arm, there is a thirty per cent chance that I will have a muscular spasm in which my left fist clenches. If I try to do something with my left hand, that cuts off the mechanism which produces spasms in that hand. But if my nerves to my left hand have almost all gone, my chances of clenching my left fist when I try may be only twenty per cent. All of this may be known to me: and it does not prevent me from intending to clench my left fist, and if I succeed, I will clench it intentionally. But my intentional clenching of my fist when I am lucky is not an effect of my action: it *is* my action.

What makes these examples so unusual is that the chances of what is intended coming about are greater if the agent does nothing. This is not the case with the vast majority of our intentional actions;

---

[23] Cf. David Pears, 'Intention and Belief', in this volume. What is intended should be described without terms implying intentionality if the claim is not to suffer from problems of triviality.

and the fact that it is not can be used by someone sceptical about the necessity of even the probabilistic belief for intention to account for the presence of the illusion that there is such an implication. It may well be that the strongest belief implications of the intention to do something are the belief that it may be possible to do it and the belief that it may be possible that what is intended come about as a result of the agent's efforts. Anything stronger need not be present in all cases of intentional action.

If we drop the belief implication, what becomes of the parallel between practical and probabilistic reasoning? What I suggest is that in the parallel I endorsed earlier, we replace 'I will ϕ' throughout by 'I will do what I can to ϕ'. When I form the intention to ϕ, my judging that there is something to be said in favour of ϕ-ing given certain reasons causes me to believe that I will do what I can to ϕ. The qualification 'what I can' means that this belief is not falsified if I find I am unable to try to ϕ (so that not even the initiating event in the neural cortex takes place), nor if any efferent nerves are severed; nor if conditions outside my body are not favourable.

It may be objected that this revision cannot be correct: since I can neither intend to do nor believe that I will do what I believe to be impossible, the qualification 'what I can' adds nothing. This objection misconstrues the role of 'what I can', or the 'if' in the equivalent 'I will ϕ if I can'. The qualification is present because the content of the belief leaves open the possibility that one will not be able to ϕ. (This is a time-relative possibility.) The qualification does *not* function by cutting down the class of conditions excluded by one's belief from those in which one does not ϕ whether or not it is possible to ϕ to those in which one does not ϕ and it is possible to ϕ. The qualification is similar to that in the sentence 'The water will do what it can to move to the same level in the two tubes': this is a weaker claim than 'The water will move to the same level in the two tubes'—and not because one allows that water will do things it cannot do.[24]

---

[24] It may be asked: if we make the qualifications just suggested, why not add also 'and if I do not change my mind and nothing unexpected happens'? But when an agent has an intention he does believe (not necessarily with *certainty* of course) that neither of these two kinds of event will occur. If this were not so, forming an intention now would not always be something that settles now for the agent the question of what he will try to do (if he can) in the future.

IV

It remains to draw together the two main threads of this paper: to connect the account of intention with *akrasia*.

On the account of intention I have outlined, intending to do something is not identified with any particular judgement, belief, or something held to be the case by the agent. There are indeed judgements involved in intending to ϕ—a prima-facie judgement in favour of ϕ-ing and a belief that one will do what one can to ϕ; yet to have an intention is not to make these judgements, but is to be in a state causally intermediate between them, a state that is a ground of a certain disposition. Such a theory allows an agent to be irrational simply in what he does without being irrational in thought. (If the akratic agent forms his intentions intentionally, then he may be irrational in the formation of his intentions, which is just a special case of irrationality in action.) By contrast, any theory which identifies having an intention with making an evaluative judgement in favour of the course of action is under pressure to elucidate two senses of 'think better': one of these will correspond to the intentionality of the *akrates*'s action, the other will correspond to its irrationality. In being free of this pressure, the dispositional theory is also free of the danger of explaining *akrasia* as a more or less complex inferential blunder. If having an intention is not making a judgement at all, forming an *akratic* intention cannot be regarded as a sign of a defective process of reasoning to a conclusion.

I do not wish to leave the impression that I think that there are no remaining general theoretical problems posed by *akrasia* (as opposed to problems about particular kinds of *akrasia*). One such problem is posed by the point upon which we touched earlier, that commonly there is some perceptual or imaginative asymmetry between the courses of action when an akratic choice is made. The question is whether we ordinarily operate with a theory which, though not a theory of the agent's reasons, is nevertheless a psychological theory, a theory according to which such imaginative or perceptual asymmetries, which relate to the object of the akratic agent's attention at the time of the formation of his intention, are required for akratic action to be possible. The supposition of such a theory would explain several phenomena. We do find *akrasia* especially puzzling when there are no imaginative or perceptual asymmetries: it is hard to understand the man who with two bottles of the same kind of wine in front of him, and with no imaginative differences between the two, chooses the one he believes to be the less good vintage. A link between imaginative or perceptual asymmetries and attention would also explain why we find akratic action hard to understand if someone is concentrating on—attending to—some statement of his reasons against the akratic course. The details and status of any such theory merit further thought. The development of an account of this theory would be part of the wider project of showing how the claim that intentional actions are events which are intelligible to us in a certain way from the agent's standpoint is to be reconciled with the fact that some actions are akratic.

IV

INTENTION AND BELIEF

D. F. PEARS

How is the statement that I intend to perform a ϕ action connected with the statement that I believe that I shall perform one? It is usually assumed that the future factual belief is part of the essence of intending, so that the first of the two statements implies the second. However, Davidson has recently made the interesting suggestion that the connection is looser than this.[1] His idea is that the first statement cancellably implicates the second.[2] This connection is set up when I say 'I intend to perform a ϕ action' in a certain context. It is not built into the essence of intending, but is only a feature of communicating intentions. That is why it can be cancelled.

In this paper I shall argue that Davidson's account of the connection between intention and belief does fit our conversations about our intentions. Nevertheless it is not an independent theory and should not be offered as a rival of the traditional theory that belief is part of the essence of intending. No doubt, the traditional theory needs to be developed with caution if it is to avoid counter-examples, but it should not be rejected. In fact, the conversational implicature appears to be founded on the essential link between intention and belief. If this really is so, the two theories are not rivals but partners and the theory of implicature should be seen as a superstructure based on the traditional theory.

I shall begin by taking Davidson's theory in the spirit in which it is offered, as a rival of the traditional theory. We need not be too concerned at the start with the precise nature and strength of the attitude associated with intending. It can be identified roughly as belief, and the details and qualifications will emerge as we proceed. However, we do need to know something about the basis of the

---

[1] Davidson, 'Intending', University of North Carolina Colloquium, 1974, printed in a slightly altered form in *EAE*, pp. 83-102.

[2] *EAE*, p. 100. Roughly, H. P. Grice's concept: see 'The Causal Theory of Perception', *Proceedings of the Aristotelian Society*, Supp. Vol. 25 (1961), 121-51.

suggested implicature. Is it like this? If A likes B, it does not follow that he will treat B well or that he believes that he will treat B well, but if he tells B that he likes him, B will be entitled to believe that he will treat him well and that he shares this belief, unless he adds a cancellation of the entitlement: for example, he might add 'I'm a sadist'. So if A adds no such cancellation, and if he is sincere in what he does and does not say, he too must believe that he will treat B well.

Davidson evidently thinks that the connection between intention and future factual belief is just like this. For according to him, when I say 'I intend to do it' my future factual belief is directly connected with my saying it and not with the intention itself. He also regards the connection as cancellable. For he says that 'adding "if I can" . . . may serve to cancel an unwanted natural suggestion of saying one intends to do something'.[3]

But why does my saying 'I intend to do it' naturally suggest that I believe that I will do it? Because 'if I say . . . "I intend to do it" . . . in the right context, I entitle a hearer to believe I will do it, and since I know I entitle him to believe it, I entitle him to believe I believe I will do it'. In short 'if I say "I intend to do it" . . . under certain conditions . . . I *represent myself* as believing that I will'.[4]

This works, as far as I can see, exactly like the announcement of personal affection. However, it does raise an important question. When A tells B that he likes him, the implicature is partly based on the fact that affection necessarily tends to produce good treatment. Hence B is entitled to believe that A will treat him well and that A shares this belief. But when A tells B that he intends to perform a ϕ action, what analogous basis is there for B's belief that A will perform one and that he shares this belief?

If 'I intend' were like 'I promise', there would be no analogous basis in this case. For the speech-act of saying 'I promise' is simply governed by the convention that it gives the entitlement directly. Davidson rightly rejects the idea that 'I intend' works in this way,[5] but he leaves a gap in his theory, a question unanswered. On what is B's entitlement to his belief based when A tells him that he intends to do it? It seems that it must be partly based on the necessary connection between an intention and the tendency to produce the intended action, just as his entitlement to the other belief was partly

---

[3] *EAE*, p. 100.   [4] *EAE*, p. 91.   [5] *EAE*, p. 90-1.

based on the necessary connection between personal affection and the tendency to produce good treatment.[6]

It is important that this connection underlies the implicature that Davidson offers as the link between 'I intend to do it' and 'I believe that I shall do it'. For it shows that the implicature theory relies *au fond* on a fact about intentions, and, if I am right, on an essential fact. So when A says 'I intend to do it', he too will be aware of this fact, and if it is an essential fact, the traditional theory will be vindicated, because A's statement will simply imply that he is going to do it. There are, of course, counter-examples which suggest that it is not an essential fact, and the traditional theory needs to be made invulnerable to them. But it is clear from the start that a full development of the implicature theory must include the very point from which the traditional theory is a natural development, and that suggests that the two theories should be seen not as rivals but as partners.

The only way to make the traditional theory invulnerable to counter-examples would be to work out a more subtle account of the future factual belief that is linked to intending. If the belief could be given a fairly weak content, the counter-examples might be evaded. Then it would be possible to preserve the traditional theory that the belief is necessarily connected with the intention itself rather than cancellably connected with its announcement. There might still be cancellable implicatures of beliefs, but only of beliefs with stronger contents than the belief that is necessarily connected with intending. In any case, the traditional theory must be seen as an answer to two independent questions, one about the point of attachment and the other about what is attached.

Let us take first the traditional answer to the question about the point of attachment, and inquire why Davidson rejects it. He uses two arguments against it. One is not meant to provide any direct support for rejecting it but only a diagnosis of its error, if indeed it is an error. The other provides direct support for rejecting it.

His first argument is that the traditional view loses its attractiveness when a certain confusion has been diagnosed.[7] He thinks that its supporters conflate two true theses about sincerity and so arrive

---

[6] But there is a difference between the two cases. It seems possible that A might like B without believing that his affection for B conferred any probability on his treating B well, but the analogous possibility does not exist for intentions.

[7] *EAE*, p. 91.

at a false one. It is a true thesis that, whatever the context, if I say sincerely 'I intend to perform a ϕ action' I must believe that I intend to perform one. It is also a true thesis that if I say sincerely to someone else 'I intend to perform a ϕ action', I must believe that I will perform one. But it is false that, whatever the context, if I say sincerely 'I intend to perform a ϕ action', I must believe that I will perform one. For though my sincerity guarantees both that I intend to perform a ϕ action and that I believe that I will perform one, the two guarantees work in different ways. The first one is independent of the context, but the second one holds only when I tell someone else that I intend to perform a ϕ action. This argument is purely diagnostic.

His second argument directly supports his rejection of this part of the traditional theory. The argument is that I can perform a ϕ action intentionally without believing that I am doing so, and, therefore, I can intend to perform a ϕ action without believing that I shall do so. He says: 'In writing heavily on this page I may be intending to produce ten legible carbon copies. I do not know, or believe with any confidence, that I am succeeding. But if I am producing ten legible carbon copies, I am certainly doing it intentionally.'[8] He then observes that, though such examples do not actually disprove the thesis, that intending essentially involves future factual belief, they make it very hard to accept.

This is a powerful counter-example to the thesis that intention essentially involves future belief. However, it is important to remember that this thesis is an answer to two independent questions, one about the point of attachment and the other about what is attached. Davidson does not allow what is attached to be weaker than belief with some confidence, and using this threshold he argues that the point of attachment cannot be the intention itself and so must be its announcement. Another reaction to his argument would be to lower the threshold in order to preserve the traditional view about the point of attachment.

Let me develop this line of thought and see whether it can be made good. First, as a rough approximation, it might be argued that a minimal future factual belief is an essential part of every intention. The agent must believe that his intention to perform a ϕ action makes it probable that he will perform one. The probability may be very low, but he must believe that it exists and that his

[8] *EAE*, p. 92.

intention confers it on his performance. If he explicitly dissociated his 'intention' from this minimal belief, he would be announcing it as something completely ineffective, and so as something more properly called 'a wish'.

This formulation of the traditional theory invites two questions. Does it need to be adapted to deal with cases in which the agent believes that his action is overdetermined? And why must the implied belief be so minimal?

The simplest case of believed overdetermination would be one in which the agent believed that even if he did nothing, an independently effective sequence of events outside his body would probably produce the result that he desired. Alternatively, he might believe that such a sequence would occur within his body. Either way, he could choose between intentionally letting events take their course or forming the intention to produce the result off his own bat, which would make an honest action of it. Now the interesting thing is that he might believe that the probability of the result would be lower if he formed the intention to produce it in the ordinary positive way.[9] So we cannot say that he must believe that his intention would confer on the result a higher probability than would have been conferred on it by the independent effective sequence of events operating without his intention. We can only ascribe to him the non-comparative belief that his intention would confer some probability on the result.

It is important that he believes this in the circumstances in which he forms his intention. For in a case in which he also believes that an independently effective sequence of events would confer a higher probability on the desired result it might occur to him that if that sequence had not been going to occur, the effectiveness of his intention would be impaired. This thought would inhibit his belief that if the sequence had not been going to occur, his intention would confer some probability on his performance. True, he could sometimes justifiably dismiss the thought; but not always. So we cannot ascribe the counterfactual belief to him in all cases of overdetermination. We can only say that he must believe that if the independently effective sequence was blocked without any impairment of the effectiveness of his intention, his intention would keep whatever effectiveness he believes it to have as things are. But that is only

[9] I owe this point and the method of dealing with it to Christopher Peacocke.

a roundabout way of saying that he must believe that as things are, his intention confers some probability on his performance.

These cases of overdetermination raise an interesting question about the correct description of the achieved result,[10] but they do not require any modification of the formulation of the agent's minimal belief. But what if the agent believed that, if he formed the intention to perform a ϕ action, his intention would initiate a sequence of events that would militate against its own effectiveness?[11] For example, there are card-games in which one gets rid of disadvantageous cards by playing them face downwards unchallenged, and one might believe that one's opponent was a thought-reader. Or, to take a loop within the body, someone might believe that the formation of his intention would produce an internal obstacle, such as nervousness.[12]

It does not seem necessary to modify the formulation of the agent's minimal belief in the light of these examples. If he believed that the events on the loop would reduce the effectiveness of his intention to zero, he simply could not form it. Otherwise, he could form it, but with a lower probability written into his implied belief. If we combine the distinguishing feature of these examples with believed overdetermination, we will get some very complex cases, but it does not seem likely that they will contain anything new.

But why is the implied belief so minimal? The reason is that if we are looking for a future factual belief that is an essential part of every intention, we have to pitch it very low. For an agent can intend to do something that he assesses as extremely difficult and he can announce his intention without qualifying it in any way, if everyone else shares, and is known to share, his assessment of the difficulty. If I say of someone that he intends to climb Mount Everest, the project is one of such notorious difficulty that nobody is misled if I omit the qualification 'if he can'.[13] The same applies when he himself says that he intends to climb Mount Everest. In such a case his intention is compatible with his own very low estimate of the probability of success, but the minimal belief is still essential.

However it would be a mistake to rest content with the universal

---

[10] When is it something done by the agent?

[11] David Charles drew my attention to this possibility.

[12] See Davidson on the opposite effect of nervousness: 'Freedom to Act', *EAE*, pp. 63-82.

[13] See H. P. Grice, 'Intention and Uncertainty', *Proceedings of the British Academy*, 57 (1971), 265.

attachment of the minimal belief. For we can regard this result as a sort of bridgehead which can be expanded by a second argument. The second argument starts from the question why the future factual belief attached to an intention is sometimes minimal and sometimes amounts to certainty. Evidently the variation depends partly on the agent's estimate of the probability of each step's following its predecessor in the development of his action and partly on the probability that he assigns to the first step, his initiation of the required bodily movement. The probability that he assigns to the first step will often be high, but thereafter there will be great variation in his estimates of the probabilities. True, certain projects will have standard probabilities, but the agent may happen to have a belief which makes his estimate of the probability in his particular case non-standard.

This explanation of the variation in the content of the future factual belief puts us in a position to argue in the following way. We may say that when someone intends to perform a ϕ action, he must have a positive belief about his future ϕ action, but the precise content of his positive belief may vary from minimal upwards. The reason why he must have a positive belief has nothing to do with his announcing his intention to anyone else. It is simply that it is an essential part of the intention itself. The reason why its precise content varies from case to case is that the agent's other beliefs may affect his estimates of the stepwise probabilities. However, there is a fairly definite constraint on the final probability that he assigns to his complete performance: if he is rational, it will be sensitive to the effect of his other relevant beliefs. So given those beliefs and his rationality, it is necessary that if he intends to perform a ϕ action, he believe with a fairly definite probability that he will perform it. Never mind that this is only a model and that in real life the assigned probability will seldom be very definite. The point is that the model allows us to vary the precise content of the attached belief without abandoning the idea that the point of attachment is the intention itself and not its announcement.

Here, then, are two arguments for the traditional view that the future factual belief is an essential part of intending. The first tries to identify a minimal belief that cannot be detached from any intention. The second tries to explain the actual variation in the precise content of the attached belief without falling back on the idea that the attachment is an example of implicature.

There is also a third argument, that the implicature theory is too social to be true.[14] This argument might start from the assumption that human intentions and their analogues in other animals must be basically alike. So if the analogue of an intention in an animal that lacks speech produces a direct effect on other things that it is doing, it is incredible that when a similar effect is produced in me by my intention to perform a ϕ action, it is not a direct effect of my intention but only of my announcement of it. Even if the effect of an intention recorded in my diary as a reminder could be explained in this way, the explanation could hardly be extended to my non-verbalized intentions.[15] It would be most conspicuously inapplicable to intentions governing a linked sequence of actions rapidly performed. How could my momentary intentions in a game of tennis have an introjected social basis?

So here are three arguments in favour of the traditional theory about the connection between intention and belief. It is important to remember that they are arguments against the implicature theory only when that theory is applied to all intentions and is offered as a rival of the traditional theory rather than as a partner of it. However, before looking at a possible form that the partnership might take, I want to ask whether the first two of my three arguments put me in a position to deal with Davidson's carbon copy counter-example.

His argument about that case starts from the premiss that I do produce the tenth carbon copy intentionally. That is unquestionably true. It is also true that 'I need not know or believe with any confidence that I am succeeding'.[16] However, there is no reason whatsoever to suppose that even in this case I could lack the minimal belief that my intention confers some probability on my performance.

This may appear to miss the subtlety of Davidson's counter-example. For I might believe that I would have been just as likely to produce ten carbon copies if I had only intended to produce nine, and the tenth was an unintended by-product. This would be a par-

[14] Grice used this argument in his reply to Davidson's paper 'Intending' at the North Carolina Colloquium in 1974.

[15] In 'Intending' Davidson identifies the formation of an intention with the making of an unconditional value judgement in favour of the project. There are objections to this identification, but even if it is correct, it does not facilitate the extension of the explanation.

[16] Davidson, 'Intending'.

ticularly interesting case of believed overdetermination, but it does not require any modification of the formulation of the implied minimal belief. The distinguishing feature of the case is that the independently effective event is actually included in the formation of the intention to produce ten carbon copies. For I cannot form that intention without forming the intention to produce no fewer than nine. It follows that I cannot believe that my intention to produce ten would have been equally effective without the occurrence of the independently effective event. So this is a case in which I could not dismiss the thought that if the independently effective event had not been going to occur, the effectiveness of my intention would be impaired. However, the earlier discussion of this point showed that it casts no doubt on the correctness of the formulation of the minimal implied belief.

There is a point that needs to be made about the principle of Davidson's argument about the case of the tenth carbon copy. The principle is that if the agent can doubt whether he is now doing what he intends to do, then *a fortiori* he can doubt whether he will do what he intends to do. I have rejected the premiss that the agent has no positive belief about his success when he is writing heavily on the paper. But I have not yet questioned the principle of the *a fortiori* argument, because, as already explained, a person may not be sure that he will even initiate an action that he intends to perform in the future.

However, it is just possible that the force of this *a fortiori* argument is sometimes cancelled by another, independent factor. It may be that the precise content of the positive belief that we require in a person who announces an intention is affected by a pragmatic consideration. Because the future is uncertain and we need to be able to rely on future factual implications, it may be that we require the agent's estimate of the probability of performance to be high when he announces an intention in advance, but less high when his action has actually been performed and he says that his performance was intentional. If we caught him at the very moment of writing and asked him whether he intended to produce a tenth carbon copy, we might still require his estimate to be high if he gave an affirmative answer. If this pragmatic consideration does operate, it may sometimes cancel the force of the consideration on which Davidson's *a fortiori* argument relies. If so, the semantics of 'intend' and 'intentionally' are less tidy than might have been hoped.

I now turn to the larger question which underlies this whole discussion: Is it possible to show that the implicature theory about the connection between intention and belief is not a rival of the traditional theory but a partner of it? Naturally, if this can be shown, it will not follow that all implicatures are reducible to implications. The point would be that in this particular case the implicature is founded on a feature of the essence of intending.

Let us start from the very special case of the tenth carbon copy intentionally produced. Even in this case the intention must involve the minimal future factual belief. In other cases the agent's estimate of the stepwise probabilities will be much higher and the final result may even be certainty. The source of this variation in the precise content of the agent's belief has been explained: it is the effect of the agent's other relevant beliefs. This yields a theory of rational intention-based belief. It remains to be shown how a theory of implicature can be constructed on this basis.

First the facts supporting the implicature theory need to be briefly described. In our deliberative conversations with one another we often say things like 'I intend to do it but I am doubtful about the last step in my plan', or, more puzzlingly, 'I intend to do it if I can'. These are evidently cancellations of some element in the associated future factual belief. So we need to know what the belief would be if it remained uncancelled, what is cancelled, and what (if anything) cannot be cancelled.

The answer to the last question is that the minimal belief cannot be cancelled, but the answers to the first two questions are less easy to give. So far I have argued that the minimal belief provides a sort of bridgehead to further, stronger beliefs. This bridgehead can be exploited in a way that is sensitive to the agent's other relevant beliefs. However, though this gives us a theory of rational intention-based beliefs, it does not give us a theory of implicature, because the agent's audience will usually be unaware of his other relevant beliefs. What is needed is shared standards of probabilities which will serve as a starting point. Cancellations will then be added if the agent's other relevant beliefs cause his estimate of the probability of performance to deviate from the shared standard. The shared standard is simply the standard probability of success that is generally assigned to types of project.[17] If Mount Everest is known to be difficult to climb, I can simply say 'I intend to climb it' without any

---

[17] This point is met by Grice in his reply to Davidson's 'Intending' (unpublished).

qualification. However, if I believe that my chances of success are even lower than the standard, I have to insert a qualification.

This conversational superstructure is convenient for economical communication and it is easily built on the basis of the theory of rational intention-based belief. The theory allows us to regard the varying probability of intention-based beliefs as a kind of sliding peg. The concept of intending does not allow the peg to move down to zero. There are also two more constraints which limit its freedom of movement within the range that is in general open to it. First, a rational agent will fix its position in a way that is sensitive to his estimate of the stepwise probabilities of achievement. This has nothing to do with conventions governing the communication of intentions. Second, these conventions impose a different kind of constraint on what the agent may say when he is communicating his intentions. When the general probability of successful execution of a type of project is known, the peg is automatically taken to move to that point on the sliding scale. So if the agent's private estimate of the probability deviates from this standard, he must say so. Otherwise, he may simply say 'I intend to perform a ϕ action'.

It follows that the implicature theory is not only compatible with the traditional implication theory but actually based on it. The implicature theory can be accepted only if it is not offered as a rival to the traditional theory. Confusion has occurred because it has not been appreciated that the belief that is an essential part of all intentions is necessarily minimal. Being minimal, it is only too easily overlooked. As a result, the attack on the traditional theory moves off in the wrong direction. It is contended that a more than minimal belief is not necessarily attached to a particular intention. But the traditional theory, far from denying this, can accept and explain it. The attack then assumes that the particular non-necessary attachment can be explained only if the belief is attached to the announcement of the intention and not to the intention itself. But the traditional theory can explain the variation in the content of the belief without abandoning the idea that the point of attachment is the intention itself. In any case, if the traditional theory were mistaken, the implicature theory would have to be based on the thesis that, as a matter of contingent fact, intentions are nearly always accompanied by minimal future factual beliefs. The implicature theory cannot stand on its own feet.

Finally, something needs to be said about the way in which the less perspicuous qualifications work. Some have a readily intelligible mechanism, but two very common ones work in a way that is far from obvious: 'I intend to try to perform a ϕ action' and 'I intend to perform a ϕ action if I can'. If the mechanism of these qualifications can be explained in a way that fits them into the theory that has been developed, that will provide some corroboration of it.

Consider first the statement that I intend to try to perform a ϕ action. A purist might argue that, since the infinitive gives the content of the intention, I am announcing a different intention from someone who says that he intends to perform a ϕ action. But that cannot be right. For it I were asked whether I had done what I intended to do when I had tried and failed, I would give a negative answer. It follows that the shift from 'to' to 'to try to' does not mark a change in intention, however strongly grammar may suggest that it does. We need some other explanation of the way in which the qualification works.

However, before we try to find one, it must be acknowledged that there are two exceptions to the thesis that the insertion of 'try to' does not produce a different intention. Someone may intend to try to perform a ϕ action simply in order to find out whether he can perform one, or simply in order to demonstrate to someone else that he cannot. In these two cases he really has done what he intended to do when he has tried and failed to perform a ϕ action. But in typical cases the insertion of 'try to' has a different effect. It qualifies the belief implication of 'I intend to perform a ϕ action', and the question is how it qualifies it.

The answer seems to be that the phrase 'to try to perform a ϕ action' gives part of the total content of the intention, which is to perform a ϕ action. Here I do not need to assume that anyone who intends to perform a ϕ action intends to try to perform one. I only need the assumption that, when the agent expects to encounter a difficulty, he can say that part of the content of his intention is to try to perform a ϕ action. But why does he specify his intention by giving what is only part of its content?

He is giving as much of the content of his intention as he can write into the implied future factual belief with the probability that is standard for ϕ actions. His point is that he can sincerely imply that he believes that it is standardly probable that he will try to perform a ϕ action, but not that it is standardly probable that he will actually perform one. He is drawing in one horn, but not the horn that grammar suggests. He does not mean that his total intention would be carried out if he tried to perform a ϕ action and failed. He means that the total content of his intention cannot be written into the implied future factual belief with the standard probability for ϕ actions.

This explanation may seem *ad hoc*, but in fact there are other cases in which the speaker makes a similar point by the same method. Consider, for example, the verb 'to regret'. A speaker may specify only part of the content of his regret, in order to make a similar point by the same grammar-flouting mechanism. Regret is an attitude that requires belief in the *fait accompli* that is regretted. But suppose that I regret saying something that may have caused another person pain, but I am not sure whether it actually did. Then instead of saying that I regret causing him pain, I may say that I regret making the remark. However, if I were asked whether the content of my regret was making the remark but not causing pain, I would give a negative answer, which would be parallel to the negative answer to the question 'Was the content of your intention trying but failing to perform a ϕ action?' Moreover, if I were asked 'Why then did you not give the whole of the content of your regret by saying "making the remark and causing pain"?' I would reply that I could not write the second conjuct into the implied past factual belief, because I did not know if I had caused pain. This reply would be parallel to the reply given in the other case: 'I could not write the whole content of my intention into the implied future factual belief with the probability that is standard for ϕ actions'.

The qualification 'if I can' may be explained in a related way. First, it is necessary to draw a distinction between what Davidson calls 'genuine conditional intentions'[18] and what I would call 'pseudo-conditional intentions'.[19] Davidson points out that in a conditional intention the word 'if' introduces a factor which would make the agent revoke, or at least reconsider, his intention, if it did not materialize. But 'if an agent cannot intend what he believes to be impossible, then he conveys nothing different by saying "I intend to do it if I can" than by saying "I intend to do it" '.[20] What then is

[18] *EAE*, p. 94.

[19] See my 'Ifs and Cans', *Canadian Journal of Philosophy* 1 (1971), 249-73, 369-91.

[20] *EAE*, p. 93. [*Editor's note*: the version of this sentence in *EAE* differs slightly from the one here cited, which is from 'Intending' as published in Yirmiahu Yovel (ed.), *Philosophy of History and Action* (Dordrecht, 1978), pp. 50-1.]

the function of 'if I can' in the specification of this intention and how does it perform it? Davidson says that it cancels the natural suggestion of 'I intend to do it', but how does it do that?

Davidson shows conclusively that when someone says 'I intend to perform a ϕ action if I can', he cannot be giving his intention a different content. Nor can we say that he is giving the part of the content of his intention that can be written into the implied future factual belief, because this time he is not giving part of the content of his intention. However, we can say that he is mentioning a condition about which he has doubts, and without which the content of his intention could not be written into the implied future factual belief with the probability that is standard for ϕ actions.

The objection that this explanation too is *ad hoc* can be answered in a similar way. When I am in doubt about the effect of my remark, I can say 'I regret causing him pain, if I did cause him pain', or 'I regret that I hit him with the water if he did walk under my window at that moment'.

So 'if I can' works as a qualification in a way that is closely related to the way in which 'try to' works. Neither of the two phrases restricts the content of the agent's intention. Both are comments on whether it can be written into the implied future factual belief with the probability that is standard for ϕ actions. The difference is that 'try to' identifies the part of the content of the intention that can be written in, while 'if I can' mentions the dubious condition whose fulfilment is required for writing in the whole of the content of the intention.

This explanation of the working of the two qualifications fits them into the theory of intention and belief that has been developed in this paper. It connects them with doubts about actual performance in a way that is consistent with the thesis that the implicature theory is based on the implication theory. For the doubts are about the precise position of the sliding peg of probability, and they exert conversational constraints on the words used to communicate the intention. However, the explanation does not allow that the lower limit to the range of the sliding peg is zero. So my general conclusion still stands: the connection between intention and future factual belief is a consequence of the semantics of 'I intend' and not of its force.

V

HUME'S PRIDE

DAN BENNETT

I

Regard now with attention the nature of these passions [Love and Hate; Pride and Humility], and their situation with respect to each other. 'Tis evident here are four affections, plac'd, as it were, in a square or regular connexion with, and distance from each other. The passions of pride and humility, as well as those of love and hatred, are connected together by the identity of their object, which to the first set of passions is self, to the second some other person. These two lines of communication of connexion form two opposite sides of the square. Again, pride and love are agreeable passions, hatred and humility uneasy. (Hume, *Treatise*, ed. L. A. Selby-Bigge (Oxford, 1888), p. 333)

Or, imagine a polarized field with six directions, thus:

Intricacies of structure of feeling, and obscurities of selfhood and causation are concealed in this figure.

II

Parallel to the Practical Syllogism is the Aesthetic Syllogism; as the conclusion of the former is an action, so of the latter it is a feeling, in particular the feeling of pleasure or displeasure (or indifference).

Pride—so far as it is an indirect passion—is a syllogism with this structure and these elements:

(1) I am pleased at: *anyone* who has the quality Q
(2) I believe: I have Q, so
(3) I am pleased at myself

The 'so' here, according to Hume's account, marks a double set of relations: an association of impressions, from the attitudinal, propositional pleasure of the major to the pleasure of the conclusion; and an association of ideas, from the idea of the pleasing quality Q to (the idea of) myself as having that quality.

According to Hume, self is the object of the passion, and pleasing qualities are the cause of the passion. Here we get tangled. Am I pleased at myself or at an idea of myself? (Rousseau contrasts *amour de soi* and *amour propre.*)

Perhaps we read the causation backwards here. Perhaps we read it in.

III

Self or person is not any one impression, but that to which our several impressions and ideas are supposed to have a reference. If any impression gives rise to the idea of self, that impression must continue invariably the same, thro' the whole course of our lives; since self is supposed to exist after that manner. But there is no impression constant and invariable. (*Treatise*, p. 251)

He goes on to say there is no self when we sleep!

Hume in Book I talks like Buddha, saying that identity through time is an illusion. So, one would expect the Buddhistic corollary, that pride is an illusion. But, I think, there is a more basic problem in the 'rationalism' of Hume's construction of the aesthetic syllogism.

IV

There is no more dangerous error than that of mistaking *the consequence for the cause*: I call it reason's intrinsic form of corruption. (Nietzsche, *Twilight of the Idols*, 'Four Great Errors')

Back in the early sixties I opposed to Donald's rationalistic view of the practical syllogism (that is the relation of reason to action) the view that the therefores, musts, and becauses of practical reasoning are actually predicates of the action, to which there is nothing causally prior.

Hume's theories of belief and value parallel my view of action, necessity, and rightness being epiphenomena of feeling. So I would argue of pride: it is my feeling of pleasure in and with myself which makes me pretty, and pleased with my house. This view is strengthened by the analogy with love—because *you* please me I find your qualities pleasant.[1]

It is indisputable that we *give* reasons for what we do and feel, but, I am saying, those various *Sprachspiel*s of offering reasons, assigning motives, justifying actions or feelings, *et alia*, are tricks consciousness plays on itself . . . , *Falschmünzerei vor sich selbst*, projections.

My account of how 'reason' partakes of our actions and feelings is more shadow-teuton, anima-projective than Donald's could ever seem.

Love of self and of other is by my assertion of that intelligence and taste I see and feel intrinsic to Donald, a function of energy not conscious of itself; a daimon, a grace, an instinct.

As for Hume; what we call knowledge of fact, knowledge of the qualities of sense, their spatial relations and their temporal sequence, is basically projective of strong feeling experienced immediately or through conditioning . . . why then not Pride a projection of feeling, employing that trick of consciousness which Hume calls the feigning of the imagination? The same mechanism as in judgements of causal connexion, temporal recurrence of the same, and value. Apart from pride in it, the it, the self, is itself a projection, a feigning of the imagination, by Hume's account.

---

[1] The remainder of this essay was added at the suggestion of the Editors.

VI

NEGATIVE ACTS

BRUCE VERMAZEN

Sometimes an agent does not do something, for example does not smoke or eat or cough, and *because* he has not done it, we want to say he has done something, has performed an act or action. It is this sort of doing or performance that I intend to cover with the term 'negative act'. And since there is no syntactic device to distinguish between not doings that are negative acts and ones that are not, I shall use the typographical device of hyphenation to mark the distinction: not-smoking, not-eating, not-coughing, etc. are all negative acts; not smoking, not eating, not coughing, etc. will generally not be negative acts, but if an ambiguous term is called for by context the unhyphenated form will be used.

My project in this paper is to take an already well-developed theory of action, that of Donald Davidson, and to show how it can be extended, with one very important modification, to cover the case of negative action. But even if Davidson's theory turns out to be inadequate on other grounds, some of what I say here will, I hope, profit anyone investigating the topic. Davidson has not published anything, as far as I know, that commits him to so much as the existence of negative acts. Other writers treat their existence as obvious, if problematic, for example Brand[1] and Goldman[2]. And at least two recent writers have argued that they do not exist.[3] Later I shall argue that certain putative negative acts, namely unintentional omissions, failures, and neglectings-to-do, do not exist (or at least should not be counted as acts), but it seems clear to me that there are some negative acts: if I intentionally pass up a chance to

---

[1] Myles Brand, 'The Language of Not Doing', *American Philosophical Quarterly* 8 (1971), 45-53.

[2] *A Theory of Human Action* (Englewood Cliffs, NJ, 1970); see especially pp. 47-8.

[3] Judith Jarvis Thomson, in *Acts and Other Events* (Ithaca, NY, 1977), pp. 212-18, and Gilbert Ryle, 'Negative "Actions"', *Hermathena* 81 (1973), 81-93.

win at cards by laying down the ten of clubs, I have done something—performed an act—describable as not laying down the ten
of clubs and as not bringing about my winning. Perhaps one reason
for the widely shared feeling that there is a class of negative acts is
that we naturally employ a kind of stress on 'not' in reading sentences like the preceding one, while, if I had inadvertently failed to
lay down the ten of clubs (and other things were equal), the stress
would not be employed. The presence of this stress is probably
neither necessary nor sufficient to demarcate the class prior to
analysis, but it is a clue to the sort of thing I am after. In his account
of action, Davidson mentions negative action, or one sort of negative action, only once: 'If we interpret the idea of a bodily movement generously, a case can be made for saying that all primitive
actions are bodily movements. The generosity must be open-handed
enough to encompass such "movements" as standing fast, and
mental acts like deciding and computing'.[4] For reasons I shall give
later, this sort is not so typical of negative action that the account
implied in the passage quoted can be extended to cover other sorts.

The main features of Davidson's view of action, as they emerge
in 'Actions, Reasons, and Causes', 'Agency', 'Freedom to Act',
and 'Intending'[5] are that an act is a bodily movement (possibly a
'null movement'), caused 'in the right way' by an appropriate pair of
a belief and a desire or pro-attitude of the agent (the person whose
body it is). The attempt to specify 'the right way' is repudiated in
'Freedom to Act' on grounds that its specification is tantamount to
the discovery of precise laws linking mental items described in a
mentalistic vocabulary with acts, a discovery Davidson has argued
(in 'Mental Events',[6] *inter alia*) is impossible. Since I agree with his
opinion here, I will not say anything about 'the right way', though I
shall assume throughout that there is one.

The belief/pro-attitude pair is appropriately related to the bodily
movement if and only if the movement is truly describable as ϕ-ing
and the agent, just before the time his body moved, had a pro-
attitude toward ϕ-ing and believed that his movement was or would
be a ϕ-ing. Since a single bodily movement is describable in many
ways, there will be some descriptions of the ϕ-ing in a particular
case that never occurred to the agent or that no pro-attitude of his

---

[4] 'Agency', *EAE*, p. 49.
[5] *EAE*, pp. 3-20, 43-62, 63-82, 83-102.
[6] *EAE*, pp. 207-25.

corresponds to. The ϕ-ing, though described in ways that don't satisfy the conditions on 'ϕ', will still be an act of his, but will be unintentional under those other descriptions.

The obvious problem with assimilating all negative acts to the case of the agent's body not moving at all as a 'right way' result of his pro-attitude toward not moving and his belief that his body would not be moving is that one can not-ϕ while doing something else that involves bodily movement. For one sort of negative act, which I shall call resisting, the rejected account has some attraction. In a case of resisting, the agent's body would be made to move in a certain way by some outside force, but the agent keeps the movement from taking place by activating the appropriate muscles. Often this will result in no gross bodily movement at all, yet we want to say that he has done something, and one of the things we shall want to say he has done is to not-move (whatever part of his body the outside force tended to move). Even in such cases, however, the not-ϕ-ing could be something other than not-moving, for example not-moving one's arm to the left, achieved by moving one's arm to the right.

The problem suggests an illusory route to a better account: perhaps the negative act is attributed to the agent because the movements he is displaying (including not moving at all) are also describable as not ψ-ing, for the appropriate ψ. I illustrate with a case of refraining, which is more difficult and more interesting than resisting.

Suppose that our agent, Andy, is confronted with a table laden with attractive hors d'œuvres, but has a pro-attitude toward not eating them and a belief that if he keeps his hands otherwise occupied, say by twisting the buttons on his vest, the movements of his body will amount to not eating the hors d'œuvres; and so he twists his buttons. Here it seems plausible to identify his negative act (not-eating) with the act he is doing instead (twisting his buttons). These are just two ways of describing his bodily movements, and they are linked to his pro-attitude and beliefs in such a way that the movements amount to acts.

One generalization suggested by the example is that an agent's act of not-ψ-ing is identical with his act of ϕ-ing, where ϕ-ing is whatever he is doing at the time he is said to be not-ψ-ing, and where 'ϕ' is a description of the action licensed by his bodily movements. But this generalization leaves out a feature of the example that, to my mind, makes the identification plausible, namely, that the agent twists his buttons *in order* not to eat. The button-twisting is a substitute for, or a stratagem toward, the not-eating. Imagine the case differently: Mickey sits at the table, refraining from the fattening morsels, and at the same time, by twisting his buttons, signals to Minnie that the time has come to leave. Here there is no temptation to identify Mickey's not-eating with his button-twisting, other than the temptation urged on us by the desire to find some bodily movement or other to figure in—to be—the negative act. And since, on Davidson's account, Mickey's button-twisting is identical with his signalling to Minnie, so too would his not-eating be identical with his signalling. This objection does not falsify the suggestion, but the awkwardness of the consequence should make us receptive to other possibilities.

Even if we limit its scope to cases where the agent does something in order not to do something else, the suggested generalization, because of its appeal to 'the time he is said to be not-ψ-ing', does not address the question when it is correct to say of him that he is not-ψ-ing, even though the example furnishes an answer. I will turn to this subject for a few pages, in order to get in a better position to address the original question. Certainly we don't want to say that a person is not-ψ-ing just in case he is not ψ-ing. Negative acts are supposed to be a class of acts, so if one is asleep and engaged in no act at all, one is not therefore not-acting. It won't help much to add the rider 'if the agent is doing something' to this last, since the agent will then be doing far too many negative acts: Andy, as he sits twisting his buttons, would also be not-sweeping the table clear of canapés, not-preparing for a Channel swim, not-attempting to cross the Sino-Soviet border, and so on. Nor will we rule out enough putative negative acts by saying that he is not-ϕ-ing at t just in case he is ψ-ing at t and his ψ-ing at t is logically or physically incompatible with his ϕ-ing at t.

The restriction we need is suggested by the example: what we count when we attribute a negative act to him is what he *intends* not to be doing. That is, it is a necessary condition of not-ϕ-ing that the agent intend not to ϕ (intend to not-ϕ). The objection will immediately occur to the reader that I am ruling out of the class of acts all those unintentional omissions, neglectings-to-do, and failures that agents are customarily called to task for. But that seems to me a welcome result. Consider two cases of omission. A night watchman is responsible for locking a certain door at 2 a.m. each day. On Tuesday of last week he forgot to lock it at that time, for he was absorbed in reading. On Wednesday he failed to lock it again, but this time he was asleep. On both occasions, we would say, he was guilty of an omission; he omitted locking the door; he neglected locking it; he failed to lock it. And since it was not intentional in either case, we might also add the qualifier 'unintentionally' to each of these characterizations. But at least in the second case, Wednesday's failure, we wouldn't want to say that he had performed any *act* at all at 2 a.m., when the omission took place, for he was asleep. Why, then, should we count his omission on Tuesday as an act? The fact that he is awake at the time doesn't seem to make the difference between action and inaction. The only act he was performing on Tuesday at 2 a.m. was reading. If it is safe to generalize from this example, omissions, failures, and neglectings that are not intentional are not acts at all. (I am unsure whether neglectings are ever intentional, so it may be that they are never acts.) We may think of them as hypostatizations of certain facts about the agent: that he omitted, failed, or neglected to do something.

I do not see how my appeal to intention can be cast in terms of the notion of intention Davidson develops in 'Intending', for there are two important features of that paper that I find obscure. He there adds to his account in the earlier papers the idea that each intentional act somehow involves an 'all-out' judgement that that act is desirable (given the rest of what the agent believes about the circumstances of acting).[7] The first obscure feature is that he does not say what causal relation the intention bears to the pro-attitude/belief pair I mentioned earlier, the 'primary reason' of 'Actions, Reasons, and Causes'. From one passage, in which he suggests that an all-out judgement may sometimes be *identified* with the corresponding intentional act,[8] one might infer that the pro-attitude/belief pair causes the all-out judgement. But if the judgement is an act, it is not clear why it is not an act of *judging*, so that the

---

[7] The notion of an all-out judgement was introduced earlier, in 'How is Weakness of the Will Possible?' (*EAE*, pp. 21-42), but was not given a definite role in the analysis of action.

[8] 'Intending' (*EAE*, p. 99): 'In the case of intentional action, at least when the action is of brief duration, nothing seems to stand in the way of an Aristotelian identification of the action with a judgement of a certain kind—an all-out, unconditional judgement that the action is desirable (or has some other positive characteristic).'

appropriate causing pair would be a pro-attitude and belief directed toward making a judgement, rather than a pair directed toward the act judged desirable. The second obscure feature is that it isn't clear what sort of entity this all-out judgement is. In the passage just alluded to, it seems to be an event (since it can be identical with an act); but at the end of 'Intending', it is said to be a pro-attitude, and so not an event. For these reasons, my discussion will deal with Davidson's pre-'Intending' reduction of intentions with which an act is done to beliefs and pro-attitudes. I hope that a clarified version of the view in 'Intending' will not make my efforts here pointless. Even if the *reduction* is invalidated by the introduction of a separate, unreduced mental item, perhaps my account can be recast as an account of what causes the separate mental item, and so have some explanatory value. Another possibility is that the role I assign to pro-attitude/belief pairs could be played by these all-out judgements.

In 'Actions, Reasons, and Causes' Davidson suggests that 'The expression "the intention with which James went to church" has the outward form of a description, but in fact it is syncategorematic and cannot be taken to refer to an entity, state, disposition, or event. Its function in context is to generate new descriptions of actions in terms of their reasons.'[9] My aim will be to unpack 'An agent not-ϕs only if he intends not to ϕ (intends to not-ϕ)' in a way compatible with this earlier view of his.

Now the sort of intending involved here is not the sort that may precede an action but lapse before the action is performed. I may intend not to cough in the break between the *adagio* and the *presto*, forget about the intention, and yet, as a result of my desires and beliefs, not cough. Here I have not not-coughed as the realization of my intention, and have (not *so*, but) also not coughed intentionally. I will call this sort of intention the prior intention (as does Davidson in 'Intending'). The intention I am interested in is the sort that makes the act in question an intentional act. It is this sort of intention, according to Davidson's earlier view, that is not a separate mental item. What makes an act intentional, he hints in 'Actions, Reasons, and Causes', is just that it be done for a reason,[10] and

---

[9] *EAE*, p. 9.

[10] 'This last point is not essential to the present argument, but it is of interest because it defends the possibility of defining an intentional action as one done for a reason' (*EAE*, p. 6).

that, in turn, is analysed in 'Actions, Reasons, and Causes' and 'Agency' as its being caused in the right way by an appropriate pro-attitude/belief pair.

So the unpacking comes to this:

(I) x not-ϕs at t only if $\sim \phi(x, t)$ and, just before t, x believes that there is some probability that $\sim \phi(x, t)$ and x has a pro-attitude toward not ϕ-ing and x's not ϕ-ing at t is caused in the right way by the belief and pro-attitude mentioned.

It seems obvious that the belief here is a necessary condition: an agent can't be completely surprised at an intentional act of his, though he may be surprised that he has succeeded (which is the reason for the belief's probabilistic nature).[11] The necessity of the pro-attitude is less clear to me, but since Davidson's catalogue of pro-attitudes ('Actions, Reasons, and Causes', *EAE*, p. 4) includes nearly everything that could get one to act, I won't explore any objections. Finally, I will take the necessity of the causal link for granted, though it, too, has been called into question.[12]

I think these conditions are not only necessary, but also sufficient for the ascription of negative acts. At any rate, their sufficiency follows from my thesis that all negative acts are intentional together with Davidson's implied equation of intentional acts, acts done for a reason, and acts caused in the right way by the appropriate pair of belief and pro-attitude. So now we have a characterization of nega-tive action compatible with much of Davidson's account. But we still haven't found a bodily movement with which to identify the not-doing. Moreover, the analysis so far ((I) with the first 'if' changed to 'if and only if') may seem to create a related puzzle: given that Davidson maintains that causation is a relation between events,[13] how can the analysis rest on a pro-attitude/belief pair causing the non-occurrence of something? What sort of event is picked out by 'x's not ϕ-ing at t'?[14]

[11] I am grateful to Michael Bratman for suggesting that an earlier formulation of (I) was inadequate. I do not know whether he would accept the present attempt. See also the discussions of the belief condition in the papers in the present volume by Christopher Peacocke and David Pears.

[12] By John Searle, in 'The Intentionality of Intention and Action', *Inquiry* 22 (1979), 253-80. See also Dan Bennett's paper in the present volume.

[13] In 'Causal Relations', *EAE*, pp. 149-62.

[14] In 'The Logical Form of Action Sentences' (*EAE*, pp. 105-22). Davidson pro-poses that every sentence about action be analysed as containing a variable, bound by an existential quantifier, whose value is the event that the action is. Thus 'John

I think that the correct answer to this last question points toward a plausible answer to the question of what bodily movement to identify with a negative act. However, I will not address the first question directly, but as a case of a more general question about causation involving the non-occurrence of events. For brevity, let me refer to the non-occurrence of an event-type as a negative event,[15] and to the occurrence of an event-type (what Davidson calls an event) as a positive event. Since negative events do not, strictly speaking, exist, they might be thought to be unimportant. But they are often spoken of as if they were causes or effects. Here are some examples:

(1) The shipment of wheat staved off a famine.
   (The shipment of wheat caused the non-occurrence of a famine.)
(2) Pete's not smoking improved his health.
   (Pete's not smoking caused his health to improve.)
(3) Pete's not smoking kept him from dying young.
   (Pete's not smoking caused Pete's dying young not to occur.)

In each pair, the sentence in parentheses is intended to be an explicitly causal equivalent of the more colloquially written one not in parentheses. The pairs exhibit, in turn, cases in which a positive event causes a negative event, a negative event causes a positive event, and one negative event causes another. I suggest that all three examples, and hence the types they exemplify, can be substantially explained in terms of causal relations between positive events. (I will explain my adverb 'substantially' in the next paragraph.) In case (1) the locution is made true by the fact that had the shipment not occurred, a famine would have occurred. And that in turn is made true by there being some third factor that would have caused the famine had the shipment not occurred—possibly the normal demands of the human body for nourishment. To generalize in a logically unrespectable but colloquially clear way, A may be said to cause not-B only if A occurred, B did not, and there is some third factor C such that, if A had not occurred and there were no

---

walks' is analysed as '$(\exists x)$ (Walks(John, x))' and 'John does not walk' as '$\sim(\exists x)$ (Walks(John, x))'. But the latter won't work for that same sentence used as a report of a negative act. If John not-walks, then there will sometimes be some event that is his not-walking.

[15] I borrow this term from Alvin Goldman, *Theory of Human Action*, p. 48.

D such that if *D* occurs, then $\sim$(*C* causes *B*), *C* would have caused *B*.[16] In case (2) the locution is appropriate because if Pete had smoked, the smoking would have caused some event incompatible with the improvement of his health, for example, its deterioration or maintenance at the same level. The generalization here is that not-*A* may be said to cause *B* only if *A* did not occur, *B* did, and *A* would have caused some other event, *C*, such that *C* is incompatible with *B*. Finally, (3) is correctly said in a case where Pete's smoking would have caused him to die young. Generalizing, not-*A* may be said to cause not-*B* only if *A* and *B* did not occur and *A* would have caused *B*.

I claim only that these causal relations between positive events *substantially* explain talk about causal transactions involving negative events.[17] They give the causal part of the story, but there is another part, probably due to the pragmatics of speech. Whenever someone is inclined to talk about a negative event as cause or effect, a causal story of the kind indicated is in the background. But something more is needed to bring about the inclination. Cases of the type of (2) raise the problem most clearly: the 6.15 train arrived on time, no earthquake of Richter magnitude 8.6 occurred, and had such an earthquake occurred, the train would have been late; but we are not tempted to say that the non-occurrence of the earthquake caused (even in part) the punctual appearance of the train. However, if the negative event in the story were the non-occurrence of rain during the rainy season, and if we knew that rain almost always made the train late, we would say that the non-occurrence of rain was (at least part of) the cause of the train's being on time. So to strengthen my generalizations to biconditionals, I would need to catalogue the pragmatic factors that make it appropriate to talk of negative events at all: someone's expectation of the negative event or of the

---

[16] The clause 'and there were no *D* such that if *D* occurs, then $\sim$(*C* causes *B*)' is necessitated by the possibility that the prevention of *B* is overdetermined. It is possible to set the situation up so that (1) *D* occurs if and only if *A* does not and (2) *D* keeps *B* from happening. In such a case, the mere supposing away of *A* wouldn't result in *B*, even though *A* is clearly preventing *B*. The clause supposes away all such substitutes for *A*. This qualification was suggested to me indirectly by an objection of Myles Brand's.

The lack of respectability I allege comes from my casual use of non-referring (apparent) singular terms. The right way to do it would be to speak of the instantiation or non-instantiation of certain event-types, and of causal relations holding between the instances.

[17] I am grateful to Malcolm MacFail for pointing out the need for this paragraph.

corresponding positive event, the importance to speaker or hearer of the event, and so on. I shall not attempt such a catalogue, since my subsequent arguments all concern cases in which the pragmatic conditions have been satisfied: talk about negative acts or other events has already arisen. What is needed is elucidation of the causal background.

The generalization drawn from case (1) makes clear what underlies the incident in which Andy twisted his buttons in order not to eat. Andy would have eaten (*ceteris paribus*)[18] had he not twisted his buttons. (The event playing the role of *C* here is a complex one, but at its core is an increase in the strength of his desire for the texture and flavour of chicken liver pâté.) So his button-twisting is correctly said to cause his not eating, that is, to cause its being the case that he does not eat, which is not the same as causing his not-eating, the negative act we are worrying about. The connection between his not eating and his not-eating is that since the former is caused by an act of his (the button-twisting), it licenses a redescription of that act as not-eating, that is, as a negative act. But since, as we saw earlier, this case exemplifies only one type of negative action, we are still without a general explanation. To borrow a term, but not its stipulated meaning, from Alvin Goldman,[19] I shall say that the case of Andy is one in which a negative act is *generated* by a positive act. The other cases that need to be covered are that in which a negative act is generated by another negative act and, most important, that in which the negative act is not generated by another act at all, but is, in Davidson's sense, primitive or basic.[20] The latter has been our real quarry all along.

A schematic account of negative acts generating negative acts can be constructed from material already furnished, but there will be a gap in it until primitive negative acts are explained. To say that a negative act generates another negative act is just to say that a negative act causes a negative event, and that the negative event licenses a new description of the causing act. From the account of causation between negative events, we know that saying that a negative act causes a negative event is warranted by the non-occurrence of the corresponding positive act and event together with the assurance that

---

[18] '*Ceteris paribus*' here and in the rest of the paper means 'if there were no *D* such that if *D* occurs, then $\sim(C$ causes $B)$'. See footnote 16.
[19] *Theory of Human Action*, pp. 20-30.
[20] See 'Agency' (*EAE*, p. 59).

the positive act would have caused the positive event. In cases where what I just called 'the causing act' is identical with some positive act, the redescription is unproblematic. Suppose that Andy, by not eating the pâté, knowingly wards off a gout attack, that is, causes a gout attack not to occur. Then his not-eating (and his button-twisting) can be redescribed as refraining from inducing (that is, not-inducing) a gout attack. The redescription is unproblematic because there is a bodily movement—the button-twisting—to serve as the ultimate descriptum. I shall call Andy's case 'displacement refraining'—refraining from something by doing something else. The gap in the account comes into view when we ask for the ultimate decriptum in a case where the negative act to be redescribed is not itself generated by any positive act, a case I shall call 'simple refraining'. I pass up the hors d'œuvres, but do nothing by way of not-eating them. As a result, I knowingly do not induce a gout attack, so I have not-induced a gout attack. But what have I *done*? What is the ultimate descriptum?

The surprising, but I hope not too surprising, answer is that there is no ultimate descriptum. We don't need one, because the clause that seems to call for one, 'x's not ϕ-ing at t is caused in the right way by the belief and pro-attitude mentioned', is just a way of saying 'had x not had the belief and pro-attitude mentioned, something else (*ceteris paribus*) would have caused him to ϕ'. The 'something else' in this case is a competing pro-attitude/belief pair. 'ϕ' probably must be a verb whose application depends on the agent's body moving in some way (again counting standing fast and mental activities as bodily movements), but 'not ϕ-ing' need not pick out an event of any sort. Positive acts are bodily movements; negative acts, when they are resistings or identical with positive acts, are also bodily movements; but simple negative acts, mere refrainings, need not be bodily movements at all. They are correctly attributed to agents in virtue of the inhibitory role played by the appropriate pro-attitude/belief pair, but they are not themselves events.

This result makes it easier to understand one final class of cases, where the following features are present: a rule, directive, law, or even an authoritative desire or wish of someone other than the agent to the effect that, or with the consequence that, the agent is to ϕ is believed by the agent to be 'in the air'; by 'an authoritative desire' I mean a desire that the agent believes held by someone who has (or who is supposed to have) a degree of authority or influence over him, for example the sheriff, a parent, a friend, or the owner of the property he is on. The agent, however, has a pro-attitude toward not ϕ-ing and no competing pro-attitude toward ϕ-ing. As a 'right-way' result of this pro-attitude and some appropriate accompanying belief, the agent does not ϕ; and here I think we would want to say he not-ϕd. The account of the causing here is not difficult, though perhaps it is a bit tortured. The causal locution is justified because, had the pro-attitude/belief pair relevant to not ϕ-ing not been present, the authority behind the directive (had it exercised its power) would have caused (*ceteris paribus*) the formation of a pro-attitude—at least acquiescence—toward ϕ-ing and so, mediately and ultimately, the agent's ϕ-ing. 'Would have caused' is perhaps too strong, but the point of calling the person or institution behind the directive or desire an authority is that *ideally* it causes such pro-attitudes; there is a normative element here that is not present in other cases. I shall call this 'disobedient refraining', although not every case in which one disobeys by refraining falls under it.

If we count negative acts among acts, then, no general definition that begins '$(x)(x$ is an act if only if' can be framed, since simple and disobedient refrainings will not count as *things* of any sort, so are not eligible to be the values of variables. A general definition would have to follow Bruce Aune's recommendation[21] and be framed in terms of the predicate 'acted' being true of an agent. But Davidson's account remains attractive for positive acts, resistings, and displacement refrainings, so perhaps the best course is to split negative acts into two groups: resisting and displacement refrainings will count as acts in the same sense as positive acts, and simple and disobedient refrainings will require a separate account, one that does not require that they be events.[22]

[21] See Aune, *Reason and Action* (Dordrecht, 1977), pp. 44-6.
[22] I am grateful to Lawrence Davis for extensive comment on an earlier version of this paper.

EVENT AND CAUSE

VII

THE STRUCTURE OF
STATES OF AFFAIRS

RODERICK M. CHISHOLM

I. INTRODUCTION

In November 1968 Donald Davidson and I took part in a symposium on the theory of action at the University of Western Ontario.[1] What emerged as the fundamental difference between us was our conception of the nature of events. He held that events are particular things, just as physical objects and persons are particular things, and I held that they are abstract objects. Or, more accurately, I held that sentences ostensibly about events, including what Davidson calls 'events as particulars,' can be reduced to sentences about those abstract objects that I called 'states of affairs.' We have subsequently debated these two points of view and the results, I think Davidson would agree, have been somewhat inconclusive.

Davidson remarked in one paper: 'it is unclear whether a viable alternative to the theory of events as particulars can be worked out along the lines proposed by Chisholm'.[2] In the present paper, which is not polemical, I shall take up one of the preliminary questions that must be answered if this challenge is to be met: What is the nature of those things I have been calling states of affairs? I hope that I can persuade Davidson that the concept is a powerful one and that he might do well consider it when he completes his theory of recurrence and possibility.

I will set forth a small primitive vocabulary consisting of locutions which it is almost impossible to dispense with in philosophy. By means of these locutions I will define the concept of a *state of*

---

[1] Davidson's contribution and mine appear in R. Binkley, R. Bronaugh, and A. Marras (eds.), *Agent, Action, and Reason,* (Toronto, 1971). Davidson's essay 'Agency' is in *EAE*, pp. 43-62.
[2] Donald Davidson, 'Events as Particulars', *EAE*, pp. 181-7; the quotation appears on p. 187.

affairs and show how it is possible to distinguish states of affairs by reference to their structure. Without confusing states of affairs with the sentences that may be used to express them, we may distinguish among states of affairs those which are *conjunctions*, those which are *disjunctions*, and those which are *negations*. And indeed we may note a sense in which it is possible to divide states of affairs into those which are *affirmative* and those which are *negative*.

Making use of this concept of state of affairs, I shall also set forth a conception of 'possible worlds' which, I think, is adequate to this concept as it has been used by Leibniz and other philosophers in the western tradition and which is considerably simpler than that presupposed by most contemporary philosophers. It does not go beyond the ontology involved in assuming that there are individuals, properties and relations, and propositions or states of affairs. It does not require us to assume that there *are* things which are 'merely possible entities'. It does not require us to say that if I have unrealized possibilities, then I exist 'in' other possible worlds. And it does not presuppose that individual things have individual essences or haecceities.

I shall make use of five philosophical concepts: that of *conceiving*, that of *accepting*, that of *obtaining*, that of *exemplifying*, and that of *de re* possibility. The latter concept is more complex than the others. It is exemplified only if there are an *x* and a *y* such that *x* is possibly such that it exemplifies *y*. It should be noted that we use the locution, '*x* is possibly *F*', and not 'possibly *x* is *F*'. I assume that, for every *x*, *x* necessarily has the universal property of being self-identical (*x* is not possibly such that it lacks the property of being self-identical). But I do *not* assume that, for every *x*, *x* necessarily has the property of being identical with *x*. If the latter assumption were true, then each thing would have a property that is essential to it and repugnant to everything else. But, as I have said, we do not presuppose that individual things have individual essences or haecceities.

II. PROPERTIES AND ETERNAL OBJECTS

We may characterize properties as being whatever is capable of being exemplified:

D1 *G* is a property   = Df *G* is possibily such that there is something that exemplifies *G*.

And I shall assume that every property is possibly such that there is someone who conceives it (every property is capable of being conceived).

'But the property of being round and square is not possibly such that there is something that exemplifies it'. The question is only terminological. I am using 'property' in a somewhat restricted sense. Its occurrence here may be replaced by another term—say, 'attribute' or 'determination.'

We may now define the concept of an *eternal object*:

D2 x is an eternal object = Df There is a property H such that (i) x necessarily exemplifies H and (ii) everything other than x is necessarily such that (a) it does not exemplify H and (b) there is something that exemplifies H.

In other words, an eternal object is a thing having an essence of the following sort: the essence is repugnant to everything else, but everything else is necessarily such that there *is* something having that essence.

Eternal objects, so conceived, are not dependent for their existence upon anything which is such that it might not have existed.

We shall assume that all properties—all things capable of exemplification—are eternal objects.

III. STATES OF AFFAIRS

We may thus characterize states of affairs:

D3 p is a state of affairs = Df p is possibly such that there is someone who accepts it; and there is something which obtains and which is necessarily such that whoever conceives it conceives p.

The definition presupposes that some states of affairs obtain and others do not. There being round squares is a state of affairs by this definition. It is capable of being accepted, and there obtains a q— for example, it being impossible that there are round squares— which is necessarily such that whoever conceives it conceives there being round squares.

I presuppose, then, that any state of affairs can be accepted. It is possible to accept the conjunction of a state of affairs with its negation. But it is *not* possible to accept a conjunction without accepting each of its conjuncts. Our acceptings force other acceptings upon us; but no accepting prevents any other accepting.

I shall assume that states of affairs are eternal objects. Hence no state of affairs is dependent for its existence upon anything that is not an eternal object. No state of affairs, then, is an 'event as particular'.

'If all states of affairs exist, what does it mean to say that some are merely possible and that others are impossible?' To say of a state of affairs that it is 'merely possible' is to say of it (i) that it does not obtain and (ii) that it is possibly such that it does obtain, and analogously for the other modal predicates that are applied to states of affairs.

IV. THREE TYPES OF RELATION BETWEEN STATES OF AFFAIRS

We now consider certain general points about the *structure* of states of affairs. To make these points, let us first introduce three relational concepts:

D4 *p* logically implies *q*   = Df   *p* is necessarily such that if it obtains, then *q* obtains.

D5 *p* involves *q*   = Df   *p* is necessarily such that, whoever conceives it, conceives *q*.

D6 *p* entails *q*   = Df   *p* logically implies *q*, and *p* is necessarily such that whoever accepts it accepts *q*.

The state of affairs expressed by 'there being Greeks' *logically implies* that expressed by 'either there being Greeks or there being Romans'. But the first does not *involve* the second (you can conceive the first without conceiving the second) and the first does not *entail* the second (you can accept the first without accepting the second). But the state of affairs expressed by 'either there being Greeks or there being Romans' *involves* that expressed by 'there being Romans', but it does not logically imply it or entail it. The state of affairs expressed by 'there being Greeks and there being Romans' logically implies, involves, and entails that expressed by 'there being Romans'.

We may characterize three further relations by making use of the qualification 'properly'. Thus *p properly* entails *q*, provided only *p* entails *q* and *q* does not entail *p*: analogously for logical implication and involvement.

I would call Davidson's attention to the fact that mutual involvement and mutual entailment provide us with intentional criteria of identity for states of affairs.

V. CONJUNCTION, NEGATION, AND DISJUNCTION

Now we are able to characterize *conjunctions*, *negations*, and *disjunctions* of states of affairs.

D7 *C* is a conjunction of *p* and *q* = Df   *C* is a state of affairs having this property *H*: it entails *p* and entails *q*, and is such that everything it entails entails something that either *p* entails or *q* entails: and everything having *H* entails *C*.

It may be observed that this definition of a *conjunction* of states of affairs is similar to Lesniewski's definition of *sum*.

D8 *p* contradicts *q* = Df   *p* is necessarily such that it obtains if and only if *q* does not obtain.

D9 *p* explicitly denies *q* = Df   *p* contradicts *q*, and *p* properly involves just what *q* involves.

This concept of explicit denial provides us with a mark of what we may call a *negative* state of affairs: a negative state of affairs is one that explicitly denies something. And so we may reject Frege's observation that 'it is by no means easy to state what is a negative judgement (thought)'.[3]

Each state of affairs and its negation are so related that one is negative and the other is not negative. We may now define *negation* this way:

---

[3] From Frege's 'Negation', in P. Geach and M. Black (eds.), *Translations from the Philosophical Writings of Gottlob Frege* (Oxford, 1952), p. 125. Frege goes on to say: 'Consider the sentences "Christ is immortal", "Christ lives for ever", "Christ is not immortal", "Christ is mortal", "Christ does not live for ever". Now which of the thoughts we have here is affirmative, which negative?' The answer is that they are all affirmative, provided that the 'is not' in the third example is read as 'is such that he is not', and that the 'does not' of the fifth example is read as 'is such that he does not'. But 'It is false that Christ is immortal' and 'It is false that Christ lives for ever' would be negative.

D10 *p* is a negation of *q*   = Df   Either *p* explicitly denies *q*, or *q* explicitly denies *p*.

Having a definition of negation, we may now define *disjunction* in a familiar way:

D11 *d* is a disjunction of *p* and *q*   = DF   *d* is a negation of a conjunction of a negation of *p* and a negation of *q*.

VI. WORLDS

What is a 'possible world'? Let us introduce the concept of 'a world':

D12 *W* is a world   = Df   *W* is a state of affairs; for every state of affairs *p*, either *W* logically implies *p* or *W* logically implies a state of affairs that contradicts *p*; and there is no state of affairs *q* such that *W* logically implies both *q* and a state of affairs that contradicts *q*.

It will be noted that I have defined 'a *world*', not 'a *possible* world'. I have avoided 'possible world', since the expression 'There are possible worlds' may suggest that there *are* certain things—worlds—somehow lying between being and non-being. But when philosophers speak of 'possible worlds', I believe that in so far as they can be understood, the concept they have in mind can be explicated by reference to those states of affairs that are here called 'worlds'. If this is so and if states of affairs are eternal objects existing whether or not they obtain, then *all* so-called 'possible worlds' exist. Hence I use 'world' and not 'possible world'.

'But you can't mean to say that all possible worlds are *actual* worlds. There is—and can be—only *one* actual world!' The word 'actual' is here ambiguous. If '*x* is actual' is taken to mean the same as '*x* exists', then all possible worlds are actual. But when it is said that only one world is actual, then 'is actual' is taken to mean the same as 'obtains'. There is—and can be—only one world that *obtains*.

Hence we should avoid the temptation to speak of 'the real world' or 'the actual world'. Let us, rather, speak of 'the *world that obtains*', or 'the *prevailing world*'.

If a world is a state of affairs, and if states of affairs are eternal objects, what could it mean to say of an individual thing that it exists 'in a world'? How could you or I exist 'in a state of affairs'?

We may *give* a meaning to this use of 'in':

D13 *x* exists in *W* = Df *W* is a world; and either (*a*) *x* has an individual essence *H* such that *W* entails *H* or (*b*) *W* obtains and *x* exists.

The definition does not imply that individual things have individual essences. It allows us to say that I exist in the prevailing world ('the actual world') even if I have no individual essence. But it does not allow us to say that I exist in any *other* world unless I have an individual essence that is implied by that world.

VII. EXCLUSION AND ELIGIBILITY

Even if I do not have an individual essence, *some* of my properties are essential to me—that is, some of my properties are such that I have them necessarily. Suppose that 'being a person' is such a property. Now there are some worlds which do not entail the property of being a person ('Some possible worlds don't contain any persons'). If I am necessarily a person, then I am necessarily such that none of those impersonal worlds obtain. Hence we may say that I *exclude* such worlds. (Or, if one prefers, one could put it the other way round and say that I am such that I am *excluded by* certain worlds.) We may single out this concept as follows:

D14 *x* excludes *W* = Df *x* is necessarily such that *W* does not obtain.

It should be noted that, from the fact that I am *not* excluded by a certain world *W*, it does not follow that I *exist in* in that world *W*.

But if I am not excluded by *W*, then I am *eligible* for *W*:

D15 *x* is eligible for *W* = Df *x* is possibly such that *W* obtains.

If I were to have an individual essence *E* such that there is a certain world *W* that entails *E*, then we could say that *W* is necessarily such that I exist. But if I have no individual essence, then we cannot say of *any* world that it is necessarily such that I exist. And we cannot even say this of 'the actual world'—that is, the world that obtains. The latter point may be put somewhat loosely by saying that this world could have obtained without me. If the world had obtained without me, then someone else would have played my role. Indeed, if neither you nor I have individual essences, then the prevailing world could have obtained with you playing my role and me playing yours. One might say, paradoxically, that you and I would have been very different but the world would have been the same; this gives us a use for the label 'existentialism'.

What if a thing has a certain property necessarily? What does this imply with respect to those characteristics that the prevailing world has necessarily? Next to nothing, I would say. Suppose, for example, that Socrates is necessarily such that he is a person. It does not follow from this either (*a*) that Socrates is necessarily such that he is a *person in this world*, or (*b*) that Socrates is necessarily such that if he exists in this world then he is a person, or (*c*) that this world is necessarily such that Socrates is a person, or (*d*) that this world is necessarily such that if Socrates exists then he is a person.

The fact that I exist only in the prevailing world—if it is a fact—does not restrict my possibilities. The unrealized possibilities of a given individual are not to be explicated in terms of the different worlds in which that individual might be said to exist. We may speak of such possibilities, using the undefined *de re* modal locution with which we began: '*x* is possibly such that it is *F*'. And so we may say, of a person who is not a lawyer, 'He could be a lawyer'. This does not tell us that he is a lawyer 'in some possible world'. It tells us no more nor less than that he is possibly such that he is a lawyer.

'But doesn't "He is possibly such that he is a lawyer" imply that he has an individual essence that is compatible with his being a lawyer?' No; the statement 'He is possibly such that he is a lawyer' does *not* mean that he has a nature that is compatible with being a lawyer. It means, rather, that he does *not* have a nature that is *incompatible* with his being a lawyer.

'If he is possibly such that he is a lawyer, and if he is not a lawyer in the prevailing world, then is it not the case that, if he *were* a lawyer, he would be a lawyer *in another world*?' This is correct. But from this fact it does not follow that he *is* a lawyer in any other world. For unless he has an individual essence, any other world could obtain without him.

VIII

CAUSATION AND EXPLANATION

P. F. STRAWSON

I

On the topics of this paper Donald Davidson has written illuminatingly and influentially. In what follows there are points of convergence with, and points of divergence from, his views. It has not seemed necessary to mark these points as such; for those views are, rightly, well known.

We sometimes presume, or are said to presume, that causality is a natural relation which holds in the natural world between particular events or circumstances, just as the relation of temporal succession does or that of spatial proximity. We also, and rightly, associate causality with explanation. But if causality is a relation which holds in the natural world, explanation is a different matter. People explain things to themselves or others and their doing so is something that happens in nature. But we also speak of one thing explaining, or being the explanation of, another thing, as if explaining was a relation between the things. And so it is. But it is not a natural relation in the sense in which we perhaps think of causality as a natural relation. It is an intellectual or rational or intensional relation. It does not hold between things in the natural world, things to which we can assign places and times in nature. It holds between facts or truths.

The two levels of relationship are often and easily confused or conflated in philosophical thought. They are confused in philosophical thought partly because they are not clearly distinguished in ordinary or non-philosophical thought. And they are not clearly distinguished in ordinary thought because making the distinction would often serve no practical purpose. Nevertheless, in so far as our philosophical purpose is to understand our non-philosophical thought, it is well that *we* should be aware of the distinction.

It is easy to point to evidence that the distinction is not clearly marked in ordinary speech. We use nominal constructions of the same general kinds—nouns derived from other parts of speech, noun-clauses, gerundial constructions—to refer both to terms of the natural and to terms of the non-natural relation. We use the same range of expressions—for example 'cause' itself, 'due to', 'responsible for', 'owed to'—to signify both the natural and the non-natural relation; or use these expressions in such a way that we may be hard put to it to say which relation is specified and thus perhaps be led to doubt whether any such distinction exists to be drawn. This is not to say that we are always at a loss as to which relation is being specified. Faced with a remark of the form 'The reason why q was that p' (for example, 'The reason why the building collapsed was that it was constructed of inferior materials') or of the form 'The fact that q is accounted for by the fact that p' ('The fact that the building collapsed is accounted for by the fact that it was constructed of inferior materials'), we need be in no doubt that it is the non-natural relation that is in question; whereas we are left in doubt by 'The collapse of the building was due to/caused by the use of inferior materials in its construction' or 'The use of inferior materials in the construction of the building was responsible for its collapse'.

There are, sometimes, relatively subtle indications of difference. Thus we might compare 'His death, coming when it did, was responsible for the breakdown of the negotiations' with 'His death's coming when it did was responsible for the breakdown of the negotiations'. His death, as referred to in the first of these sentences, is certainly an event in nature. It came when it did. But his death's coming when it did did not come at any time. It is not an event in nature. It is *the fact* that a certain event occurred in nature at a certain time. Are we then entitled to conclude that the phrase 'the breakdown of the negotiations' refers, in the first sentence, to an event in nature and, in the second, to the fact that that event occurred, and that the phrase 'responsible for' signifies, in the first sentence, the natural and, in the second sentence, the non-natural relation? We are not entitled to draw any such conclusion. For it simply need not be true of the ordinary language-speaker either that he means to speak consistently at one level or the other or that he mixes levels. It is often simply that he does not distinguish the levels, because he has no need to.

An exhaustive examination of ordinary usage on this point would be a possible exercise and one neither uninteresting nor unprofitable. But it is not, I think, indispensable. So I shall forego it.

A little more must be said, however, of a preliminary kind, about the distinction I have drawn, or suggested, between the putatively natural relation of causality, said to hold between things in nature, and the non-natural explaining relation, said to hold between facts or truths. The latter description may seem obscurantist or at least provocative. I do not mean, in adopting it, to deny any connection between this relation and natural facts. On the contrary, my aim is to emphasize a certain connection with certain natural facts, namely, natural facts about our human selves. As a first approximation, one could say that the non-natural fact that the explaining relation holds between the fact that p and the fact that q expands into the natural fact that coming to know that p will tend, in the light of other knowledge (or of theory) to induce a state which we call 'understanding why q'. The non-natural relation between the truths is mediated by the connection which, as a matter of natural fact, we give them (or they have) in our minds. This is why, as a variant on calling the relation non-natural, I call it rational. But the objects so related are obstinately intensional objects, not assignable to a place or time in nature, though of course the thinking of them, the reporting of them, and the objects they are about may all be so assigned. (Since the objects related by the explaining relation are not found in nature, the relation between them is not found in nature either: the relevant natural relation is between events in our minds. But we cannot report *these* naturally related events without reference to the non-naturally related objects.)

Against this it has of course been said that facts are part of the natural world, forming a rather comprehensive category which includes events, conditions, and the like. Linguistic evidence can be called on both sides of this debate. But it is not a very profitable debate except in so far as it makes us aware, once more, of the absence of practical need to mark clearly and consistently a distinction which it nevertheless behoves *us* to draw. Once this is recognized, the debate itself can be amicably and trivially terminated by each side allowing the other some rights in the word.

Once we are clear about the distinction I am drawing, we can avoid certain tangled ways of speaking which seem to have gained currency in recent philosophical writing. Thus we sometimes read of an event 'under such-and-such a description' being the cause—or being the explanation—of some other event or state-of-affairs. But both these ways of talking, whether of cause or explanation, must be thoroughly confused if there is in truth such a distinction as I have drawn. Suppose a particular happening or a particular condition of things, A, is the cause or part-cause of another particular happening or condition of things, B. Then if causality is a natural relation, a relation which holds in nature between A and B, that relation holds however A and B may be described. Of course it is not true that we can choose any uniquely applicable descriptions of A and B that take our fancy and still be confident that the fact that there occurred or existed an event or condition answering to our A-description will explain the fact that there occurred or existed an event or condition answering to our B-description. If what we are after is an explanation, we must select appropriate facts about A and B. Selecting an appropriate fact about an event or condition may involve choosing among different possible descriptions of the same event or condition. It does not involve choosing among different descriptions of the same fact. The fact is, in this connection, something to be stated, not described.[1] So whether what is at issue is the reporting of a causal relation or of an explaining-relation, it is misleading, and a mark of confusion, to say that one thing, under such-and-such a description, either causes or explains another. If the distinction I have drawn is sound, the situation is, rather, first, that A causes B *simpliciter*; and, second, that the truth of some statement including some description of A explains the truth of some statement including some description of B (or, in other words, that some A-involving fact explains some B-involving fact).

But then what makes descriptions suitable to figure in such statements? Or, in other words, what makes the selected facts the right facts to stand in the explaining relation? And what is the connection between the suitability of the descriptions, the rightness of the facts, and the causal relation itself, the relation which, we presume, holds in the natural world, when it does hold, between particular events and conditions, however described? Surely there must be such a connection. Surely the power of one fact to explain another must have some basis in the natural world where the events occur and the conditions obtain and the causal relations hold. We must think this on pain of holding, if we do not, that the causal relation itself has no natural existence or none outside our minds; that the belief in such

---

. [1] Though it is, of course, possible to describe facts; as when we say of such-and-such a fact that it is widely known or insufficiently appreciated.

a relation is simply the projection upon the world of some subjective disposition of ours, the disposition, perhaps, to take some facts as explaining others.

Now this is, in part, the doctrine that Hume held, though the subjective disposition he saw as thus projected was different from that just mentioned. But of course this was only a part of his doctrine. For he also held that there was indeed a natural basis which existed independently of the disposition in question, a basis for the disposition to operate on. Only this basis was not something that was intrinsically capable of being detected or observed or established *in any particular case*. It was only the observation of the repeated holding, in like particular cases, of certain other relations which *were* intrinsically capable of being detected in the particular case, that could ground the attribution of the causal relation, in any one individual case, as something holding irrespective of any subjective disposition of ours. So the causal relation regarded as holding between particular 'objects' (as Hume would call them) has a quite unique character; it is a dependant of generality; it is not, one is tempted to say, something actually present in the particular situation involving the particular objects at all. Or, to put the point in another way, causal generalizations are not generalizations of particular instances of causality; rather, particular instances of causality are established as such only by the particularizing of causal generalizations.

This famous and ingenious solution has become and—in spite of later sophistications—has in essentials remained what the greatest of Hume's critics called 'the accepted view'. It may be worth repeating that critic's summary of the accepted view. It is, he says, the view 'that only through the perception and comparison of events repeatedly following in a uniform manner upon preceding appearances . . . are we first led to construct for ourselves the concept of cause'.[2] Never mind that this summary omits the boldest element in Hume's doctrine, namely his diagnosis of the source of the illusory belief in necessary connection in nature; for that diagnosis has not generally found favour and forms no part of the view as generally accepted.

The received view has not been universally received. It has been attacked from different angles. Kant's own counter-argument, where clear, is clearly unsuccessful; and indeed it seems to me that

[2] *The Critique of Pure Reason*, B 240-1.

no direct attack, no attack which concentrates on the highly general notion of cause, or on that of necessity, is likely to be successful. Nevertheless there is a family of points, none of them novel, which, rightly organized, may radically change the face of the received view, and put it, as it were, in its place. I am fairly sure that I have not succeeded, in what follows, in finding the right organization of these points. Nevertheless I shall assemble them; or some of them.

II

Before I begin to assemble these points, it will be well to indicate the general line I propose to follow. The received view, I shall maintain, is partly right and partly wrong. It is true that there is no single natural relation which is detectable as such in the particular case, which holds between distinct events or conditions and which is identifiable as the causal relation. Neither is there a plurality of relations observable in particular cases, holding between distinct events or conditions and identifiable as specific varieties of a general type of relation, namely the causal. In this respect, the notion of causality differs from another categorial notion, that of an individual substance, with which it is traditionally, and rightly, associated. Both notions are highly abstract. Neither belongs to the vocabulary of particular observation. But whereas there is a host of expressions for specific kinds or varieties of individual substance which do belong to the vocabulary of particular observations—so that, of particular dogs and tables, men and mountains, one can say that each is an observable instance of such a kind—there is no evident parallel for this in the case of causality, thought of as relating distinct particular events or circumstances.

On this negative point, then, the traditional view is justified. But it is a grave error to attach to this negative point the importance that is traditionally attached to it. It is a grave error to take this negative point as a starting point in the elucidation of the concept of cause. It is the error of premature generality. Though the notion of cause, *understood as a relation between distinct particular events or circumstances*, finds, in the observation-vocabulary, no footing which exactly parallels that which I have just illustrated in the case of the notion of substance, yet the notion of causation in general does find a footing or, rather, a foundation, and a secure foundation, in the observation-vocabulary. There is an enormous variety, a great multiplicity, of kinds of *action* and *transaction* which are directly observable in the particular case and which are properly to be described as causal in so far as they are varieties of *bringing something about*, of producing some effect or some new state of affairs. Why then is there no parallel with the case of substances? The reason is this. When, as often, in reporting such observable actions or transactions, we employ a two-place predicate, a transitive verb, appropriate to the type of transaction in question, the two places are not filled by the designations of distinct particular events or circumstances. At least one of them is filled, and often both are filled, by the designations of particular substances. Typically, though not exclusively, such a predicate signifies some specific exercise of causal power by an agent, animate or inanimate; and often, though not always, an exercise of such a power *on* a patient.

Nothing, then, could be more commonplace than the observation, in particular cases, of specific varieties of the bringing about of effects by things. The observation-vocabulary is as rich in names for types of effect-producing *action* as it is in names for types of substances. Indeed the two kinds of name—for types of substance and types of action—are indissolubly linked with each other. Thus one thing, say, acts to bring about an effect, a new state of affairs—perhaps in another thing—by a characteristic exercise of causal power; and in observing such a transaction one already possesses the explanation —at least the immediate explanation—of the new state of affairs. There is no question of dissolving the transaction into a sequence of states of affairs—a sequence of 'distinct existences'—and wondering whether, or in virtue of what, the sequence constitutes a causal sequence. One has *observed* the change being *brought about* in some characteristic mode. Someone who observes the outcome, but not its bringing about, may seek an explanation of the outcome; and to him the outcome can be explained by mentioning the observable, but by him unobserved, action of bringing about the outcome. In these cases, then, explanation rests directly on observable relations in nature.

But, of course, explanation is not always so easily had. And when it is not, there begins, or may begin, the search for causes; guided partly by those models of bringing about, of the exercise of causal power, which nature presents to gross observation, and partly by that observation of regularities of association of distinct existences which is dear to the holder of the received view. If, by theoretical construction or minuter observation, we can discover or postulate copies or images or analogies of our grosser models to link the mere regularities of conjunction, then we are satisfied, or provisionally satisfied, that we have reached the level of explanation; that we have found the cause. Even in those cases where the observation-vocabulary supplies us with verbs of action or undergoing, so that in a sense we already understand effects by observation of their grosser modes of production, we may have motives for seeking a deeper, or more general, understanding and hence for investigating the micro-mechanisms of production, the minuter processes which underlie the grosser. It is true, no doubt, that in the evolution of sophisticated physical theory, the use, and the utility, of our gross models diminishes and finally, perhaps, wears out altogether. At this point also the notion of cause loses its role in theory; as Russell said that it would and should. But that is a point which none of us occupies for much of the time and few of us occupy at all.

III

Now to start to fill in this outline. Hume tracked down to a subjective source what he took to be the distinctive feature of our confused conception of causality as a natural relation. That distinctive feature he usually referred to as the idea of necessary connection. But he allowed that it bore other names of which he said that they were virtually or, as he put it, 'nearly' synonymous. His list of nearly synonymous terms includes 'efficacy', 'agency', 'power', 'force', 'energy', 'necessity', 'connexion', and 'productive quality';[3] to which he might have added 'compulsion' without straying far outside the bounds of his notion of near-synonymity. In tracking the idea down to its subjective source he of course followed, or claimed to follow, his leading principle: seek the impression from which the idea is derived. But, curiously enough, in the *Treatise* Hume ignored the most obvious direction in which that principle might have led him. If we concentrate on the trio 'power', 'force', and 'compulsion', and ask from what impression the idea discernible in them all is derived, the most obvious answer relates to the experience we have of exerting force on physical things or of having force exerted on us by physical things—including here the bodies of other

---

[3] *A Treatise of Human Nature*, I. III. xiv.

people as physical things.⁴ We push or pull, or are pushed or pulled, and *feel* the pressures or the tugs, the force, compulsion, or power we exert or have exerted upon us. Here is as immediate an experience as could be desired: an impression of force exerted or suffered. (The very word 'impression' has here its own ironical resonance.) In a dismissive footnote in the *Enquiry*⁵ Hume appears to respond to the point by seeking to atomize the total experience: isolating a pure bodily sensation as a single element merely accompanying, succeeding, or preceding other simple impressions of sense. But so to atomize is to falsify; as Hume systematically falsifies the phenomenology of perception in general.

Here then is a source of one of the ideas which Hume scornfully links together as 'nearly synonymous'. Of course, however, we do not limit the application of the idea of force to those mechanical transactions, those pushings or pullings, in which we ourselves, or our fellows, are engaged as agents or patients. We extend the idea to all such transactions. Is there, as Hume suggests in the footnote referred to, an element of anthropomorphic projection in this extension? Perhaps so. In a great boulder rolling down the mountainside and flattening the wooden hut in its path we see an exemplary instance of force; and perhaps, in so seeing it, we are, in some barely coherent way, identifying with the hut (if we are one kind of person) or with the boulder (if we are another): putting ourselves imaginatively in the place of one or the other. But whether or not such an element of projection underlies, or lingers on in, the extended application of the notion is a matter of no consequence. For the point is that in these mechanical transactions, these pushings and pullings or knockings down or over, these manifestations of force, we have examples of actions, of natural relations, which, whether entered into by animate or inanimate beings, are directly observable (or experienceable) and which, being observed (or experienced) or appropriately reported, supply wholly satisfactory explanations of their outcomes, of the states of affairs in which they terminate. We see the boulder *flatten* the hut. The outcome is the state of the hut, the state of being flattened. We see the man *pick up* the suitcase and *lift* it on to the rack. That is the explanation of the suitcase's being on the rack; that is how it got there.

⁴ The point is elegantly made by Austin Farrer. See *The Freedom of the Will* (London, 1960), p. 184.
⁵ *An Enquiry concerning Human Understanding*, VII. ii, final footnote.

I am suggesting, then, that we should regard mechanical transactions as fundamental in our examination of the notion of causality in general. They are fundamental to our own interventions in the world, to our bringing about purposed changes: (we put our shoulders to the wheel, our hands to the plough, push a pen or a button, pull a lever or a trigger). Entering into them ourselves, we find in them a source of the ideas of power and force, compulsion and constraint. Ourselves apart, they include observable natural phenomena, actions or relations directly detectable in the particular case, the observation of which supplies explanations of the states they end in. Finally, much of the polymorphous language of gross causal action and relation falls into this category: as 'push', 'pull', 'lift', 'put', 'remove', 'open', 'close', 'bend', 'stretch', 'dent', 'compress', and so on.[6] It is not then to be wondered at that such transactions supply a basic model when the theoretical search for causes is on; that we look for causal '*mechanisms*'; that, even when it is most clearly metaphorical, the language of mechanism pervades the language of cause in general, as in the phrases 'causal connection', 'causal links', and 'causal chain'.

Consideration of the notions of attraction and repulsion, fundamental in physical theory, confirm this claim. In the first place, the sense of mechanical interaction as being paradigmatically explanatory goes a long way to accounting for an initial reluctance to accept the idea of action at a distance, and the associated inclination to posit some medium through which impulses are transmitted. Second, even when the reluctance is overcome, it is still the model of pushing and pulling which is indirectly at work. There is indeed a double indirectness here. For, though the presence of the push-pull notions is etymologically obvious in the words 'attraction' and 'repulsion', the application of these words in the case of physical action at a distance is surely mediated by their already analogical application in the case of beings capable of desire and aversion, who are said to be 'drawn to' or 'repelled by' the objects of these emotions. The French word for magnet, after all, is *aimant*.

Closely connected with the model provided by the mechanical interaction of solid bodies is that supplied by the behaviour of fluids. This again pervades the figurative language of cause in

[6] Cf. G. E. M. Anscombe, 'Causality and Determination', reprinted in Ernest Sosa (ed.), *Causation and Conditionals* (Oxford, 1975), pp. 63-81.

general, as when we speak of the *sources* from which consequences *flow*. More specifically, it provides a preliminary model in the theory of *current* electricity: current *flows* under *pressure*, encounters *resistance*, and so on.

In general, then, the search for causal theories is a search for modes of action and reaction which are not observable at the ordinary level (or not observable at all, but postulated or hypothesized) and which we find intelligible because we model them on, or think of them on analogy with, those various modes of action and reaction which experience presents to gross observation or which we are conscious of engaging in, or suffering, ourselves. Such a statement calls for qualification. I do not wish to draw too sharp a line between observation and theory. Refined observation will notice powers and propensities which grosser observation passes over. Refined observation shades into theory. Again, one theory may itself provide the basis of analogy for another; as the gravitational theory applied to the solar system supplied the model for a theory of subatomic structure. And finally, as already suggested, in the most sophisticated reaches of physical theory the models seem to wear out altogether. Equations replace pictures. Causation is swallowed up in mathematics.

IV

In making, as I have done, so direct a transition from the topic of observable production of particular effects to the topic of the search for general causal theories, it may seem, and with reason, that I have passed too quickly over too much. For, it may be said, it is vital to distinguish between the theoretical enquiry into the causes of some general phenomenon and the demand for explanation of the occurrence of some particular incident or the obtaining of some particular state of affairs; and the mere reference to the observable production of effects constitutes no adequate treatment of the latter topic even in those cases where such observation of causal action is available.

There is point in this. For though some observable production of an effect, by some particular manifestation of causal power or liability, may yield an immediate explanation of the effect, there is often still room for the question why that particular manifestation occurred, why the type of which it was an instance was then and there realized. To meet the point, it is necessary and sufficient to return to the topic of concepts of types of substance and their link with concepts of types of action and reaction (or of obstruction or resistance to action). The existence of the link—the thoroughgoing dispositionality of our substance-concepts—is a philosophical commonplace. Yet such is the persisting power and influence of the Humean theory of causation that the importance of this commonplace in its bearing on that topic is regularly missed or underrated.

Our concepts of types of individual thing or substance, then, are concepts of things with characteristic dispositions to act or react in certain ways *in certain ranges of circumstances*. Emphasizing that last phrase, we might say, with pardonable exaggeration, that all action is reaction. But of course we may observe or learn of some action or reaction of a thing without knowing which of a characteristic range of action- or reaction-triggering circumstances operated in the particular case; or without knowing the detail of those circumstances; or without knowing enough of the surrounding circumstances even to be able to choose a satisfactory classification of the observed behaviour from among those types of behaviour to which substances of the kind in question are prone. In all these cases a demand for explanation is in order. This is a demand for the filling-in of gaps in our knowledge. But the gaps, one is tempted to say, are, or often are, like blanks in an already prepared proforma. We know in advance the range of possible fillings; for we know what type of thing we have to deal with. It is not that we first acquire the concepts of types of thing and only then, and only by repeated observations of similar conjunctions of events or circumstances, come to form beliefs about what kinds of reaction may be expected of such things in what ranges of antecedent conditions. Rather, such beliefs are inseparable from our concepts of the things.

It will not do to exaggerate the scope of the point; nor have I exaggerated it—or at least not greatly—in the formulation just given. It would be absurd to deny, and I have not denied, that we learn by experience, as we say, about the propensities of things of different types and, indeed, about the propensities of individual specimens of those types; most notably the latter when the type is the type of fellow human beings. But the learning takes place in a pre-existing, in an already prepared, framework of conditional expectation. There is no point, in our self-conscious existence as beings aware of a world

of objects and events, at which we are equally prepared, or unpre-
pared, for anything to come of anything; and hence no process,
whereby we emerge from this condition, such as that described by
Hume: observation of constant conjunctions generating mental
compulsions which we then project upon objects in the form of the
delusive notions of efficacy, agency, power, force, necessary connection, and the like.

But surely, it might be said, it is at least true that it is observation
of regularities which suggests or confirms that enriched conception
of the powers or propensities of things which we owe to experience?
No doubt there is truth in this. But it goes no way to show that the
notion of causal action or reaction, as embodied in the myriad
specific forms which it takes in our common and theoretical vocabularies, is derived from experience of bare regularities of succession
or that it is, as far as all objective content is concerned, reducible to
such regularities—the idea which Hume first sketched and which
Mill and subsequent writers have refined. To think that such a derivation is necessary or possible is to get things the wrong way round.
And to see this it is sufficient to bear in mind two points already
implicitly or explicitly made.

The first is the thoroughgoing dispositionality of our ordinary
pre-theoretical concepts of things and their qualities. With this dispositionality, the *generality*, which is the core of the reductive conception, is already given. It is not given in a form which supplies
any comfort to the reductionist. This it could only do if the relevant
concepts of thing and quality dissolved into, or were constructed
out of, a complex of wholly non-dispositional concepts (of sense-
quality) plus generalizations relating them. But the relevant concepts
of thing and quality do not so dissolve and are not so constructed.
They are basic conceptual stock; and to think otherwise is to mis-
represent us as being theorists before we have the means of theorizing. It is internal, then, to the relevant concepts of thing and quality,
the concepts which belong to our basic, pre-theoretical stock, that
those things, or the bearers of those qualities, regularly act and
react in such-and-such ways. *This* is the conceptual setting in which
dispositionality carries generality within it. It is on this basis that
observation of regularities can help us to enrich our primitive conceptions of the powers and propensities of things—those primitive
conceptions without which we would have no conception of the
things themselves. And this is why the received or traditional

account of causal action and reaction can, with unusual aptness, be said to put the cart before the horse.

Or, rather, this is one reason. The other, also previously suggested, is that mere regularities of succession do not of themselves satisfy us that we have found causes. The symptoms displayed at successive stages of a disease may exhibit as high a degree of regularity as could be desired. The birds flying inland portend the coming storm. Many other phenomena are quite reliable indications of yet other phenomena to come. But it is only if we can more or less dimly conceive of the antecedent and the subsequent phenomenon as being connected in some way more or less remotely assimilable to, or analogous to, the models of causal action and reaction which we already possess, that we are disposed to regard the former as the cause of the latter. To those of a more curiously enquiring turn of mind—to the *natural* natural scientist—such a dim and vague conception of a causal link will not be satisfactory. He wants to know the detail of the link, the inner mechanism of the connection. He wants to know *how* it works. Only then is he satisfied that he possesses a full understanding of the matter. Not, of course, that the interest in such understanding is purely theoretical. For it is by means of these enquiries that we extend our own control over nature, our own power to bring about or avert effects we desire or fear.

The general point I have been urging in the immediately preceding paragraphs is that, though we do indeed learn much about the operation of causality in the world through the observation of regularities of succession, we do so only because the general notion of causal efficacy and causal response, of effects being brought about in a variety of specific ways, is already lodged with us, is already implicit in a wide range of concepts of thing, quality, action, and reaction which belong to our basic stock of concepts of the observable. This is why Kant is fundamentally right against Hume; although, partly because he also shared the almost universal fault of treating the topic at an excessively high level of generality, his particular arguments are defective. Nevertheless, he had a secure grasp of the central point, which it would perhaps not be unacceptable to express in more or less his own words by saying that the concept of causal efficacy is not derived from experience of a world of objects, but is a presupposition of it; or, perhaps better, is already with us when anything which could be called 'experience' begins.

V

I remarked earlier that the notion of mechanical action, directly experienced or observed, and the more general and indirectly derived notion of physical force (attraction and repulsion) play a fundamental part in the elaboration of causal theories. They provide models of the explanatory. But at an early stage of human theorizing we find another supplementary model at work. (The supplementary model is itself connected with the mode of derivation which I suggested for the generalized notions of physical attraction and repulsion.) I refer to the model of human action and motivation. It is not by reliance on an observed constant conjunction between motive and movement that we know why we are acting as we do act. Any such idea is quite absurd. We have, in general, immediate knowledge of what we are up to, of what we are doing or trying to do. Such knowledge is a species of immediate causal knowledge: knowledge of our desires and aims as moving us to try to fulfil or achieve them. In so far as we can assign any effect in the world to the act of an agent, himself (or herself) actuated by such motives as we know in ourselves, we feel that we can to that extent understand it. In so far as we conceive certain effects, desired or feared by us, to be within the power of certain agents, we also conceive it to be within *our* power to influence the production or avoidance of those effects to just the extent to which we can supply those agents with appropriate motivation. Our primitive, and not so primitive, theorists, aware of their own powers of agency and of the motives behind their exercise, aware, also, of vast effects in nature, dreaded or hoped for, but quite beyond their own powers directly to avert or produce, seem to have found it utterly easy and natural to attribute these effects to the exercise of powers by superhuman agents who, capricious as their acts must often have appeared, were actuated by motives not wholly alien or wholly inscrutable. Hence they sought to propitiate these agents by honours and offerings, by sacrifices and worship—doing what they could to get the gods on their side.

This was early science: a Kuhnian paradigm, now out of fashion and unlikely to come in again;[7] not in itself unreasonable, although,

---

[7] Perhaps we can find a lingering trace of it in the sense, on the part of some of the ecologically minded, that we have, as a species, been guilty in this century of *impiety* towards Nature; for which we shall be made, and are being made, to pay. A sentiment to be encouraged.

in comparison with some later theories, poor in its yield of practical successes. Its importance in the present connection is obvious enough. For neither our knowledge of the causal efficacy of motive in general nor the theoretical extension of this model of causal efficacy to the sphere of the superhuman can with any plausibility be represented as resting on Humean foundations, that is on the observation of 'events repeatedly following in a uniform manner upon preceding appearances'. To say this is not, of course, to deny that we can learn about human motivation, or even fancy that we can learn about divine motivation, from experience. But, of this kind of learning, as of learning an enriched conception of the powers and propensities of non-animate things, it must be said that it presupposes an awareness, both general and specific, of causal propensity; and it should further be added that experience in this area normally works through a distinctive kind of advance in self-understanding or empathetic understanding, of which nothing resembling a Humean account can possibly be given.

VI

Theories of superhuman agency, never alone in the field, ultimately gave place, of course, to theories which, except in the field of human or animal action, made no reference to motives. The successor theories owed their succession to their greater success. The gains from improved knowledge of causal propensity and causal power are not only improved understanding, but increased certainty of prediction and increased power of control. We have already seen how the notions of generality and normality of action and reaction are inseparable from those of causal propensity and power, themselves inseparable from the notions of types of substance or of natural kinds and of the qualities in respect of which individuals of the same kind may differ from each other; and it is easy to appreciate how practical and theoretical pressure alike will tend to drive enquiry in a certain direction: in the direction of an advance from mere regularities to invariabilities, from propensities to strict laws. For the demand for explanation is generated not only by ignorance of what characteristic circumstances induced a characteristic response or of what characteristic exercise of causal power produced a charactersitic effect. It is generated also, and with greater poignancy, when the expected response or effect is not forthcoming, although the characteristic circumstances or excercise of power were observed to obtain or to occur; or, again, by the mere observation of differences in reaction to similar circumstances between things with similar general propensities.

These pressures arise, then, at the level of ordinary observation; and, as already remarked, we can go some way to refining our conceptions of the powers and propensities of things while remaining at that level. But we cannot go all the way to meet the theoretical pressure for strict law while remaining at that level. We can indeed say with confidence that when the brains are out, the man will die and there an end; or that a smart blow with a twenty-pound hammer will break an ordinary glass window. But these truths are insufficiently general to satisfy the theoretical pressure. To reach propositions which are sufficiently general and also have the character of strict law, we must abstract from the level of ordinary observation, abstract from all the complexity of circumstance characteristic of particular situations and confine ourselves to the terms of a particular physical theory. The procedure is reasonable, indeed necessary. But it does point to a great gap between our ordinary causal explanations of particular events and circumstances and the notion of explicit appeal to strict law.

This is a point on which Mill, for example, appears to have been thoroughly confused, and to have confused his followers. Consider his account of the cause, 'philosophically speaking', as 'the sum total of the conditions, positive and negative, taken together; the whole of the contingencies of every description, which being realized, the consequent invariably follows'.[8] A man, say, falls down a flight of stone steps as he begins the descent. The steps are slippery and the man's mind is elsewhere. This is a sufficient explanation of his fall. But of course not every preoccupied man falls down every flight of slippery steps he descends. There is absolutely no question of our formulating or envisaging exceptionless laws, framed in terms of *this* order, to cover all such cases: no question of invoking 'contingencies' of various descriptions with the aim of achieving such a result. We do indeed suppose there to be exceptionless and truly general mechanical laws which bear on the case; but these are laws framed in terms of a quite different order, the relatively abstract terms of a physical theory. We have no prospect of knowing, and no interest in enquiring, in precise detail, just *how* these

[8] *System of Logic*, III. V. iii.

laws apply in such a particular case as that described. So Mill's account is quite curiously wide of the mark so far as ordinary causal explanation is concerned.

Having said so much, I may seem under some obligation to answer two questions about theoretical laws: how are such laws established? and how are they applied in practice, that is, how are they *used* to achieve desired effects? For such laws certainly *are* established, or come to be accepted as established; and they certainly *are* put to use—now as never before. These questions belong to the philosophy of science and of applied science; and anything like a generally adequate answer to them is beyond both my competence and the scope of this paper. But perhaps it is enough, for present purposes, to point out that the establishing of such laws requires, first, the framing of hypotheses and, second, that the hypotheses be tested, and perhaps given specific quantitative form, *in carefully contrived observational situations*, that is situations so contrived that exact knowledge is possible of those features in the situation to which the putative law relates. (How such hypotheses themselves come to be framed I have earlier suggested in pointing to the role of models or analogies derived from ordinary observation of causal efficacy and to the progressive attenuation of their influence in the course of theoretical advance.) As for the practical application of such laws, this is again a matter of careful contrivance: of ensuring, as far as possible, that the conditions we produce answer to certain exact specifications *in respect of those features to which the law relates*. It is then a necessary truth that if we have succeeded in this, if the law in fact holds, and if we have done our calculations correctly, then the conditions we have produced will themselves produce, *as far as the relevant features are concerned*, the outcome we intend.

So much—and I know it is all too little—about the role of exceptionless law. Thinking, as we do, of the natural realm at a variety of different levels, or from a variety of theoretical and practical viewpoints, we may suppose that there is one level at which general, exceptionless, and discoverable law reigns throughout that realm. We are authoritatively told that there is another level—a lower or minuter level of physical theory—at which it does not; at which the most we can expect is probabilisitc law. What I have been lately concerned to suggest is that at the level of ordinary causal explanation of particular events and circumstances, the level at which we employ the common vocabulary of description rather than the technical vocabularies of physical theories, there is no reason to think that our explanations presuppose or rest upon belief in the existence of general, exceptionless, and discoverable laws frameable in terms of that common vocabulary; and that, further, there is no reason to think that our explanations are, for this reason, in any way deficient. I think I have, earlier on, said enough about the way in which the notion of causal action and reaction, of causal efficacy and propensity, is embodied in our common concepts to explain, if explanation is needed, how and why this is so.

VII

Before concluding, I wish to mention one odd philosophical consequence of adherence to the received view—or to an essential element in the received view—of causality; or, which is virtually the same thing, of neglect of the ways in which the notion of cause is actually embodied in our ordinary ideas of things. This essential element of the received view is the doctrine that, as far as its objective content is concerned, the notion of cause is reducible to that of invariability of association of types of occurrence or circumstance. The favoured terminology for handling this latter notion is the terminology of necessary and sufficient conditions. Thus we have such formulations as the following: if circumstances of a certain type, X, obtain, then the occurrence of an event of a certain type α is necessary and sufficient for the subsequent occurrence of an event of a certain type β. This scheme is clearly equivalent to: if circumstances of a certain type, X, obtain, then the occurrence of an event of a certain type β is sufficient and necessary for the prior occurrence of an event of a certain type α. Suppose circumstances of type X do obtain and particular events of types α and β do occur in that order. So far as necessity and sufficiency are concerned, we have no reason for calling the α-type event a, or the, cause of the β-type event rather than vice versa; no reason, indeed, for distinguishing between cause and effect at all rather than recognizing a symmetrical relation of, say, mutual causal dependence. Yet we seem to have an obstinate prejudice in favour of the view that there is such a distinction, and that, while causes may precede or be simultaneous with their effects, effects never precede their causes; and, further, that this is not to be understood as simply the consequence of a trivial verbal stipulation. So the received doctrine presents us with the problem of justifying, or at least explaining, our obstinate adherence to this view.

Once we turn our backs on the received doctrine, however, and consider together both the modes in which the notion of causality is embodied in our ordinary ideas and the association of this notion with that of explanation, we see that the supposed problem is quite spurious. Consider the two basic and connected models of (1) the exercise of mechanical power by a physical agent and (2) the motivation of human action; and note how the first model is present in the very naming of the second. Recall how the state of affairs which ensues upon the exercise of mechanical power—the pushing or the pulling—is explained by reference to that exercise; and how human action is explained by reference to the motives behind it. Recall again how any display of natural propensity is explained by the typical circumstances which excite it, to which it is a response or reaction. Here are natural asymmetries enough, and to spare, to show that the notion of priority which would, on the received view, appear as a trivial or whimsical addition to our concept of causal dependence, lies in fact at its very root. One might think it extraordinary that philosophers could manœuvre themselves into a position at which so fundamental a feature of so fundamental a concept should appear as problematic; but perhaps, on second thoughts, one should recognize the fact as one of the glories of the subject.[9]

And now to conclude. If we take in our hand, as Hume would say, any volume, such as an old-fashioned novel or a book of traveller's reminiscences, which contains extended passages of narrative-cum-descriptive writing, we may not find in those passages

[9] Of course it is always open to ingenuity to describe imaginary situations in terms which encourage us to think of reversed causality as a possibility; but such descriptions generally owe their persuasive power to a perverse exploitation of concepts, such as those of observation or copying, which belong to our ordinary scheme. Evidently observation and copying involve causal dependence. Equally evidently it is impossible to copy or observe what has not yet come into existence. But the imaginary situations in question are described in terms which irresistibly put us in mind of these ordinary acts or relations while placing their pseudo-objects in what is, relative to them, the future. The essential feature of the trick is to describe isolated cases of the imagined kind, in order to play them off against the normal conceptual background.

This is not to deny that it may be possible to describe imaginary cases which do not thus exploit ordinary causal concepts and yet similarly invite us to invert the ordinary temporal order of *explanation*. But so deep are the natural roots of the common concepts of *causal efficacy* and *causal dependence* that, even if we accepted the invitation, it is unclear that we should regard ourselves as thereby employing, with inverted temporal application, those very concepts.

many occurrences of the word 'cause'; but we shall find the pages stiff with verbs, transitive and intransitive, referring to a myriad modes of causal action and reaction. An account in such terms carries with it, in general, a sufficient explanation of the circumstances recorded—of why such-and-such a thing happened, of how such-and-such another came to pass. Sometimes, in such a text, causality will figure under its general name: for example, when the notion or question of explanation or of mode of production of some particular circumstance is, for one reason or another, *explicitly* to the fore. And, of course, in a quite different kind of text, or of context, causality may figure under its general name in connection with the search for, or the discovery of, the *general* mechanism of production of some *general* type of effect; as when we speak of the cause of malaria or of cancer.

Should we then finally say—to end where we began—that 'cause' does name a relation which holds in nature between distinct existences; or should we deny this and call it rather the name of a general categorial notion which we invoke in connection with the explanation of particular circumstances and the discovery of general mechanisms of production of general types of effect? I do not think it matters very much which we do. I think we may be obscurely and confusedly drawn towards the former alternative by the fact that there do undoubtedly and observably occur in nature the many types of causal action and reaction which I have repeatedly insisted on. This is not, of course, a good reason for espousing that alternative. On the other hand, when we properly invoke one particular fact or conjunction of facts in explanation of another; and when the particular events or circumstances mentioned in the statement of the explaining and the explained facts are distinct existences; then, although the relation holds only because the particular events and circumstances are of the kinds described in the explaining and explained propositions, there seems no particular harm in saying that those particular events and circumstances, however described, do in fact stand in a particular relation which may be called causal.

IX

A WORLD WITHOUT EVENTS?[1]

IRVING THALBERG

Practitioners of analytical or 'descriptive' metaphysics have been debating vigorously of late as to whether we should assume there are events. For instance: Should we suppose that causal relationships hold between events; that actions are events; and that the doctrine of materialism would be true if mental events were in fact identical with various brain processes? We need not go into those issues. Nor is there any problem about the meaning of our key noun. Nearly all opposed theorists appear willing to define 'event' broadly.[2] Thus, along with either dramatic or gradual alterations of things—the crash-landing of a jumbo jet, the growth of a redwood—most litigants will admit 'unchanges' as events. These unchanges may be quite diverse: states like the frozen condition of a pond; homogeneous processes, either steady or intermittent, such as the constant glow or the periodic blinking of a searchlight; perhaps even the onset, the ending, and other assorted high points of a state or process. But however narrowly or liberally we construe our favoured term, we will run into philosophers who declare 'there are no such things as . . . events', and especially no ' "concrete events" in addition to states of affairs';[3] 'there is no such thing as

[1] I am grateful to Donald Davidson for many fruitful discussions of a wide range of problems about actions and events. On this particular essay I have received valuable comments from my colleagues Daniel Berger, Myles Brand, and Douglas Stalker. When I read an earlier version of the paper at Syracuse University in November 1978, I benefited from the reactions of José Benardete, Peter Van Inwagen, Margery Naylor, and Philip Peterson. Richard Feldman and Edward Wierenga kindly sent me a pre-publication copy of their 'Thalberg on the Irreducibility of Events', published in *Analysis* 39 (1979), 19-25. It was also extremely helpful to talk over the main issues with Arnold Levison, and to read several of his works-in-progress which deal with event theory.

[2] See Davidson, 'Agency', *EAE*, p. 49; N. Wilson, 'Facts, Events, and their Identity Conditions', *Philosophical Studies* 25 (1974), 313; J. Kim, 'Events as Property Exemplifications', in M. Brand and D. Walton (eds.), *Action Theory* (Dordrecht, 1976), p. 159 f.; B. Aune, *Action and Reason* (Dordrecht, 1977), p. 31.

[3] R. Chisholm, *Person and Object* (LaSalle, Ill., 1976), p. 115.

an event distinct from a fact';[4] and 'events as *particulars* do not exist'.[5] By a 'concrete' or 'particular' occurrence, state, or process, these nay-saying writers mean any event which can be recorded, and assigned temporal and presumably spatial co-ordinates. Examples would be: the belly-landing of United Airlines Boeing 747 flight 218 at Stapleton Field, Denver, at 12.55 pm, 21 November 1978; Chicago's Lincoln Park lagoon remaining iced over from New Year until mid February, 1979 and the kick-off of this winter's Super-bowl game.

I have a simple question for no-event metaphysicians (henceforth abbreviated 'NEMs'). I want to know what sort of cosmos they envisage—which explains the 'uneventful universe' of my title. Generally, what would things be like if there were no concrete happenings, states, and the like? In order to decide, I must briefly set forth what the leading pro-event metaphysicians (PEMs) have postulated, and why. My twin labels of course imply no doctrinal uniformity among NEMs and PEMs respectively, beyond either rejection or acceptance of individual events.

I. MODELS FOR THE NEM'S POSITION

You might tell a credulous, sheltered young person that there are no dragons, or dinosaurs, and in all likelihood no flying saucers from outer space. Dragons have never existed. Dinosaurs flourished once, but are extinct now. Reports of flying saucers are terribly controversial. Surprises are possible, however. It could turn out that there are dragons, dinosaurs, and flying saucers.

When the NEM refuses to acknowledge particular events, is he making this kind of claim? No; he cannot mean that there never have been any crash-landings, frozen conditions, blinkings, kick-offs—or that such changes and unchanges very probably won't occur.

Here is a different analogy. A friend of mine who had joined a spiritualist commune in Scotland recently sent me the group's magazine. One contributor announced 'an explosion of data on the subtler aspects of human existence—from photography of radiatory energies around life forms, to out-of-body travel, psychokinesis, clairaudience, clairvoyance, etheric surgery, exotic healing, and

---

[4] Wilson, op. cit. 317.
[5] T. Horgan, 'The Case Against Events', *Philosophical Review* 87 (1978), 29.

awareness in plant life'.[6] Another wrote that initiation into the group

means to consciously participate in the creative enfoldment [*sic*] of the goals . . . of the planetary lord. This planet is a living being . . . the custodian of that . . . cosmic energy which . . . is . . . responsible for the . . . evolution of consciousness of this world. . . . Initiation . . . is the conscious evocation of the fire of will . . . [that] transcends the dualities of space and time. It simply *is*, and . . . shatters whatever forms are not in resonance [*sic*] with what it is.[7]

These pronouncements may be sincere and inspiring. But have we the slightest inkling how to interpret phrases like 'radiatory energies around life forms' and 'awareness in plant life'? What does it mean to say our globe is 'a living being' equipped with a 'will' that 'transcends . . . space and time'? Although we might be emotionally stirred by the musings of these occultists, we can make no clear sense of them.

I believe this is not the kind of reaction that NEMs have to talk of events. The NEM understands as well as PEMs and ordinary folk do what it is for crash-landings and similar concrete events to take place. His complaint is surely not that the notion of an event is unintelligible.

I want to try out one more model for the NEM's thesis. It is from philosophical psychology, where it still generates debate; however, I deploy it here for illustrative purposes only. I am alluding to the contention of many down-to-earth theorists that we should not reify 'the mind' and its alleged denizens. On this view, we should not say that there are such items as stabs of pain, cavalcades of sense data, or thrusts of volition. Nor should we hypostatize mental departments or faculties like cool reason, rebellious passion, steadfast will, or grumpy, guilt-ridden conscience. And if we are 'into' psychotherapy, we must not assume that terms like 'id', 'ego', 'superego', 'libido', and 'defence mechanism' stand for bits of machinery or tiny people within us. The anti-mind philosopher would urge us to jettison this burdensome theoretical luggage—this array of elusive objects, agencies and happenings allegedly lurking inside us. Why not just report the whole *person's* mental-cum-behavioural career? Instead of puzzling over her or his unobservable

---

[6] D. Keys, 'Transpersonal Growth and Global Integration', *Onearth* 4 (1977), 10.
[7] F. Duquesne, 'Findhorn and Initiation', ibid. 20 f.

imagery, thoughts, volitions, and unconscious impulses, we can say that the visible, tangible woman or man we have before us is suffering from headache; that he is carefully, smugly, or indignantly calculating his income tax; that he is in perceptual contact with numerous medium-size dry goods in his environment; that he is bicycling attentively or recklessly. These random samples hardly furnish us a full story of anyone's psychological existence; but they suggest how we might be able to describe it without summoning up a mind replete with contents and faculties.

In a clear sense, the anti-mind theorist is saying there are no minds. Yet he is far from asserting that people are mindless—that nobody ever aches, worries, rages, deliberates. Rather, he prefers to construe these mental phenomena as states and happenings which involve flesh-and-blood, active people—not an elusive inner theatre and its spectral players.

This outlook sounds more like the NEM's denial of concrete events—including, naturally, those very mental-cum-behavioural episodes and states which are championed by anti-mind philosophers. This model also diverges significantly from the case of occult energies and entities. Opponents of the traditional 'mind' story would never hold that the 'ghost in the machine' doctrine is utterly, glaringly confused. Besides Descartes, many other philosophical giants—Locke, Leibniz, Berkeley, Hume, Mill, Russell—have worked out appealing variants of the dualistic hypothesis. Such theories seem marvellously cogent, almost self-evidently true. If they are really unintelligible, the nonsense must be heavily disguised, requiring sedulous argumentation to unmask. With exceptions that I shall discuss immediately, I think this is roughly the attitude of NEMs toward the doctrine of particular events.

II. IS EVENT ONTOLOGY BLATANTLY INCOHERENT?

One sympathizer with the NEMs has claimed to detect nonsense hidden just below the surface of a leading PEM's theory. Examining Donald Davidson's 'event' analysis of action sentences, Bruce Aune tries out the example 'John walked into the door'. Now I must quote Aune at length, but without his paragraphing. Aune remarks:

According to Davidson, this sentence has the form of '$(\exists x)(Wxj \ \& \ Ixd)$' [colloquially: 'There is an event x such that x is a walking by John, and x is an into-the-door event—a collision with the door']. But suppose, consistently with Davidson's theory of action, that John's walking here is identical with his amusing Mary. Since his act of amusing Mary is *an* act of amusing her, and since it is also identical with the act that, according to the formula above, is *into* the door, we can then infer that '$(\exists x)(Axjm\ \&\ Ixd)$'. But the vernacular equivalent to this statement is 'John amused Mary into the door'. Clearly, this result is absurd . . .[8]

Must we interpret the second Davidsonian formula so comically? I would offer a more long-winded but charitable reading: 'There is an event x such that x is an event featuring John which amuses Mary, and x is an into-the-door event'. This may be unidiomatic, but it is far from unintelligible.

Aune is prepared with another case which he thinks will enable him to derive a contradiction, rather than nonsense, from Davidson's event analysis of action sentences. Of his example, 'Jones travelled slowly'. Aune comments:

this statement cannot be interpreted as '$(\exists x)(x$ was a travelling by Jones and x was slow)'. . . . [A] modifier like 'slowly' cannot be detached from its verb and converted into a simple predicate true of events. If Jones's travelling were identical with his walking, then, if Jones walked extremely fast [*sic*], the proposed analysis would require us to say that his action was, without qualification, both slow and fast. Since saying this would be absurd, some other analysis must be found.[9]

Before we agree, we should recall Aune's action sentence. Isn't it elliptical? In any context where adverbs like 'slowly' and adjectives like 'slow' are used, we can point to some standard—of comparative velocity here. So I would spell out Aune's example in some contexts as follows: 'There is an event x such that x is a journey of Jones, x is slow by comparison with most aeroplane, rail, and automobile trips over the same distance, and x is rapid by comparison with most foot journeys'. If my phrase 'by comparison' disturbs you, then say: 'event x is a slower travelling than most aeroplane trips, and x is a faster travelling than most hikes of that length'.

---

[8] Aune, *Action and Reason*, pp. 29 f.; see M. Cohen, 'The Same Action', *Proceedings of the Aristotelian Society* 70 (1969-70) 77 f.; J. Annas, 'Davidson and Anscombe on "the Same Action"', *Mind* 85 (1976), 254; R. Trenholme, 'Doing Without Events', *Canadian Journal of Philosophy* 8 (1978), 183 n. 19.

[9] Aune, op. cit., p. 29; cf. Davidson, 'The Logical Form of Action Sentences', *EAE*, pp. 106 f.; Trenholme, op. cit. 182.

Awkward, perhaps, but not 'absurd'; consequently we have no reason yet to join the NEMs.

Actually Aune declares himself officially neutral in the NEM-PEM quarrel. Another disputant, Russell Trenholme, unequivocally lines up with the NEMs, and produces a somewhat different type of example against PEMs. Allegedly it will refute an event analysis of causal statements. Trenholme first asks us to accept the premiss 'Stubbing his toe caused John to walk slowly'.[10] Now Davidson and most other PEMs hold that only events stand in causal relations. So I gather that Trenholme believes PEMs would symbolize his premiss '$(\exists x)(\exists y)(x$ is a toe-stubbing by John, and y is a walking by John, and y is slow, and x caused $y)$'. However that may be, the rules of elementary logic permit us to delete any conjunct of such a conjunctive assertion. But here is the catch: if we erase the conjunct about y's slowness, we can deduce a false conclusion from our presumptively true premiss. For Trenholme reads the shortened conjunctive statement—minus 'y is slow'—as the causal assertion 'Stubbing his toe caused John to *walk*'.[11] Yet evidently we do not want to say that the walking event y resulted from the toe-stubbing event x.

Again we should look at the original anecdote. Wasn't Trenholme's premiss that as a result of injuring his foot, our peripatetic hero slowed down? John was breezing along; but as soon as he damaged his toe, his place diminished to a hobble—and his hobbling was slower than his antecedent ambulation. In symbols, my causal report would be: '$(\exists x)(\exists y)(\exists z)(x$ is a toe-stubbing by John, and y is a hobbling by John, and z is a [somewhat earlier] walking by John, and y is slower than z, and x caused $y)$'. Now if we amputate the 'slowness' conjunct, we still have a true causal assertion, namely that the toe-stubbing produced John's hobbling. But for this mishap, he would be walking normally.

If this sounds too context-dependent, we could symbolize Trenholme's anecdote: '$(\exists x)(\exists y)(x$ is a toe-stubbing by John, and y is a slowing-down [a deceleration] by John, and x caused $y)$'. This seems closer to what Trenholme's causal utterance means. However, it contains no 'slowness' conjunct for Trenholme to delete; so

[10] 'Doing without Events', p. 177; and see Trenholme, 'Necessity and Causality', *Journal of Philosophy* 72 (1975), 447.

[11] Trenholme, loc. cit., emphasis added; see J. Watling, 'Are Causes Events or Facts?', *Proceedings of the Aristotelian Society* 74 (1973-4), 162.

that the inference he proposes will not go through. But whichever reading PEMs opt for, they may continue believing that events cause events.

Before we shrug off the accusation that event ontology is incoherent, we must look at one last species of counter-example. It also hinges on adverbs; but unlike 'slowly', we cannot transform these into standard predicates of events. Terence Horgan's case is: 'Sebastian almost strolled'.[12] Horgan defies PEMs to formalize this alleged event report 'so as to reveal that . . . [it] entails "Sebastian didn't stroll"'. Clearly I ought to avoid the very tough, and for us extraneous, problem of how to formalize psychological statements —for instance, reports of Sebastian's intentions, preparations, and abstentions. I feel the same about adverbs and statements which seem patently modal, such as 'Possibly Sebastian walked'. Therefore I will replace Horgan's example with a non-psychological and non-modal analogue: 'Sebastian's drink almost spilled'.

How would PEMs render this? My guess is: '$(\exists x)(x$ was a tipping of Sebastian's drink to angle n, and x was *not* a spilling of Sebastian's drink, but if x had been a tipping of Sebastian's drink to angle $n + m$, then x would have been a spilling of the drink)'. This clearly entails '$(\exists x)(x$ was not a spilling of Sebastian's drink)'. If you dislike my counterfactual 'if-then' conjunct, you may revise that part of my statement to your taste. In order to decide whether the ontology of PEMs is incoherent, we should not have to work out the logical form of counterfactual utterances.

III. ARE EVENTS SUPERNUMERARY?

The critical literature is loaded with more ostensible counter-instances to the event theories of Davidson and other PEMs. I think alert, uncommitted readers will discover these to be as inconclusive as the ones we have tested. At any rate, the cases we have grappled with so far were designed to prove that we *cannot* postulate events: that PEMs risk nonsense or inconsistency; that they must accept invalid inferences; and that they will be unable to draw valid inferences like 'Sebastian almost walked, therefore he did not walk'. Next I want to evaluate another line of argument by NEMs: that we *need not* acknowledge happenings, states, and processes.

[12] Horgan, 'The Case Against Events', 46 f.; see Aune, *Action and Reason*, pp. 29, 32.

Why not? PEMs are warned that it is simply gratuitous to assume that events form an additional category alongside physical objects—including human beings—and certain other entities. In short, NEMs claim that an eventless world already provides us with all we need to reconstruct the goings-on and the conditions postulated by PEMs.

Here emerges a significant resemblance between our controversy and the previously mentioned debate over 'minds'. The anti-mind theorist could, for purposes of argument, suppose that the doctrine of an inner theatre brimming with 'ideas' and their cohorts is free of disguised nonsense, contradiction, and similar flaws. Yet he might contend that these quaint psychic items are only excess baggage; we can adequately account for, and perspicuously describe, a person's mental life without the aid of this mumbo-jumbo. I think that if we are sympathetic to this outlook in philosophical psychology, we should give a careful hearing to the NEM's 'superfluity' objection regarding events.

The most compact version of this complaint which I recall is in a paper by Paul Ziff on the logical structure of English sentences. Ziff laments that

quantificational logics are not equipped to cope with adverbs in any simple way . . . Adverbs . . . operate on verbs, as does 'slowly' in 'He ran slowly'. Since the conspicuous operation in quantificational logic is . . . predication . . . [o]ne must cast 'slowly' in the guise of 'is slow', which means conjuring up an entity to fill the bill in 'x is slow'. . . . [W]e shall count such things as a run that was slow. One could then represent . . . 'Something ran slowly' as '$(\exists x)(\exists y)(Pxy \ \& \ Ry \ \& \ Sy)$', where '$Pxy$' stands for '$x$ performed y', 'Ry' for y was a run' and 'Sy' for y was slow'. Thus we construe running as a relation between a person and a run he performs . . . [However, this is] a *façon de parler*. We are not required to suppose that somehow runs have an existence of their own apart from things that run. [13]

I am unsure what Ziff's ontological position is. But this kind of reasoning seems to misconstrue the outlook of PEMs. So perhaps the superfluity indictment is unfounded. PEMs have not set changes and unchanges 'apart from' changing and changeless objects. Consequently they do not have to dream up a weird transaction or 'relation between a person and a run he performs'. A PEM like

[13] P. Ziff, *Understanding Understanding* (Ithaca, NY, 1972), pp. 50 f.; originally published in H. E. Kiefer and M. K. Munitz (eds.), *Language, Belief and Metaphysics* (State University of New York Press, Albany, NY, 1970), p. 32; some notation adjusted to fit ours.

Julius Moravcsik takes pains to emphasize the mutual 'dependency' of object and event; for example, he says you might re-identify a paring knife which you are now looking at as 'the same knife with which I cut an orange an hour ago'.[14] You establish the implement's continuing identity by reference to such events as slicings and observings. These events, on the other hand, you pinpoint through the objects, the living creatures, and the nearby physical landmarks which figure in the events.

The same kind of 'symmetrical dependence' informs Davidson's *Weltanschauung*; he remarks that 'substances' or objects are noteworthy because 'they survive through time', and of course 'the idea of survival is inseparable from the idea of surviving certain sorts of change'.[15] Neither Moravcsik nor Davidson fancy—as Ziff puts it —'that somehow runs have an existence of their own apart from things that run'. Thus PEMs are not espousing a doctrine like the 'mind' philosopher's baroque theory, which indeed propagates all manner of superfluous independent entities. For that matter, the mystifying 'relation between a person and a run he performs' had a counterpart in the Cartesian scheme. Traditional mentalists picture us—or the minds we somehow own—contemplating, perceiving, accepting, dismissing, perchance repressing this or that content. However, PEMs do not in this way segregate events from objects; accordingly, they are dispensed from building any sort of pontoon bridge which brings object and happening together. The redundancy accusation has not yet been justified.

IV. CAN WE DERIVE EVENTS FROM OTHER ENTITIES?

We must set forth the redundancy charge in more detail. When NEMs urge us not to open up a special category of events, most of them believe we are already supplied with more than the familiar material objects and human agents which all sides recognize. A few NEMs begin with an abundantly stocked ontological warehouse.

What is on hand? We must be specific, and consider a representative NEM. At the start I quoted the unequivocal statement from Roderick Chisholm's latest book that there are no ' "concrete

---

[14] J. M. E. Moravcsik, 'Strawson on Ontological Priority', in R. J. Butler (ed.), *Analytical Philosophy*, Second Series (Oxford, 1965), p. 116.
[15] Davidson, 'The Individuation of Events', *EAE*, pp. 173 f.

events" in addition to states of affairs'.[16] For short, let us talk of SoAs, and inquire how they diverge from concrete goings-on.

The great Chicago Fire is, or was, a notorious and exemplary particular blaze. It had a fairly precise beginning in the lumber yards on 8 October 1871—according to legend, because Mrs O'Leary's bovine kicked over an oil lantern. Tireless volunteers extinguished it many catastrophic hours later. During the interim, it reached very high temperatures as it swept through most sections of the metropolis, ravaging more than seventeen thousand structures. How different is the Chisholmian SoA of Chicago burning! The SoA has no spatio-temporal origin, and cannot be touched off or snuffed out. It is not flaming, or hot—or cold either. It destroys no neighbourhoods and injures nobody. It might have only a shadowy form or 'being' on the fringes of our cosmos.[17] It would retain its 'being' even if Chicago never once caught fire. Or so I gather from the way Chisholm discusses his own examples of SoAs: 'Socrates being mortal', 'there being unicorns', 'Brutus killing Caesar', 'Truman being re-elected President', 'an incumbent President being re-elected', and 'Jones being robbed'.[18] Such SoAs 'are abstract entities which exist necessarily and which are such that some but not all of them occur, take place, or obtain . . . [They] are in no way dependent for their being upon the being of concrete, individual things. Even if there were no concrete, individual things, there would be indefinitely many [SoAs].'[19]

Although they are aloof from 'concrete, individual things', SoAs appear to be tailor-made for human cognitive, affective, and conative undertakings. Chisholm declares: 'the mark of a [SoA] is . . . that it is capable of being accepted'; and he encapsulates this 'mark' in a definition: '*p* is a [SoA] = *Df*. It is possible that there is someone who accepts *p*'; most generally, 'a [SoA] is whatever may be considered or entertained'.[20] My example would be a nostalgia buff, too young to have observed the historic conflagration, who can still direct his thinking at the SoA of Chicago burning.

Our relationship to SoAs differs from the hook-up between a Cartesian mind and its bizarre contents. The latter are totally private; they belong exclusively to that mind. SoAs may be publicly unobservable; however, a single SoA may be the target of many

[16] *Person and Object*, p. 115; see also pp. 122, 124, 128.
[17] Ibid., pp. 119, 130.　　　　[19] Ibid., p. 114.
[18] Ibid., pp. 123-35.　　　　[20] Ibid., p. 117.

people's thinking. Chisholm supposes that the SoA of 'Brown being elected mayor' is the formal or 'intentional object' of both Jones's fear and Smith's efforts. Jones is apprehensive toward the SoA, and Smith is acting with the goal of 'bringing about' the SoA.[21] Their opposed attitudes and purposive behaviour 'would have this common [intentional] object even if Brown were not elected mayor'—in which case 'Jones's fears would have been unfounded and Smith's efforts unsuccessful'.[22]

We could say more about SoAs, but I want to consider how they make particular events supernumerary. The idea is that when a SoA occurs, takes place, or obtains, we have all we need. Of course we must learn what this 'occurring' is like. Chisholm's latest account focuses on the concrete individual or individuals, and the relational or non-relational 'property' which figure in the SoA. His view seems to be that a given SoA occurs whenever the individual or individuals acquire the property; they are then said to 'concretize' the SoA, and presumably they anchor it to their spatio-temporal position. Chisholm's illustration runs: 'that [SoA] which is *Brutus killing Caesar* was concretized in 44 BC by the set consisting just of [the individuals] Brutus and Caesar'.[23] A non-relational case is 'that [SoA] which is Smith being ill': Chisholm writes that it 'implies Smith to have the property of being ill'; and this SoA gets concretized when Smith is burdened with 'the property of being ill'.[24]

The occurring, or concretization, of a SoA was designed to eliminate particular events. Ironically, the most obvious result of our exposition is that SoAs themselves are metaphysical dead wood. All that seems to matter for occurring is concretization, and we have that whenever one or more individuals possess an attribute. You might as well forget 'that [SoA] which is *Brutus killing Caesar*', and 'that [SoA] which is Smith being ill'. It is sufficient for this particular homicide that Brutus and Caesar acquire the relational property, and for this particular bout of poor health that Smith is afflicted by 'the property of being ill'. SoAs may be indispensable for other purposes, but we can explain concrete goings-on as effectively with properties and individuals alone.

Not unexpectedly, this is the upshot of a similar theory developed by another NEM, Neil Wilson. His doctrine is 'a "no event"

[21] Ibid., pp. 116 f., 164 f.   [23] Ibid., p. 125.
[22] Ibid., p. 117; see p. 123.   [24] Ibid.

theory', and I already quoted his slogan that '[t]here is no such thing as an event distinct from a fact'.[25] Specifically, Wilson believes 'an event is a truncated fact'.[26] What is a fact, then? Wilson reports that 'the fact is constituted by an individual [or set of individuals], a property and a time'; his example is 'the fact that Columbus discovered America in 1492'.[27] Wilson's truncation theory takes an agreeably homespun form. He suggests:

if you . . . subtract one or more constituents of a fact, then, if all goes well, what you are left with is an event . . . If we leave out the agent we can get the discovery of America in 1492 . . . But . . . the action [the relational property] cannot be dropped . . . Language just won't permit it . . . ' What Columbus did to America in 1492' is [still] a description of an action . . .[28]

Does Wilson mean that these 'constituents' are enough for a fact? I doubt it. Take the individual substances Columbus and Alaska, the relational property of discovering, and the year 1482. By even the most restrictive criteria, all these constituents 'exist' in 1482, although Columbus was nowhere close to Alaska at the time. But if constituents suffice for the corresponding fact, we would be obliged to count it as a fact that Columbus discovered Alaska in 1482. This would also yield far too many truncations having the status of events.

Should Wilson say that events are unmutilated facts? Again I doubt it. The event of Columbus reaching the West Indian island of Hispaniola is over and done with. This is grotesquely obvious if you date the event 1492. But isn't it still a fact that Columbus got to Hispaniola in 1492? The temporal mismatch between event and fact is all the more striking if we accept another claim of Wilson's about facts. He argues: 'A fact is a true proposition . . . It is a true proposition that Socrates died in 399 BC. It is a fact that Socrates died in 399 BC. The foregoing sentences say the same thing. Hence . . . we may as well conclude that "fact" is synonymous with "true proposition".'[29] Call Wilson's proposition 'S'. On some popular accounts of what it is for a proposition to be true, if S is true at all, then S is true always. For instance, S was true long before 399 BC, and will be true for ever after. But the event of Socrates dying did

[25] 'Facts, Events, and their Identity Conditions', 317.
[26] Ibid. 304 f., 312, 314.
[27] Ibid. 311; my apologies to Native Americans!
[28] Ibid. 311 f.   [29] Ibid. 305.

not happen prior to 399 BC, and has not continued happening subsequently. Of course there is a rival theory about truth—the view
that it makes no sense to add temporal specifications when we say
that S is true. One analogy would be the unintelligible expansion 'S
is true in Athens, and in Tokyo also'. A more direct parallel might
be: '7 was a prime number last April, and will remain so the rest of
the year'. If events are untruncated facts, and such facts are true
propositions, then on the atemporal view of truth, we cannot
meaningfully date and otherwise situate events in our chronological
framework. Time references could only appear within the description
of a fact-event like Wilson's 'fact that Socrates died in 399 BC'; but
the fact-event would be dateless or eternal. That is a high price to
pay just for maintaining Wilson's event = fact = true proposition
hypothesis.

This brings us back to Wilson's 'constituents of a fact'. If Wilson
only added that the individual constituent or constituents must
acquire the property constituent 'at' or 'in' the temporal constituent,
his theory would be invulnerable to my frivolous counter-instance
of Columbus discovering Alaska in 1482. For Columbus and
Alaska did not then, or ever, possess this relational property. So
amended, Wilson's analysis of events would parallel Chisholm's
explication of how SoAs become 'concretized' when concrete individuals 'have the property'. And it will not have escaped the attention of *cognoscenti* that both men's theories boil down to the
familiar 'property exemplification' analysis of particular events
championed by Jaegwon Kim.

Plainly we must inquire whether Kim's ontology, and *ipso facto*
my versions of Chisholm's and Wilson's, can give us what we need
to replace or to reconstruct particular events. It is irrelevant that
Kim disavows the goal of NEMs.[30]

V. EXEMPLIFICATION

I shall only glance at Kim's latest formulations. Like Chisholm and
Wilson in the works I cited, Kim decomposes happenings and states
into a triad of elements: 'a substance (the "constitutive object" of
the event), a property [which the substance] . . . exemplifies (the
"constitutive property") . . . and a time'.[31] Kim continues: 'an

---

[30] Kim, 'Events as Property Exemplifications', 162.   [31] Ibid.

event exists (occurs, if you like) . . . just in case the substance *x* has
[or exemplifies] the property *P* at time *t'*.

If our ontological radar is functioning, we will ask what is astir.
We can meekly allow properties to go by unchallenged. But we
ought to wonder about exemplification, and hence about concretization. What is their status? Is a secret category in the warehouse
open for them? We ought to be doubly suspicious when Kim, perhaps inadvertently, refers to 'the *event* of *x*'s having *P* at time *t'*.[32]
His tell-tale slip ought to embolden us to question whether '*x*'s having *P*' may be something extra, over and above *x* and *P*—but
especially whether this secret addition is itself event-like.

Chisholm is waiting with a partial reply. He denies that he is
ontologically committed to concretizations or 'occurrences' of
SoAs—which we have equated with individuals exemplifying properties. Chisholm takes a causal assertion: 'The third occurrence of
[the SoA of] Jones being robbed contributed causally to his illness'.
Chisholm's analysis and commentary read:

'There is a time *t* such that: Jones being robbed occurs at *t*; Jones being
robbed is such that at *t* it has been concretized exactly three times; and
Jones being robbed contributes to Jones being ill' . . . [T]ruths . . . like [this
one] ostensibly pertain to the particular occurrences of [SoAs] . . . But . . .
each . . . can be construed as pertaining just to individual things, properties
and [SoAs].[33]

Technically speaking, Chisholm is right. NEMs have ascribed no
ontological status to exemplifications, 'occurrences', or concretizations as long as they refuse to quantify over such phenomena—
refuse to say 'There is an exemplification ['occurrence'] *x* such that
. . .'. NEMs can also forgo give-away noun phrases like 'the exemplification of *P* at *t*' and 'the third occurrence of the SoA of Jones
being robbed'. But aren't these merely evasive manœvres? They
hardly elucidate the NEM's analysis of particular happenings and
his claim that they are not among his basic entities.

Neither Chisholm nor Kim deals with the charge that the property-
exemplificationist has smuggled in an undeclared category, and
that it looks event-like. *x, P,* and *t* may be uneventful; but when
you go on to say that *x* concretized a given SoA, or that *x* had or

[32] Kim, 'Causation, Emphasis, and Events', *Midwest Studies in Philosophy* 2
(1977), 103; my emphasis.
[33] Chisholm, *Person and Object*, pp. 135 f.

exemplified *P* at some juncture, aren't you announcing a substance-property-time get-together? Outside the philosophical arena, you might say that a revolutionary leader exemplified ruthlessness and great stamina while in command, or that a new test vehicle displayed its road-handling qualities all winter. These analogues sound like reports of more or less long-term events. So NEMs who favour the property-exemplification analysis might deign to tell us why '*x* exemplified *P*' may not be interpreted similarly.

Two defenders of Chisholm, Richard Feldman and Edward Wierenga, only say:

'we have . . . no reason to think that if a [SoA] obtains then there is a concrete event which is the occurrence of that [SoA] . . . Chisholm's theory . . . says that there are no such things. True sentences purporting to involve reference to particular occurrences . . . are provided with paraphrases that are about [SoAs] and their properties [such as the property of occurring].[34]

These writers seem unaware of the issue: How plausible is it to assert (i) that SoAs occur, or that properties get exemplified, (ii) 'that there are no such things' as occurrences of SoAs or exemplifications of properties? No doubt NEMs will declare (i) and (ii) mutually compatible. But must we accept this on their authority? Shouldn't NEMs allay our doubt with some reasons?

VI. SIMPLER 'NO EVENT' THEORIES

While awaiting enlightenment, I should remark that not all NEMs and fellow-travellers start with the rich supply of materials we have been inspecting. Some theorists do not load themselves down with SoAs, properties, concretizations, or exemplifications. Bruce Aune, whom I quoted in section II, is particularly unburdened by such things. Aune considers it an 'open question whether we need to acknowledge such entities' as the PEM's 'events, actions and states'.[35] If we side with NEMs, Aune thinks we can devise an ontologically frugal 'theory of agents'; he says its

subject matter will be rational agents rather than the supposed acts that agents perform . . . [I]t will employ predicates where an action [event] theory employs referring singular terms. Thus, instead of saying that

---

[34] R. Feldman and E. Wierenga, 'Thalberg on the Irreducibility of Events', *Analysis* 39 (1979), 13.

[35] Aune, *Action and Reason*, p. 45.

John's act of hitting Tom caused Mary's anger . . . [we] might say . . . that Mary was angry *because* John hit Tom . . . [S]ince . . . predicates are not referring terms, they do not commit [us] to actions or events.[36]

I am befuddled: what are we committed to when we report that John struck Tom? Besides the aggressor, John, and his victim, isn't there a punch involved in this mini-drama? As we noted in section III, John's haymaker would not be another agent like John, or an object like Tom's black eye. Are such 'predicates' as the transitive verb 'hit' applicable whenever John and some appropriate person or object merely exist? Or must there be a display of fisticuffs? Aune says no more about his 'predicates' than Chisholm and Kim say of concretization and exemplification. I continue to suspect undeclared goings-on.

Horgan, an avowed NEM, offers a more detailed linguistic solution than Aune's. Horgan appeals to the truth of so-called action statements instead of the non-referentiality of action 'predicates'. We are to imagine that Jones apologizes to someone by uttering suitable words. In this context, Horgan says,

we need not assume that there exists an entity (or two . . . related entities) answering to the descriptions 'Jones's saying "I apologize"' and 'Jones's apologizing'. Rather, we need only recognize that the following statement is true: 'Jones said "I apologize", and thereby he apologized' . . . So action theory can dispense with the notion of redescribing an action [or event], and also with actions [and events] themselves.[37]

Many PEMs would hold that a single action or event has been described first as the uttering of certain words, then redescribed as a ritual act of politeness. Other PEMs would discern two separable but synchronous, conventionally related events. No matter. What puzzles me is more basic: Does Horgan want us to consider it a brute, *sui-generis* fact—a given—that the statement about Jones, and similar assertions, just are true, and their contraries false? Are we that keen to get rid of particular events? If not, perhaps we should at least contemplate the possibility that Horgan's statement 'Jones said "I apologize", and thereby he apologized', is true because it matches up with Jones's past social capers. The statement would be untrue if Jones were alive but comatose in the past. Must he not have said, and—by virtue of the canons of language and etiquette—thereby done something? But then we seem to be

---

[36] Ibid., p. 44.   [37] Horgan, 'The Case Against Events', 37.

reintroducing actions and events as more basic than Horgan's 'true statement'.

While we are looking over the ontology of NEMs who get along without SoAs, properties and exemplification, we should not forget Trenholme. He endorses and embellishes a proposal of E. J. Lemmon to the effect that 'events be treated as [reduced to] space-time regions'.[38] I shall not attempt to comprehend, or to reproduce, Trenholme's intimidating formal apparatus. But I think it will complement our misgivings about the property-exemplification and linguistic theories of NEMs if we investigate the concept of 'time' and 'times' which they nonchalantly bring in.

VII. 'TIMES' AND EVENTS

Suppose I am deluded about the eventfulness of property-exemplification, predicates and truth. I would still wonder if NEMs are importing contraband events when they introduce moments and periods of time. I shall explain by means of Chisholmian fable. We report that the SoA of Jones being robbed occurs at the same instant as, or at an earlier time than, some other SoA takes place. The latter might be the SoA of the night watchman checking Jones's apartment house. Equivalently, we can talk about Jones exemplifying the property of getting robbed while, or before the night watchman exemplified the property of patrolling. This is a handy method of temporally situating garden-variety processes and conditions; but it is adaptable to such purported non-events as concretizations and exemplifications.

My conjecture, which I cannot prove, is that when PEMs and plain folk date an event, using expressions like 'on 8 October 1871', their prepositional or adverbial phrases retain this kind of meaning. Instead of placing events in a heterogeneous sequence, the dating method inserts them among periodic and uniform goings-on— regular changes of solar illumination, of seasons, of planetary positions. Here I am merely gesturing at, but not attempting to vindicate, an extremely widespread conception of temporal discourse.

What significance does this conception have for NEMs? I think the onus is on them to show that when they situate concretizations

---

[38] E. J. Lemmon, 'Comments on D. Davidson's "The Logical Form of Action Sentences"', in N. Rescher (ed.), *The Logic of Decision and Action* (Pittsburgh, 1967), pp. 95-100; and Trenholme, 'Doing Without Events', 182-5.

or exemplifications at times, they are not also tacitly presupposing a framework of events. I certainly would not beg the question at issue in this paper, and assume that there are particular happenings and states, over and above substances and properties. For the same reason I cannot assume that concretizations and exemplifications are event-like. But I can fairly shift the burden of proof to NEMs. All I have to say is that the PEM's deployment of 'at the same time as', 'during interval *t*', and similar terminology makes clear sense, given his world view. The challenge to NEMs will be: What do they mean when they talk so confidently of dates and other temporal matters? It they are not smuggling in events, what are they conveying?

When I fleetingly voiced similar doubts in a previous essay,[39] Feldman and Wierenga produced two alternative rebuttals. If I have understood, they believe NEMs could either insist 'that times are irreducible, or else . . . reduce times to things other than events'.[40] To what 'things'? Listen:

We might fix the referent of the expression 'Time 1' by saying that it shall refer to now (the present moment). A short time later we might establish the referent of 'Time 2' in a similar way. A unit of time would then be the interval between Time 1 and Time 2. Such a system might be awkward to use unless a unit of time coincided with some regular and natural occurrence. [But] such a connection does not seem to be a logical requirement for reference to times. So it is implausible to think that we can't refer to times without somehow referring to events.[41]

Both proposals only reinforce my scepticism. We won't even raise eyebrows over the 'short time later' and 'the interval between Time 1 and Time 2'. The answer 'that times are irreducible' sounds dogmatic. PEMs can at least set forth the specifics of what they mean when they place one event in the chronological web of others. So for PEMs 'at time *t*' is not totally resistant to analysis. Why then should they knuckle under to this pronouncement? Perhaps the NEM owes them an explanation. As for the 'baptizing' strategy outlined by Feldman and Wierenga, it runs into trouble immediately. Recall the best-known account of 'now', 'the present moment' and tensed language generally. This is the 'token reflexive' analysis

---

[39] 'The Irreducibility of Events', *Analysis* 38 (1978), 1-9.
[40] Feldman and Wierenga, 'Thalberg on the Irreducibility of Events', 19.
[41] Ibid. 16.

elaborated by Hans Reichenbach.[42] In brief, Reichenbach equates 'now' with 'the time at which *this token* is uttered'. Thus if you report, aloud, with smoke signals, or otherwise in writing, 'Jones is getting robbed now', you mean that while you are producing these very noises or marks, Jones is being deprived of his possessions. What you are announcing is simultaneous with your announcement —with your utterance of a particular physical token of 'Jones is getting robbed now'. The same goes if you proclaim: 'Time 1 is now'. You would be fixing an instant or interval or time by reference to your issuing of this token. So you pinpoint Time 1 through an event: your act of christening Time 1!

My objection presupposes a token reflexive analysis of 'now' and its kin. NEMs might devise a cogent alternative which brings in no speech acts. Until then, is it 'implausible to think we can't refer to times without . . . referring to events'?

VIII. OUR FAILURE TO DISLODGE EVENTS

Our first goal was to understand what NEMs are denying. The closest model we found was in philosophical psychology: the anti-Cartesian's rejection of publicly unobservable minds and their eerie contents. In section II we weighed objections that an event ontology will engender nonsense, contradiction and faulty reasoning. We were unpersuaded. The rest of our inquiry dealt with the complaint that, like minds and their denizens, events are surplus theoretical baggage. Can we derive all the concrete goings-on we need from other, uneventful entities? Perhaps; but each tempting alternative ontology seemed either inadequate or tainted with eventfulness. NEMs have not yet mapped their promised land, their world without the basic category of events.

[42] Reichenbach, *Elements of Symbolic Logic* (New York, 1947), pp. 284-7.

PHILOSOPHY OF PSYCHOLOGY

X

IS THE MENTAL SUPERVENIENT ON THE PHYSICAL?

HARRY A. LEWIS

In several papers Donald Davidson has suggested that mental characteristics are dependent or supervenient on physical characteristics,
in the same way that moral properties are supervenient on descriptive, or semantic properties of sentences in a formal system on
syntactical properties. As he puts it in 'Mental Events': 'Such
supervenience might be taken to mean that there cannot be two
events alike in all physical respects but differing in some mental
respect, or that an object cannot alter in some mental respect without altering in some physical respect.'[1] Davidson cites G. E. Moore
as his predecessor in the claim about moral properties: Moore has
been followed by R. M. Hare and others.[2] The idea that some such
loose form of dependence might obtain more widely, where hitherto some philosophers have sought for reduction by law ('bridge
laws') or definition, can be found in several recent writings.[3]
'Supervenient' is not always the preferred term, but I shall follow
Davidson's choice of word (in preference to 'dependent', 'consequential', or 'emergent').[4]

---

[1] Davidson, 'Mental Events', *EAE*, p. 214; see also 'The Material Mind', *EAE*,
pp. 253-4, and 'Replies to David Lewis and W. V. Quine', *Synthèse* 27 (1974), 345.

[2] R. M. Hare, *The Language of Morals* (Oxford, 1952); and, for example,
J. Kovesi, *Moral Notions* (London, 1967). Moore's exposition can be found in 'The
Conception of Intrinsic Value', in *Philosophical Studies* (London, 1922).

[3] For example, J. A. Fodor, 'Special Sciences (or: The Disunity of Science as a
Working Hypothesis)', *Synthèse* 28 (1974), 97-115; G. P. Hellman and F. W.
Thompson, 'Physicalism: Ontology, Determination, and Reduction', *Journal of
Philosophy* 72 (1975), 551-64; and J. Kim, 'Supervenience and Nomological Incom-
mensurables', *American Philosophical Quarterly* 15 (1978), 149-56.

[4] Peter Geach has suggested to me that the term 'supervenient' entered our
philosophical vocabulary by way of Latin translations of Aristotle, *Nicomachean
Ethics* 1174B31-3, where (in Ross's English) pleasure is described as 'an end which
supervenes as the bloom of youth does on those in the flower of their age'. Indeed
Robert Grosseteste's Latin uses 'supervenire' at this point. (See R. A. Gauthier
(ed.), *Aristoteles Latinus* XXVI. 1-3 (Leiden and Brussels, 1973).)

The interest of supervenience is considerable. It seems likely, as Jaegwon Kim says, that 'belief in reducibility often derives from belief in supervenience, and not the other way around'.[5] It is easy to see how belief in supervenience could make reducibility seem plausible. For example, if every instance of goodness can be characterized in descriptive terms that report that in which its goodness consists, the fallacious inference to the conclusion that there is one set of descriptive terms that characterize every instance of goodness will be (and arguably has been) tempting. However, I believe there is good reason to proceed cautiously in admitting new claims to supervenience: and perhaps even the old ones are not beyond question. I shall indicate several reasons for scepticism. Claims that one kind of characteristic is supervenient on another may readily lapse into triviality or falsehood. If they avoid those hazards such claims may none the less imply that there are laws or entailments linking the subvenient to the supervenient properties, or so some critics have said: I shall examine this line of criticism. Finally I shall speculate on the reasons one might have for asserting, or denying, the supervenience of the mental on the physical.

I

The claim to supervenience in the case of evaluations, moral or aesthetic, surely reflects an important insight. If one butterfly is beautiful, another one just like it could not be ugly.[6] If St Francis was a good man, another man who acted as St Francis did, in similar circumstances, would also be good.[7] The attempt to capture this insight in a general formula can readily obliterate it, however. For example, 'any two objects alike in all non-moral respects would be alike in all moral respects' is trivially true if there are no two objects alike in all non-moral respects: and indeed there are not. Likewise it is a truism that there cannot be two events alike in all physical respects but differing in some mental respect, because it is a truism that there cannot be two events alike in all physical respects.[8] Clearly likeness in all non-moral (or physical) respects is more than was intended; likeness in those respects *relevant* to the

---

    [5] 'Supervenience and Nomological Incommensurables', 154.

    [6] The example is from Wittgenstein's *Zettel*, trans. G. E. M. Anscombe (Oxford, 1967), para. 199.

    [7] Hare, *Language of Morals*, p. 145.

    [8] Davidson's suggested criterion for identity of events (defended in 'The Indi-

supervenient property is all that is needed. But another form of triviality threatens if we say this in so many words: 'if *a* is like *b* in all respects relevant to goodness, and *a* is good, *b* is good too' is another truism. In fact it reflects the universalizability that R. M. Hare found in all descriptive judgements.[9]

A similar view, that supervenience belongs to every judgement, is expressed by Julius Kovesi:

When we evaluate something we can make the following three assertions about our evaluation:

(*a*) If I say: '*x* is good' I cannot say '*y* is exactly the same as *x* except that *y* is not good; this is the only difference between them', because there is no extra quality or property called 'good'.

(*b*) If I say '*x* is good', I cannot say '*y* is exactly the same as *x* but *y* is not good', because in this case I cancel my reasons for saying that *x* is good.

(*c*) If I say '*x* is good' I must be able to say that *any x* which has the same revelant qualities or properties as *x* is also good, because we judge *x* to be good for having those qualities or properties. . . .

These assertions however can be made about any rational activity that makes use of language; we can, for instance, make these three assertions about judging something to be a tulip.[10]

I accept this, but I do not infer that supervenience is a wholly empty notion. To be sure, if the 'relevant' qualities of (*c*) included goodness, (*c*) would be trivial. But in cases of goodness at least, we say that an object is good by virtue of some *other* qualities it has. Moreover. as Kovesi has earlier remarked, the same does not appear to hold for the quality we call 'yellow': supervenience is not quite universal.[11] It is one thing to accept these points, another to find a formulation of supervenience that captures them without lapsing into triviality. No doubt such a formulation should include the requirement that the sets of subvenient and supervenient properties are distinct. (The criteria for distinctness of properties may be unclear, but I should wish to argue that any formulation of supervenience will incorporate that kind of unclarity.) Some further restriction on the two classes seems to be required, however. The idea that needs to be expressed is the one implied by Kovesi when he says, 'there is no

viduation of Events', *EAE*, pp. 163-80), namely identity of causes and effects, surely yields this as a truism.

[9] *Freedom and Reason* (Oxford, 1963), pp. 10-13.
[10] *Moral Notions*, pp. 158-9.
[11] Ibid., p. 7.

extra quality or property called "good"', or 'we judge x to be good for having those qualities or properties'. In other words, the supervenient property *consists* (case by case) in the presence of subvenient properties. Any account that meets the bill will require fine discriminations in the metaphysics of properties.

II

If triviality threatens general claims to supervenience (whatever the properties in question) falsity threatens them too. Again I shall take evaluations, aesthetic and moral, as paradigms. Imagine that we are able to characterize the determinable properties relevant to a particular judgement without begging the question. St Francis was good, perhaps, because he was kind and self-effacing.[12] If we can identify the determinables under which being kind and self-effacing fall, say d_1 and d_2, we may infer that anyone like St Francis in respects d_1 and d_2 would be good. However, such judgements are defeasible by further contrary evidence, and in order to ensure the truth of our generalization from the case of St Francis, the possible categories of contrary evidence must be mentioned as relevant to our judgement of St Francis. There are two difficulties about this, however. One is that it is most implausible to suggest that we canvass all such categories in making the original judgement. The other is that *moral* evaluation, at least, is not based on any antecedently identifiable set of subvenient properties: we cannot list a priori the determinables whose determinate forms will settle each moral question. (It is arguable that in *aesthetic* evaluation the 'supervenience base' can be specified, for example as perceptible properties.)[13] The generalization that the claim to supervenience implies may thus be false, but the attempt to head off falsehood may once again yield triviality.[14]

It is not surprising to find that the notion of property causes difficulty for the formulation of the supervenience relation. Further

---

[12] It may be objected that 'kind' and 'self-effacing' are already morally coloured. As Jonathan Dancy has pointed out to me, a very general term of appraisal like 'good' often rests in this way on other moral terms. But if they are supervenient in turn on other terms that are non-moral, and supervenience is transitive, only complication, and not difficulty, is introduced by this fact.

[13] The expression 'supervenience base' is due to Kim, 'Supervenience'.

[14] Jonathan Dancy helped me to see the relevance of the defeasibility of moral evaluations, and of the openness of the (alleged) supervenience base of moral judgement.

grounds for caution in the use of that notion are provided by another source of falsehood in claims to supervenience. The formulations mentioned above invite us to entertain the possibility of another object or event that shares all (relevant, subvenient) properties with the first: such another should then share the supervenient properties. But for many examples of determination, this will not hold. Winning a race is determined by other properties, but if two people share all those properties, neither is the outright winner. The value of a rare postage stamp supervenes on its physical properties but is also determined by its uniqueness: the existence of another physically indiscernible stamp would lower its value. Biological fitness has been alleged to be a supervenient notion: but fitness is partly determined by the frequency of a particular genotype in a population, and frequency, like uniqueness, is not a property of individuals at all.[15] (As Frege would say, it is a second-level property—a property of properties.) Such examples present more difficulty for a doctrine that physical properties determine all others, but they also increase the doubt whether any general account of supervenience will capture the variety of cases. 'Brute facts' come in so many shapes and sizes that it is misleading to lump them all together as 'properties', whether of objects or events.[16]

III

Davidson holds that supervenience is compatible with the absence of reducibility, by law or definition, of supervenient to subvenient characteristics. His position goes further than that, because he denies that there are psychophysical laws. Laws may be universally quantified conditionals; reducibility presumably requires biconditionals linking the two theories. And yet any definition of supervenience requires that it guarantees some universally quantified conditionals. Must those consequences be regarded as natural laws or truths of definition? And if they have that status, can reducibility be denied? Davidson offers an argument from cases against any

---

[15] I am indebted here to Jonathan Hodge, Paul Jakubovic, and Peter Long. The supervenience of fitness is proposed by A. Rosenberg, 'The Supervenience of Biological Concepts', *Philosophy of Science* 45 (1978), 368-86. S. P. Stich, in 'Autonomous Psychology and the Belief-Desire Thesis', *The Monist* 61 (1978), 573-91, by the use of science-fiction examples of replication of human beings, reveals ways in which our uniqueness is relevant to mentalistic ascriptions.

[16] Cf. Anscombe, 'Brute Facts', *Analysis* 18 (1958), 69-72.

claim that supervenience entails reducibility: 'Dependence or supervenience of this kind does not entail reducibility by law or definition:
if it did, we could reduce moral properties to descriptive, and this
there is good reason to *believe* cannot be done; and we might be
able to reduce truth in a formal system to syntactical properties,
and this we *know* cannot in general be done.'[17] If we accept this in
all particulars, we must accept that supervenience does not entail
reducibility. But that involves assent to the thesis that at least one
of the moral/descriptive and truth/syntax relations is a case of
supervenience, and that reducibility is impossible in that instance.
It is worth exploring the question further, then, for several reasons.
Some might reject parts of the thesis just mentioned; some hold
that supervenience involves laws or truths of definition that none
the less do not allow reduction because they are conditional, not
biconditional, in form; and it could still be held that the impression
that supervenience entails laws or truths of definition is the result
of an error of formulation, a failure to capture in an adequate
phrase what is none the less a truth.

An argument that supervenience involves a form of entailment of
supervenient by subvenient properties has been presented by Simon
Blackburn. He is considering the position of a 'moral realist' who
holds that moral properties are supervenient on naturalistic properties, but also that there is no moral proposition whose truth is
entailed by any proposition ascribing naturalistic properties to its
subject.

> He [the moral realist] has to say that the truth of a moral proposition con-
> sists in the existence of a state of affairs, which it reports; that the existence
> of this state of affairs is not entailed by the existence of other, naturalistic
> facts; yet that the continuation of these facts entails that the moral state of
> affairs continues as it is.[18]

As Blackburn remarks, such a position seems very mysterious, if
not actually inconsistent. It looks as if supervenience demands that
absence of change in naturalistic properties entails absence of
change in moral properties, and so some statement of naturalistic
properties entails a moral proposition.

Our own previous discussion alerts us to one facet of this argu-

---

[17] Davidson, 'Mental Events', p. 214.
[18] 'Moral Realism', in J. Casey (ed.), *Morality and Moral Reasoning* (London,
1971), at p. 110.

ment. 'A remains $N_1 \ldots N_k$' (where '$N_1 \ldots N_k$' reports naturalistic properties) is not the same proposition as 'A does not change in any naturalistic property' unless we add the clause '"$N_1 \ldots N_k$" is a complete naturalistic description'. And it looks as if any entailment is not from 'A remains $N_1 \ldots N_k$' alone, but from the conjunction of that with the added clause. That conjunction, however, is no straightforward ascription of naturalistic properties: for the added clause is not a naturalistic fact, but a general statement about naturalistic facts—a conceptual observation.

Are the generalizations that supervenience involves rightly to be called entailments? Several of the philosophers who have discussed the topic have been exercised over the nature of the modality involved in asserting that supervenience holds.[19] It is agreed that supervenience is a matter of meaning: if moral properties supervene on naturalistic properties, that is a matter of the meaning of the words expressing moral properties. Blackburn, like Hare, talks of logical impossibility in such cases. When a property M is supervenient upon properties $N_1 \ldots N_n$, Blackburn says that 'it is logically impossible that two things should each possess the same properties from the set $N_1 \ldots N_n$ to the same degree, without both failing to possess M, or both possessing M, to the same degree'.[20] Let A and B have all the same properties from $N_1 \ldots N_n$, say $N_a \ldots N_k$, and let A possess M fully. Then we may infer that B possesses M fully. I submit however that this does not show that B's possessing $N_a \ldots N_k$ *entails* B's possessing M. The 'logical impossibility' mentioned in the definition cannot be imported in this way: a formal fallacy is involved. You might as well say that since it is logically possible for A and B to be entirely alike and A to be clever and B not clever, A's being like B *entails* B's being clever. Indeed it does, but only conjoined with the suppressed premise, 'A is clever'. B's possessing the subvenient properties does not of itself entail that B possesses M fully: however the fact that A possesses M fully and that B is like A in the N-respects can be said to entail that B possesses M fully. But here the premiss makes essential use of of 'M'—it is not (for example) a mere naturalistic fact. The modality, whatever it is, belonging to supervenience itself cannot be 'detached' and applied to the generalizations that are licensed by an attribution of the supervenient property.

---

[19] Notably Moore 'Conception of Intrinsic Value', p. 265.
[20] 'Moral Realism', p. 106; cf. Hare, *Language of Morals*, p. 145.

Kim uses reasoning like Blackburn's to draw the conclusion that 'if M supervenes on N, each property in M which is instantiated has a general sufficient condition in N', and he adds, 'I don't see how such generalizations could fail to be lawlike'.[21] However, the generalization that states the sufficient condition is a logical consequence (by virtue of supervenience) of an instance: since it is given only by way of instances it is misleading to talk of a 'general sufficient condition in N'.[22] Only through finding a property in M was the generalization discovered: the condition in N is parasitic on an attribution from M. If that attribution is contingent, it is odd to find any necessity, natural or logical, in a consequence drawn from it. The logical or conceptual necessity involved in supervenience is not inherited by the generalization, as argued above. And I see no good reason to think of such generalizations as laws, if their provenance is understood. To keep that provenance clearly before us, we should best express them thus (where M supervenes on N, P is a property in M, Q an N-maximal property—here I use Kim's framework): 'Because a has P and Q, anything that had Q would have P'. A form of words like this offers no temptation to think of 'if anything has Q it has P' as a natural law. Scepticism is reinforced if one notes that in some agreed examples of supervenience, the idea of independent observation of supervenient and subvenient properties is unintelligible, since we see the supervenient *in* the subvenient. (Aesthetic evaluation is an example.)[23]

In discussing supervenience, we do well to pay close attention to the notion of property, as I suggested earlier. It may be that in some uses 'property' approximates to 'natural kind', and the inference that any matching of properties is lawlike may seem plausible. But Kim uses a broad notion of property that allows sets of properties to be closed under Boolean operations, and to be sorted into maximal consistent sets. It is arguable that lawlikeness can be

[21] 'Supervenience', 153.

[22] Kim's abstract and general account of supervenience is as vulnerable as any to the charge of triviality, but his feeling (he does not present it as an argued conclusion) that the generalizations are lawlike does not seem to depend on the aspects of his account that lay it open to this charge.

[23] In 'Physicalist Materialism', *Noûs* 11 (1977), 321, Hellman and Thompson offer another argument for psychophysical laws, based on their formulation of the thesis that the mathematical-physical facts determine all the facts. This formulation draws on concepts of model theory, and may be paraphrased as: the physical facts determine all the facts if and only if, in all structures compatible with the laws of physics, any two models that agree on the truth values they assign to the propositions

undermined by such operations (so that an '*N*-maximal' property could never occur in a law).[24]

If the generalized conditionals involved in supervenience do not have the status of entailments or laws, any suggestion that reducibility by law or definition is a corollary of a claim to supervenience must fail too, since that requires generalizations that are biconditional in form but share that status. Even if formulations of supervenience are defective in other ways, they do not show any inconsistency in the view that whereas there are no psychophysical laws, the mental is supervenient on the physical.

IV

How could we settle whether the mental is supervenient on the physical? Davidson calls the view that it is a 'dogma', which suggests that he would agree with Kim that 'our belief in supervenience is largely, and often, a combination of metaphysical convictions and methodological considerations', rather than hold that it can be the result of reflection on examples or of detailed argument.[25]

I have been accepting that moral judgement is a model of supervenience. But the differences between evaluative and psychological judgements and the respective supervenience bases are striking. Difficult as it may be to formulate a definition of supervenience, we readily see how it must be true that if this cup is beautiful, another just like it would have to be beautiful too—and we understand this as a significant claim. I can find no parallel for the ready appeal of claims like this in the realm of psychological attribution. 'If John is running, anyone undergoing the same physical process as John would be running'—this seems evident enough, but only because the idea of someone's body going through the motions

that use the physical vocabulary also agree on the truth values they assign to the propositions expressed in the psychological vocabulary. But I cannot see that their argument amounts to more than this: if the physical and psychological vocabularies are distinct, the only way in which a fact about the models of the physical propositions could constrain the interpretation of psychological propositions would be for bridge laws to be added as axioms to the physical theory. I see this argument as having force only for one who accepts their way of expressing dependence. (I am grateful to Steven Savitt for drawing my attention to the work of Hellman and Thompson.)

[24] Cf. Fodor, 'Special Sciences'.
[25] Davidson, 'Replies to David Lewis and W. V. Quine', 345, Kim, 'Supervenience', 154.

without his running seems absurd. 'If John is thinking of Cambridge, anyone else in just the state he is in would be thinking of Cambridge.' That seems trivial, if we take 'state' one way, or false, if we take it another (since we have no reason to believe that indiscernible physical events in one person's brain and another's constitute the same thought—even the most doctrinaire reductionist supposes that we may all be wired up differently). In the absence of any immediate appeal in examples like these, the difficulties canvassed earlier for accounts of supervenience crowd in. What is to count as a relevant physical difference between two cases? How much of the environment of the person (for example, the ground on which he runs, the book he sees) is to be included in a physical description?

In evaluative judgements, moral or aesthetic, there is an epistemological link between supervenient and subvenient properties. Typically, in moral judgement, we consider properties that are nonmoral on which we base our evaluations; in aesthetic judgement, we may not notice other properties, but our perception of them enters into our judgement (in the way that perception enters into recognition of a familiar face that we could not begin to describe). Does anything correspond to this in our ascriptions of psychological properties? In first-person ascriptions, usually not; in third-person ascriptions, the grounds are perceptible behaviour. Let us assume that behaviour can be described in physical terms: even so mental characteristics could not be said to be determined by behaviour alone. Mutually indiscernible patterns of behaviour may over short periods be compatible with quite different mental facts.[26] If the supervenience base is taken to be a person's behaviour over a long period—his lifetime, say—we leave practical discovery behind us and enter the realm of abstract theorizing. The idea of any two people exhibiting indiscernible patterns of behaviour even for an hour strains credulity. But there is still the first-person ascription to account for. It is already apparent that our reasons for mental ascriptions are not to be identified as a set of physical subvenient properties belonging to behaviour. This conclusion is secured if the claim is that mental characteristics supervene—even in part—on microphysical characteristics, for the latter play no role in everyday observations of mental properties, our own or others'. In this paper I have made little reference to the supervenience of the semantic on

[26] As Davidson remarks 'The Material Mind', p. 252.

the syntactical, cited by Davidson: if this is a genuine example, it shares with evaluation the feature that we come to know the supervenient by way of the subvenient properties. So in this regard the mental stands apart from Davidson's other examples.

To indicate a difference between the relation of mental to physical characteristics and other alleged instances of supervenience shows at best that the case for the supervenience of mental on physical is not to be proved by citing the others as parallels. It would be more satisfactory to find a direct method of settling the question. I shall explore briefly three related lines of attack that I find promising.

The first line is implicit in much of the discussion of this subject that I have mentioned. It is to try to describe counter-examples to the supervenience thesis. In the forms that Davidson gives to it, counter-examples would involve pairs of events physically indiscernible but mentally discernible, or (following his second formulation) a mental change that was not accompanied by a physical change. Counter-examples of the first kind seem all too easy to find, or to imagine, provided only physical indiscernibility is construed in such a way as to admit the very possibility of two indiscernible events. If we are wired up differently from one another, presumably the two events would have to happen in the same person. It is the more plausible that there could be two such events if their descriptions do not involve relations with the outside world (for example, if they were perceivings, the material object of perception might enter into the description). To keep within the framework of Davidson's position, let us assume that both events (under their mental aspect) possess intentionality. I can see no direct argument to show that counter-examples of this type exist, but part of my difficulty lies in the notion of *determinacy* of the mental aspect that the notion of the determination of the mental by the physical involves. If Davidson is right to say that no tighter notion of 'correct' mental ascription is available to us than is consistent with the 'evolving' theory of an interpreter—why should not the theory evolve a little between the first event and the second? (What pressures on mental ascriptions could guarantee supervenience?)[27]

The second formulation appears to resist counter-examples. Could there be a mental change without a physical change? A change

---

[27] Cf. Davidson, 'Mental Events', p. 223: 'the constitutive ideal of rationality partly controls each phase in the evolution of what must be an evolving theory'.

is at least a change in predicates or properties, but we must rule out as spurious examples of mental change in me such things as a change in your beliefs about me. Could *I* change mentally without changing physically? Within the framework of Davidson's 'Mental Events' the answer is a straightforward 'no', because the mental changes there considered are causes or effects of physical (physically describable) events, and so have themselves physical descriptions that reveal them as causes or effects, and therefore as changes. If we restrict our attention to such events, the thesis of the supervenience of the mental on the physical is revealed as a corollary of Davidson's other views in the philosophy of mind. But I do not see any way of extending this argument to all mental events except by showing that any mental event stands in causal relations to physical events.[28]

The fact that the two formulations fare so differently suggests that they are far from equivalent. To speak of pairs of physically indiscernible events, both of which are changes, is not the same as to speak of individual changes.[29] Indeed, it appears that the formulation in terms of individual changes may give a hint as to how to capture the elusive notion of 'consisting in'. Instance by instance, the properties relevant to the possession of a supervenient property are those in which the supervenient property consists in that instance. 'Consists' is a mereological metaphor, and points us towards ontology. Just as this table is made of wood, that table of metal, we might suggest that this case of thinking is made of such-and-such physical events, that case of others. But in the way that both tables by virtue of their physical nature fulfil the same function, so both collections of physical events may answer to the same mental description. Perhaps we may take identity as a limiting case of being made of—my axe is (made of) this sharp stone; my thinking is (made of) that physical event. If this is acceptable, the case for supervenience in the second formulation is strengthened, since it gives a sense to 'this mental change consists in that physical change', and so to 'this instance of a change in mental properties

---

[28] The task of showing this is one that Davidson declines to attempt at p. 224 of 'Mental Events'.

[29] I note a similar diversity in the two formulations of supervenience offered by Blackburn ('Moral Realism', p. 106). One speaks of changes in a single thing, the other of the similarity of two things.

consists in that physical change'. (I recall that for a change to be mental is for it to have a mental description.)

Some philosophers have proposed that *all* other properties are supervenient on microphysical (or mathematical-physical) properties. The form that this proposal has been given is very general: roughly, that all the physical facts determine all the facts whatever.[30] There is the familiar risk of vacuity. For the same reason, such broad formulations cannot capture the idea that any particular mental fact consists in some suitably confined collection of physical facts. The state of your body, or the state of the body of the human being closest to the antipode of my present position on the earth, is as relevant to my current mental state as is the present state of my own body, according to such accounts. Even a thoroughgoing holist will accept that some physical facts are more relevant than others to each mental fact. But if we assume that the proposal can be given a non-vacuous formulation, it has interesting metaphysical implications. No Platonic forms determine the properties of objects independently of their physical structure; no Fregean senses fix the meanings of our sentences.[31] To reject such 'downward' determination, however, does not commit one to accepting 'upward' determination of all properties by physical properties. The background to claims of supervenience for value judgements does not direct our attention to ultimate physical properties. To the extent that the doctrine that the mental supervenes on the physical does so, it loses the intuitive appeal of those other cases. I believe that the way forward lies in respecting the differences between the alleged cases of supervenience. This would mean that arguments for supervenience would draw on special features of the concepts in question, rather than on a global metaphysical commitment.

The special feature that invites attention in the connections

[30] See Hellman and Thompson ('Physicalist Materialism' and 'Physicalism: Ontology, Determination, and Reduction', *Journal of Philosophy* 72 (1975), 551-64), Kim ('Supervenience', 154-6) with the formulation attributed to Terence Horgan on p. 155.

[31] At Plato, *Phaedo* 100[d] Socrates denies the supervenience of beauty in these words (as translated by Tredennick): 'If someone tells me that the reason why a given object is beautiful is that it has a gorgeous colour or shape or any such attribute, I disregard all these other explanations—I find them all confusing—and I cling simply and straightforwardly and no doubt foolishly to the explanation that the one thing that makes that object beautiful is the presence in it or association with it . . . of absolute Beauty.' (I am grateful to Peter Long for drawing my attention to this passage.)

between mental and physical properties is the causal relation, once a stumbling block for dualism and now a prominent element in Davidson's thought. It would be widely agreed that the physical indiscernibility of two events would ensure identity of causal role.[32] If we could show that identity of causal role is sufficient (although not necessary, *pace* familiar forms of reductionism) for identity of mental characteristics, we should have an argument for the supervenience of the mental on the physical. I believe that such an argument could be mounted, but I cannot undertake the task now. Until an argument is offered, and shown to survive the criticisms of hitherto published forms of the thesis presented here, we should remain sceptical.[33]

[32] Waiving triviality, of course. But attending to causes and effects might give a way of isolating an interesting subset of the physical properties.

[33] In addition to the particular debts noted above, I should like to acknowledge a general debt to Donald Davidson, who first drew my attention, through his teaching, to the interest and potential significance of supervenience. I have profited from discussions of earlier versions of this paper in England and Australia, and from conversations with Greg O'Hair and Raimo Tuomela.

XI

DAVIDSON'S MINIMAL MATERIALISM[1]

J. J. C. SMART

Davidson has argued very ingeniously for a materialistic ontology of the mental. His argument proceeds from a preliminary lemma to the effect that the mental is anomalous, that is, that there are no laws about mental events as such, and this preliminary lemma is of fundamental importance in its own right. Davidson turns the tables neatly on those philosophers who have tried to use the anomalousness of the mental as an argument *against* materialism.

The argument has the following three premises, of which P3 is the important lemma of which I have just spoken[2]:

P1   There is causal interaction between the mental and the physical. Thus on some particular occasion the incidence of light rays on my retina may cause me to see a glass of beer and to desire to drink it, and my desire may cause me to lift the glass.

P2   Where there is causality there must be a law, though the events may not be described as falling under the law in the same sort of vocabulary as is used in the causal statement itself.

P3   There are no strict laws whereby mental events (described in the vocabulary of the mental, that is, of the propositional attitudes) can be related to one another or to physical events.

From P2 it follows that there are laws under which particular causal interactions between the mental and the physical fall. By P1

---

[1] This paper was written while I was a Fellow at the Center for Advanced Study in the Behavioral Sciences, Stanford, California, USA.
[2] Davidson, 'Mental Events', *EAE*, p. 208, 'The Material Mind', *EAE*, pp. 249-50, and 'Psychology as Philosophy', *EAE*, p. 230.

this last statement is not empty and so is not merely trivially true. By P3 the law relating a particular mental event to its cause or effect cannot use the mentalistic vocabulary, but must describe the event purely physically. So any individual mental event has a physical description and falls under physical laws. There are no general psychophysical laws, but any individual event described mentalistically is identical to some physical event.[3] There are 'token' identities between the mental and the physical but no 'type' identities.[4]

Later on I shall comment briefly on premiss P2, but for the moment I shall focus attention on P3. Whereas Davidson takes P1 as obvious and P2 as (I think) nearly so, P3 is a thesis for which he argues at some length and with much subtlety. Indeed his argument for P3 may be thought even more interesting and challenging than the final argument to the materialistic conclusion.

The materialism to which Davidson argues is a 'minimal materialism', as David Lewis has called it.[5] It is compatible with the existence of irreducible or 'emergent' biological laws. It is thus a more modest sort of materialism (or physicalism)[6] than that which some of us would wish to propound. For this stronger physicalism I myself rely partly on plausibility considerations in the light of total science as we know it today, and partly on rebutting a priori or intuitive philosophical arguments against physicalism. However it would be possible for a philosopher, perhaps Davidson himself if he so wished, to proceed from minimal materialism to a stronger materialism by making use of such plausibility considerations and defensive arguments.

In fact Davidson does not appear to be interested in proposing a wide-sweeping metaphysical theory or to be concerned with the unity of science. At least in the articles with which I shall be concerned in the present paper, Davidson is concerned with the mental as narrowly concerned with the propositional attitudes, such as beliefs, desires, hopes, and fears. Occurrent experiences such as the having of an itch, of a memory image, or of a visual sense datum

---

[3] Davidson, 'Mental Events', p. 224, 'The Material Mind', pp. 248-9, and 'Psychology as Philosophy', p. 230.

[4] 'Mental Events', pp. 212-15, 'The Material Mind', pp. 253-4, and 'Psychology as Philosophy', p. 230.

[5] David Lewis, 'Radical Interpretation', *Synthèse* 23 (1974), 334.

[6] I prefer 'physicalism' to 'materialism', since physics may need to postulate non-material entities such as space-time points and perhaps also, as Quine has urged, mathematical objects, such as sets.

are not obviously propositional in nature. If Davidson's argument does not touch these occurrent experiences, then if it is taken to be an argument for materialism in general there is a serious lacuna in it. It is these occurrent experiences that have often been supposed to provide the greatest difficulty for the materialist.

It is true that in 'Mental Events' (*EAE*, pp. 211-12) Davidson has argued that the havings of pains or after-images and the like, and even such obviously physical events as the collision of two stars in space, fall within his criterion of the mental, because they have a mentalistic description. Consider a certain collision of two stars. Let '*P*' be some predicate true of this collision, and true also of other collisions, but such that '*P* at time *t*' is uniquely true of this particular collision. But *t* may be the time that some intentional event occurred, such as 'Jones noticing that a pencil starts to roll across his desk', to use Davidson's example.[7] So even more intuitively 'physical' events than itches and the havings of after-images and the like will turn out to have a mentalistic description. The danger is indeed to prevent a Spinozistic characterization of *all* events as 'mental'. In 'Mental Events' Davidson views this with equanimity. So long as no intuitively mental events are *not* captured by his criterion, his argument for the identity of (token) mental events with (token) physical events, goes through. However, I am not so sure that this Spinozism is harmless.

Consider a typically physical event, a collision (E_1) of two billiard balls which causes another physical event, a rebounding (E_2). There may well be purely physical laws of the form 'Events of sort E_1 are followed by events of sort E_2'. (Actually the laws of elastic collision are a bit more subtle than this, but the simple formulation here will do for my present purposes.) Now E_1 and E_2 have purely physical descriptions, without intentionality, and it is these 'extensional' descriptions that are the normal ones and that are used in the laws. On the other hand the normal or usual descriptions of mental events, such as coming to desire a glass of beer, are done in terms of the propositional attitudes. It is by no means clear that the normal or common-sense descriptions of the havings of pains, itches, images, or sense data are intentional or make reference to propositional attitudes. Hence I do not think that Davidson has proved materialism for these events. I believe that these events are material, but it needs a different sort of argument to make this plausible.

---

[7] 'Mental Events', p. 211.

Quite apart from its possible utility in the proof of minimal materialism, Davidson's thesis of the anomalousness of the mental is of great importance in its own right. It has profound implications for the philosophy of the social sciences, including among these social and humanistic psychology. It shows why these subjects can never aspire to be sciences with proper laws and tight explanations. As Quine had argued earlier,[8] the language of the propositional attitudes is not suitable for scientific purposes. Davidson gives further reasons why this is so. Of course this does not mean that the language of the propositional attitudes is not admirably suited to other purposes. We need not devalue Gibbon's *Decline and Fall of the Roman Empire* because it uses language that is unsuitable for scientific purposes. What other language could a historian use? It is just that our intentional language is unsuitable for a science of psychology which must go (via functionalism no doubt) towards neurophysiology. Such a view of psychology has been worked out by K. V. Wilkes in her excellent book.[9] All this may be found distressing by social psychologists and the like, but as R. S. Peters has pointed out,[10] there are lots of useful empirical investigations that can be performed in the fields of social psychology and educational psychology, for example, without the psychologists in these fields having to aspire to strict laws or tight theoretical frameworks.

Davidson argues for the anomalousness of the mental from three partially separable but interdependent sorts of consideration. These are: (*a*) The holism of the mental; (*b*) the indeterminacy of belief and desire; (*c*) the indeterminacy of meaning and translation.

Let me discuss (*a*) first. As Davidson says, 'Too much happens to affect the mental that is not itself a systematic part of the mental.'[11] There are no laws to the effect that (to quote Davidson again) 'If a man wants to eat an acorn omelette, then he generally will if the opportunity exists, and no other desire overrides.'[12] We cannot tell in advance whether the clauses 'the opportunity exists' and 'no other desire overrides' are true. There is no way of improving this generalization in the way in which statistical laws in classical physics can be improved. Nor is the acorn-omelette thing like an

[8] *Word and Object* (Cambridge, Mass., 1960).

[9] *Physicalism* (London, 1978).

[10] 'Chairman's Remarks', in S. C. Brown (ed.), *Philosophy of Psychology* (London, 1974), pp. 56-8.

[11] 'Mental Events', p. 224.

[12] 'Psychology as Philosophy', p. 233.

irreducibly statistical law in quantum mechanics. Such a quantum-mechanical law cannot be improved on, but it is part of a tight network of theory which explains why such improvement is impossible.

I am not sure that the considerations of the previous paragraph have all that much *specifically* to do with the mental as defined by Davidson, that is, with intentionality. I am inclined to say also, 'Too much happens to affect the biological that is not a systematic part of the biological.' I would not go so far as to say, as I used to, that there are *no* laws in biology.[13] But I would still say that in many of the central parts of the subject specifically biological laws do not loom large, and biologists are concerned with applying strict laws of physics and chemistry to defeasible and cosmically parochial generalizations about certain terrestrial structures. The conduction of nerve impulses up a neuron can be explained electrochemically, but as is sadly shown by the existence of certain pathological disorders, the possible presence of poisons, and other sorts of possible troubles, there are no strict laws of nerve conduction in what (to use Davidson's language) might be called the 'constitutive' language of physiology, which is quasi-anatomical. Indeed perhaps some reasoning on the same lines as this part of Davidson's argument for the materiality of the mental could be given for the physicality of the physiological, thus extending the argument from a minimal materialism to a much stronger materialism. It would be less interesting, of course, because there is less controversy about the physicality of the physiological than there is about the materiality of the mental.

Similarly there is a certain anomalousness of the technological, which is testified to by the engineers' joke of 'Murphy's Law' (that if anything can go wrong it will go wrong). Could there be laws about clocks and watches, or even about clocks or watches of a given make and type? No, because such clocks or watches, even if of the same make and type, are not so alike as all that. Recently I dropped my watch while changing to play squash, whereupon it began to behave somewhat oddly. Well, should we say that all watches of make and type X, which do not get dropped, do Y? The trouble with this is that there is no limited list of such qualifications that need to be put in. Still, we do have rough statistical general-

---

[13] For example, in 'Can Biology Be an Exact Science?', *Synthèse* 11 (1959), 359-68. There is a good discussion of these issues in David L. Hull, *Philosophy of Biological Science* (Englewood Cliffs, NJ, 1974), Ch. 3.

izations such as 'usually the minute hand of my watch (or of any watch of make and type X) revolves once every hour plus or minus two minutes'. Such generalizations are not nomological (since, for example, it is physically possible that every such watch should have been dropped on a changing-room floor) but they are not entirely useless. Nor, of course, as Davidson recognizes, are such rough truisms as 'When Jones wants to eat an acorn omelette, etc., he generally does so.'

However some of Davidson's reasons for asserting the anomalousness of the mental are ones that cannot be invoked in the case of the anomalousness of the horological, or more generally, of the technological. Some of these reasons have to do with Quine's thesis of the indeterminacy of translation. Suppose we say that a person has a belief that it will rain. Here we are saying that the person is in a certain relation to a proposition, that is, a class of inter-translatable sentences. If translation is indeterminate, if there is 'no fact of the matter' (as Quine would say) about which sentences are translatable into which, then there is no fact of the matter as to what propositions are believed to be true. Similarly a desire is the desiring true of a proposition, and so there will be no fact of the matter as to what are the desires a person has. There is something about our language of belief and desire, hope and fear, and so on, which will for ever prevent it having the character of determinate factuality that would be needed for there to be a nomological theory of these mental states. Reliable prediction of human behaviour can come only from scientific psychology, which avoids reference to intentional states. Psychology must become neurophysiological, or at the least it must refer to functionally defined entities whose precise neurophysiological embodiment in any particular case may be unknown. This scientific psychology will not attempt to explain human actions as flowing from intentional states, but will cut human behaviour up in very different ways from those of common sense. Consider for example experiments on the recognition and classification of shapes and other sorts of psychological concern so ably discussed by K. V. Wilkes in her *Physicalism*. This sort of scientific psychology is not 'psychology' as defined by Davidson, and it avoids his strictures precisely by eschewing intentionality.

Indeterminacy of translation can be understood most easily if we consider ourselves in the situation of having to investigate the language of a people whose language and customs are entirely new to us. In interpreting the utterances of such a speech-community we make certain assumptions. Davidson holds that we need to credit the persons in question with a large degree of consistency and rationality. Allowing for explicable error we try to interpret the foreign utterances so that as much as possible they turn out to be true.[14] According to Quine,[15] this 'principle of charity' is due originally to Neil Wilson. We cannot ascribe too much inconsistency and other forms of irrationality to the foreigner. As Davidson says, 'Global confusion . . . leaves nothing to be confused about'[16] and translation depends on 'a constitutive ideal of rationality'.[17] This means that we appeal to a framework of ideas quite different from those that occur in the nomological net of scientific thought.

Two things about Davidson's view here might worry us slightly. First of all, we might ask why the constitutive ideal of rationality should preclude laws in human psychology. It might be said that economics bases itself on a similarly idealized conception of economic man, and yet without the idealization it would become less, not more, theoretical and nomological. But how truly nomological is economics? It is perhaps this 'ideal' character of economics that explains why economics is of such doubtful value in enabling us to predict what will happen in real life. Secondly, we might ask whether people might not actually *be* approximately rational and consistent in their patterns of belief and desire. In which case might not a particular choice of translation scheme actually reflect psychological reality, so that there would be 'a fact of the matter' in interpreting another's words? Consideration of this second query will lead us to consider an argument that Davidson puts forward in 'Psychology as Philosophy'. Here he gives evidence which seems to indicate that there is a limit to any empirical determination of the beliefs and desires of a more or less rational agent. Davidson considers an idea from a paper 'Truth and Probability' (1926) by F. P. Ramsey.[18]

This paper of Ramsey's was a brilliant pioneering work in decision theory and for many years it was neglected, perhaps because it was ahead of its time. A person's actions clearly depend not just on the intensities of his desires but also on the strengths of his beliefs. We

[14] Davidson, 'Replies to Lewis and Quine', *Synthèse* 27 (1974), 346.
[15] 'Comment on Donald Davidson', *Synthèse* 27 (1974), 328.
[16] 'Mental Events', p. 221.
[17] Ibid., p. 223.
[18] Published in F. P. Ramsey, *The Foundations of Mathematics* (London, 1931).

need to find out some way of disentangling the two, of separating out values from subjective probabilities. In order to get a scale of subjective probability, Ramsey proposes the following method. We begin by defining a subjective probability of 1/2. Suppose that *A* is a proposition that the event in question occurs. Let *B* be the proposition that something very nice happens to Jones, and let *C* be the proposition that something horrible happens to Jones. Then Jones assigns a probability of 1/2 to *A* if he is indifferent between 'If *A* then *B* and if not-*A* then *C*' on the one hand, and 'If *A* then *C* and if not-*A* then *B*' on the other hand. This determination of a subjective probability of 1/2 provides a sort of Archimedean point from which Ramsey is (on certain assumptions) able to scale values (or strengths of desires) and subjective probabilities (or degrees of belief) generally, the former on an interval scale and the latter on a ratio scale. Unfortunately Davidson discovered that the required assumptions do not obtain, so that Ramsey's decision theory is not able to yield correct empirical predictions. Davidson did an experiment (with Merrill Carlsmith) which showed that even without reward or feedback but by the mere fact of making choices, a subject's pattern of preferences will change with time. It will also become more consistent in a way that Davidson found inexplicable.[19] The problem is not, so it seems, just that experiments or decisions change the pattern of the decisions. Application of a voltmeter to a circuit very slightly changes the potential difference it is designed to measure. Physics knows how to tolerate and allow for such problems. The difficulty in the case of values and subjective probabilities appears to be that we can give no operational or theoretical meaning, independent of the measurements themselves, to the assertions we want to make. This makes the case different from that of the voltmeter. The upshot of all this is that we are inclined to treat inconsistency as merely apparent, and once more we are driven back to interpreting behaviour by means of the constitutive idea of rationality. In fact Davidson holds[20] that Ramsey's problem of sorting out values and probabilities is really the same problem as that of radical interpretation of language. A man's beliefs, he says, cannot be ascertained unless we understand his language, but equally we cannot understand his language unless we ascribe beliefs to him.

[19] 'Psychology as Philosophy', p. 236.   [20] Ibid., p. 239.

In 'Radical Interpretation' David Lewis modifies the principle of charity as used by Davidson and includes a few other plausible constraints on radical interpretation. He here assumes a minimal materialism rather than argues for it in the manner of Davidson. However, he has elsewhere argued for a stronger form of materialism or physicalism.[21] Lewis formulates the problem of radical interpretation as 'Given . . . the facts about Karl as a physical system, solve for the rest.'[22] Here 'the rest' covers Karl's beliefs, desires, and the interpretation of his language. Lewis holds that there are limits to the extent of any such ineliminable indeterminacy, so that it is not too worrying philosophically. Any more radical indeterminacy, which must be distinguished from the indetermination by evidence such as occurs in physics, can be got rid of by suitable constraints on translation. The only question, he thinks, is whether it can be eliminated under the constraints on radical interpretation that he has listed, or whether it can be eliminated only by finding further constraints.[23]

In the present context we can concentrate too much on the thesis of indeterminacy of translation.[24] Quine's earlier criticisms of the analytic-synthetic distinction ought to be enough to show the way to the anomalousness of the mental.

Suppose that we grant that Davidson's argument for the anomalousness of the mental is successful. What about his further deduction of minimal materialism? The other premiss that could be attacked is P2. Davidson holds that 'when events are related as cause and effect, they have descriptions that instantiate a law'.[25] I am willing to accept this principle, with the necessary qualifications, which Davidson is also willing to make, that are needed in order to deal with quantum-mechanical indeterminacy. But I am willing to accept this principle because I already am a physicalist. It is not

[21] 'An Argument for the Identity Theory', *Journal of Philosophy* 63 (1966), 17-25; 'How to Define Theoretical Terms', ibid. 67 (1970), 427-46; and 'Psychophysical and Theoretical Identifications'; *Australasian Journal of Philosophy* 50 (1972), 249-58.

[22] 'Radical Interpretation', 331.

[23] 'Radical Interpretation', 343. I should like to thank David Lewis for helping me to state his position more correctly than I would otherwise have done.

[24] On Davidson's approach there is less indeterminacy than on Quine's because Davidson's use of convention *T* assures uniqueness of quantificational structure, and because of Davidson's use of a wider principle of charity. However compare further remarks by Quine in 'Comment on Donald Davidson', 326-7.

[25] 'Mental Events', p. 215.

clear that a traditional 'anomalous dualist' would accept this principle. Hence though Davidson's argument has (I think) a true conclusion, it is possible that some philosophers might feel that it is in a way circular. Indeed it may be the case that though Davidson's principle is true it is not believed to be true by many of those who actually use causal language. It is likely that causal language grew up in an animistic context. Something is thought to happen because some god or spirit desired it to happen. In giving and receiving explanations men have often acted more like analogue computers than like digital computers.[26] Of course I believe that whether or not we behave rather like analogue computers we are still mechanisms explicable by natural laws, together with the plans of our construction, but this indeed is something that those who need to be convinced by Davidson's argument might very likely reject. They would also, I expect, dislike the comparison with analogue computers, though I think that it is helpful in understanding the popularity of animistic forms of explanation.

To sum up, then, I like Davidson's argument for the anomalousness of the mental, and I am disposed to agree that a truly scientific psychology cannot use the language of the propositional attitudes. From this corollary Davidson produces a most ingenious argument for minimal materialism. I find this argument congenial but have given some reason for thinking that it may be found to have a sort of circularity by some of those against whom it is presumably directed. This is not surprising. I do not think that there are any really knock-down arguments in philosophy: we need to fall back somewhere on considerations of relative plausibility.

[26] See H. Putnam, *Meaning and the Moral Sciences* (London, 1978), p. 86.

DAVIDSON'S VIEWS ON PSYCHOLOGY AS A SCIENCE[1]

PATRICK SUPPES

More than two decades ago Davidson and I together conducted several experiments on decision making. We have not talked much about psychology for many years and, as will be apparent from my remarks in this short article, our views about psychology as a science and, indeed, our views about science in general, diverge. All the same, I find what Davidson has to say about psychology enormously interesting and stimulating. I have confined my comments to three articles, 'The Material Mind' (*MM*), 'Thought and Talk' (*TT*), and 'Psychology as Philosophy' (*PP*).[2] Certainly other articles of Davidson's are relevant to the themes advanced in these three, but the limitation is not unreasonable for the restricted purposes of my analysis.

I regard *MM* as a classic that should be required reading for a variety of folk, and I strongly agree with its final sentence: 'There is no important sense in which psychology can be reduced to the physical sciences.'

On the other hand, I do not agree with many of Davidson's more detailed arguments and conclusions. I have selected five theses that I think are defensible and that more or less contradict views that Davidson has advanced in one place or another in one of the three articles, including the printed discussion of *PP*.

Before turning to the first thesis, there is a general methodological point I want to make about the three articles and my comments. Nothing is proved in detail. The arguments are not complete. In arguing that psychological concepts are not connected in a lawlike way with physical concepts, Davidson likes to take as a parallel

[1] I have benefited from a variety of critical remarks by Philip Staines and my wife, Christine, on an earlier draft.
[2] Published in *EAE*, pp. 245-59; *Inquiries into Truth and Interpretation*, (Oxford, 1984), pp. 155-70; and *EAE*, pp. 229-39.

example the semantic impossibility of giving within a fairly rich language a definition of truth for that language (*MM* pp. 249-50). But there is an important methodological difference about this example. *Circa* 1980 it can be confidently described in a few sentences because the underlying semantic theory was given such a satisfactory and explicit form much earlier by Tarski and others. Davidson's arguments (or mine) are not cast out of the same mold, and I miss in his arguments and analysis the formulation of problems and issues he cannot solve. It is hard to believe he regards his arguments as definitive for fixing, as Kant might put it, the possible limits of any future psychology. On the other hand, he gives few if any hints about how he thinks the arguments can be made more formal and explicit. I hope that he and I may agree that this is work yet to be done.

I turn now to the five theses.

(1) It is common in physics as well as in psychology to study systems that are not closed, that are not deterministic, and that are holistic in character.

I have mentioned in this first thesis three properties that Davidson (*PP*, pp. 229-30) gives to discriminate physics from psychology. A casual perusal of the *Physical Review* would substantiate the claim that determinism is as dead in physics as it is in psychology. (Even Einstein never really seemed to believe in determinism.) The present strong interest in astrophysics—some physicists regard it as the most promising current area of research—and the widespread renewed interest in theories of space provide evidence enough that physicists do not deal primarily with closed systems. A concern with holistic theory is found in current views on the beginnings of the universe or, to take a less exotic example, in the great emphasis on field theories in physics for the past quarter of a century.[3]

---

[3] Following is a quotation from a currently fashionable book (S. W. Hawking and G. F. R. Ellis, *The Large Scale Structure of Space-Time* (Cambridge, 1973): 'In fact it may not be possible to isolate a system from external matter fields. Thus for. example in the Brans-Dicke theory there is a scalar field which is non-zero everywhere' (p. 64). Here is C. Truesdell, in *Essays in the History of Mechanics* (New York, 1968) on the rather small importance of experiments for the development of rational mechanics. This passage says some of the things about mechanics that Davidson says about psychology. I cite it as part of my general argument that Davidson tends to separate physics and psychology methodologically and theoretically more than I think is warranted. 'Without *experience*, there would be no rational mechanics, but I should mislead you if I claimed that experiment, either now or 200 years ago, had greatly influenced those who study rational mechanics. In this con-

In *MM* (p. 245), Davidson sets aside the indeterminism of quantum mechanics (but not of astrophysics) as part of a fanciful tale about complete physical specification of a person, but in *PP* (p. 231) he declares as irrelevant the possibly irreducible probabilistic character of microphysics. In another passage (*MM*, p. 246), he says that the assumption of determinism for macrophysics is not essential to his argument. I hope that in the future he will elaborate on this point, for it seems to me that from today's perspective it is only potted physics, of the sort taught undergraduates, that is deterministic. There is even a substantial literature on the indeterminism of classical mechanics.[4] From a purely psychological standpoint, microphysics does seem relevant because of the enormous sensitivity of the visual and olfactory senses to essentially a quantum of light in the one case and a few molecules in the other. These two examples are easily multiplied because of the near-molecular level of many physiological phenomena that obviously interact with psychological states.

For these and other reasons I shall in the sequel discuss quantum mechanics as a relevant physical theory.

Perhaps the best argument against closed systems in physics is the prominent place in quantum mechanics given to disturbances of a system due to measurement. To put the case in most extreme form, it might be said that there may well be closed systems in physics but we shall never be able to observe them. Moreover, parallel to what Davidson says about psychological phenomena (*PP*, p. 230), quantum phenomena are observed in terms of macroscopic concepts that are foreign to microconcepts. To use G. E. Moore's concept of supervenience (as Davidson does in *MM*, pp. 253-4), we might argue

nection experiment, like alcohol, is a stimulant to be taken with caution. To consult the oracle of a fine vintage at decent intervals exhilarates, but excess of the common stock brings stupor. Students of rational mechanics spend much effort thinking *how materials might possibly behave*. These thoughts have not been fruitless of information on how some materials do behave. Real materials are not naive; neither are they irrational' (p. 357).

[4] For a beautiful instance, see D. Gale, 'An Indeterminate Problem in Classical Mechanics', *American Mathematical Monthly* 59 (1952), 291-5.

King Oscar of Sweden's prize was given to Henri Poincaré for his work on the *n*-body problem in classical mechanics, in so far as it solved Laplace's problem of the stability of the solar system. What Poincaré's and subsequent results showed is that the necessarily infinite series methods of solution prevent us from having a satisfactory deterministic solution of even the three-body problem.

for the supervenience, from a human standpoint, of the microphysical with respect to the macrophysical. One of the benefits of having a more formal version of Davidson's arguments on these matters would be being able to examine the extent to which a structurally similar argument could be made for the relation between quantum mechanics and classical physics.

It is a favourite theme of mine—I do not have time to expand' upon it here—that physics is becoming like psychology. In this sense, some of the pessimism Davidson expresses about psychology I would extend to contemporary physical theory, but this is not the point he wants to make. His grounds for differentiation of physics and psychology in terms of closed systems, determinism, and holistic properties are, I believe, hard to make a case for in detail. In his wide-ranging criticism of the possibility of fundamental psychological theory, or at least fundamental theory about propositional attitudes, Davidson has thrown out the physical baby with the psychological bath water. He seems to want to impose a standard for fundamental scientific theory that is satisfied neither by physics nor by psychology.

(2) Much of modern physical theory is intensional in expression, and the reports of physical experiments are intensional accounts of human activity that cannot properly be expressed in extensional form.

Thus, once again I accept much of Davidson's thesis about psychology, but it is not a thesis that strongly differentiates psychology from physics. I certainly grant that the concepts that are intensional in psychology are often different at the theoretical level from those in physics. Thus there is no natural place in physical theory for concepts of purpose and desire, but there is a natural place for a concept closely related to belief, that of probability, and if we adopt a thoroughly subjective view toward probability, the same concept would apply to belief that applies to the expression of probability in physics. The important point, however, is that the use of probability concepts in physics is essential to almost all modern theory and is, at the same time, thoroughly intensional in character. Many familiar examples show that probability statements create intensional contexts. We may calculate in a given theory that the probability of two events A and B being identical is some number between 0 and $1/2$, but without calculation the probability that A is identical to A

is 1.[5] Moreover, so distinguished a physicist as Eugene Wigner traces the problem of measurement in quantum mechanics all the way back to the (intentional) consciousness of the observer.

Perhaps the more important point is that in the standard accounts of physical experiments the use of intensional language is widespread and, in my view, uneliminable. Philosophers of science have generally neglected the details of actual experiments or the language in which experiments are reported. Let me give a couple of examples of such intensionality.

Here is Henri Becquerel in 1896 (1964 translation): 'I then attempted to transmit a new activity to these substances by various known procedures. I heated them in the presence of the photographic plate without heating the latter, and I obtained no impression.'[6] Becquerel is perhaps especially apposite to quote because his classic experiments on establishing the existence of radioactivity constituted a major step in building the current edifice that has destroyed the classical deterministic view of physics.

Here is Ernest Rutherford in 1900 using the plain man's concept of expectation (reprinted in 1964): 'If the radiation is of one kind, we should expect the rate of discharge (which is proportional to the intensity of the radiation) to diminish in geometrical progression with the addition of equal thicknesses of paper. The above figures show this is approximately the case.'[7]

I can see little difference between the theoretical status of trying to infer something about the probabilistic structure of beliefs of an individual and the probabilistic structure of decay in radioactive atoms. Neither structure is amenable to direct observation; both require elaborate and subtle experimental procedures of an intentional kind to test significant aspects of theoretical claims.

(3) Animals have beliefs.

In *TT* Davidson gives several different arguments why dogs and other mammals that do not talk cannot have beliefs. On page 170, he succinctly summarizes his main points: (1) The idea of belief

---

[5] I have expanded upon this point in my 'The Essential but Implicit Role of Modal Concepts in Science', in K. F. Schafner and R. S. Cohen (eds.), *Philosophy of Science Association 1972: Proceedings* (Dordrecht, 1974), pp. 305-14.

[6] 'On the Invisible Radiations Emitted by the Salts of Uranium', in A. Romer (ed.), *The Discovery of Radioactivity and Transmutation* (New York, 1964), p. 17.

[7] 'A Radio-active Substance Emitted from Thorium Compounds', in Romer (op.cit.), p. 27.

comes from the interpretation or understanding of language; (2) a creature that has beliefs must have the concept of belief; (3) a creature that has beliefs must also have the concept of error of belief and thus the concepts of truth and falsity. I find these arguments unpersuasive and I shall try to say why. There is, however, a more general issue I want to comment on first. Certainly most plain men believe that dogs, monkeys, and other primates have beliefs and are capable of thinking about a certain range of problems. As some philosophers in the recent past might put it, it is analytic that animals have beliefs because of this widespread common opinion and common acceptance of the 'fact' in casual conversation and the like. I certainly do not oppose going against the grain of the plain man when scientific theory demands it. There are plenty of examples of importance to be cited that require it. But to go against the grain requires a detailed theory with an articulation of concepts in a systematic structure. This, it seems to me, Davidson has not provided.

A dog waits at the door. We say that he expects his mistress to arrive, or we may say that he believes that his mistress will arrive soon. A cat meows at the door. We say that he thinks it is time to be fed. The monkey grabs a stick in order to reach a banana outside the cage. We may say that he grabs the stick and uses it because he expects to be able to reach the banana, or, put another way, he believes that he can reach the banana. It seems to me that we can stipulate, in order to agree with Davidson (not that I do), that the concept of belief arose in connection with the interpretation of language, but that does not mean at all that its use is now restricted to a linguistic context. We could, on the same principles, say that there can be no proper non-human physical concept of force, because we can maintain with Jammer[8] and others that the initial primitive concept of force is that of muscular force. There have been occasional attempts in the history of physics to exclude the concept of force and to reduce mechanics to pure kinematics, but these attempts at elimination seem to me as unsuccessful as those aimed at a similar elimination of the concept of belief for animals.

It simply is the case that people talk about beliefs, thoughts, and expectations of animals in the style of my simple examples, and it seems to me there is a natural and straightforward interpretation of

[8] *Concepts of Force: A Study in the Foundations of Dynamics* (Cambridge, Mass., 1957).

these uses that places them outside the restrictive framework that Davidson would like to impose on the concept of belief.

Let me now try to deal more directly with Davidson's main points cited above. The analysis just given, favoured by animal-lovers everywhere, he may set aside as being mistaken and in need of a fundamental revision, for which he has written the prolegomena. That his own views require revision, in order to be viable as a relevant theory, seems to me to be most directly seen by considering an array of data from developmental psychology, including those on language acquisition. A variety of data shows indisputably that only gradually does a child master either language comprehension or language production, but his intentional motor behaviour is well developed much sooner. I would say that as the child learns to crawl about, he early develops beliefs concerning what is and is not feasible, what be ventured and what not. If we turn to his language productions of single-word utterances around 22 months, it is difficult to hold that at this stage his beliefs have the properties Davidson alleges are necessary for belief. It is even difficult for me to believe that these properties are there when he is 36 months and babbles away in two-, three-, and four-word utterances. What general concept of belief does he have? What concept of truth? On the holistic theory of language, meaning, and interpretation advanced in *MM* (pp. 256-7), it is not easy to see how a child could acquire beliefs at all. Short of his giving us the details of an actual theory of language acquisition and cognitive development, it is hard not to be sceptical of Davidson's views about the necessary relation between belief and language.

(4) There are theoretically derived statistical laws of behaviour.

I have already argued that it is not just psychology but physics as well that at a fundamental level is based only on statistical laws. If there were more space, I would expand upon my argument to include the case of classical physics, once errors of observation are included in the theoretical analysis. But the real point is that fundamental physics in the latter half of the twentieth century, as opposed to the first half of the nineteenth century, is almost wholly statistical in character at a fundamental level. Sometimes, however, Davidson goes further, as, for example, in *PP* (p. 233) and in the subsequent discussion of his paper (pp. 239-44), to suggest that the kind of statistical laws that are characteristic of quantum mechanics cannot be achieved in psychology. As he puts it, 'The statistical laws of physics are serious because they give sharply fixed probabilities, which spring from the nature of the theory.' (A similar passage is found in *MM*, p. 250.) It is my claim that there are many examples of such serious statistical laws in psychology. Some of the best are to be found in mathematical theories of learning. This is not the place to present a detailed axiomatic formulation with derivation of theoretical statistical laws and accompanying evidence of their empirical correctness. However, I do want to make the point that the number of both theoretical and experimental papers on these matters is enormous, even though there is much that is still lacking to have the theory as adequate as we would like.

Although the subject-matter here is different from that of physics, the techniques of theoretical derivation of results and the use of general probabilistic tools of analysis are very similar. As an example, a simple model of all-or-none learning that may be thought of in terms of either conditioning or insight is easily described informally. Learning is a two-state Markov process depending on a single learning parameter c; if we call the states U for unlearned and L for learned, the transition matrix is

$$\begin{array}{c c c} & \text{L} & \text{U} \\ \hline \text{L} & 1 & 0 \\ \text{U} & c & 1-c. \end{array}$$

The probability of a correct response in the state L is 1, and the probability of a correct response in the state U is p. It is also assumed that the initial state is U with probability 1. The mean learning equation giving the mean probability of a correct response p_n on trial n is then easily derived:

$$p_n = (1-c)p_{n-1} + c,$$

whence

$$p_n = 1 - (1-p)(1-c)^{n-1}.$$

All probabilities, for example, the distribution of last error, not just the mean learning curve, are a function of the two parameters of the model, c and p. Let E be the random variable for the trial of last error. Then the distribution of E is:

$$P(E=n) = \begin{cases} bp & \text{for } n=0 \\ b(1-p)(1-c)^{n-1} & \text{for } n>0 \end{cases}$$

where

$$b = \frac{c}{1-p(1-c)} \cdot [9]$$

It is possible that Davidson will argue that this example falls outside of that part of psychology with which he is concerned, the part that makes essential use of intentional (and therefore intensional) concepts. The explicit classification is only hinted at in various passages by Davidson (for example, *PP* pp. 229-30, and discussion of *PP*, p. 240), and general reservations are not stated in *MM*, which was published before *PP* and *TT*. As I classify matters, the applications of the all-or-none learning model to concept learning of children fall within an intentional framework. In the first place, the concepts learned were elementary mathematical concepts that are a part of the curriculum the child is taught intentionally to learn and remember and that come to be a part of his beliefs about the world. Secondly, the experiments referred to were concept experiments in the following sense: no stimulus displays of sets, isosceles triangles, or the like were repeated, and thus no reductive theory of fixed stimulus-response connections could explain the learning. Thirdly, the theory does not postulate an observable point at which learning or insight occurs; only the pattern of responses is observable. The expected trial of learning, as opposed to trial of last (observable) error, is easily computed in theory but it cannot be directly observed. Obviously this simple example does not postulate a very complex internal pattern in the learner, but it is easily extended to models that do.[10]

(5) Experimental tests of decision theory do not require an interpretation of speech.

[9] Detailed application of this model, and more complicated extensions to the learning of elementary mathematical concepts by children, is given in P. Suppes and R. Ginsberg, 'A Fundamental Property of All-or-None Models, Binomial Distribution of Responses Prior to Conditioning, with Application to Concept Formation in Children', *Psychological Review* 70 (1963), 131-61, and P. Suppes, *On the Behavioral Foundations of Mathematical Concepts*, Monographs of the Society for Research in Child Development 30 (1965), pp. 60-96.

[10] See, for example, P. Suppes, 'Facts and Fantasies of Education', Phi Delta Kappa monograph reprinted in M. C. Wittrock (ed.), *Changing Education: Alternatives from Educational Research* (Englewood Cliffs, NJ, 1973), pp. 6-45.

From the standpoint of quantitative theory in psychology, I find Davidson's remarks about decision theory puzzling. He mentions Ramsey's early work, casually describes an experiment of his own with Carlsmith (*PP*, pp. 235-6), and discusses briefly the transitivity of preference. The number of theoretical and experimental papers on these matters is very large. It is hard to think of a matter that has been more thoroughly investigated in various ways than the putative transitivity of indifference of preference. It is easy enough to agree with his remarks that we could improve decision theory by incorporating into it a theory of communication, but remarks of this kind about improvement can be made for almost any physical theory as well. The question is, rather, how he wants to evaluate scientifically the massive psychological literature on decision theory. It will be useful to focus on a single issue—Davidson's claim in *TT* (pp. 162-3)—that we cannot properly understand the choices an individual makes in expressing his preferences without relying on talk about these choices. Here is what Davidson has to say on the matter:

What is certain is that all the standard ways of testing theories of decision or preference under uncertainty rely on the use of language. It is relatively simple to eliminate the necessity for verbal responses on the part of the subject: he can be taken to have expressed a preference by taking action, by moving directly to achieve his end, rather than by saying what he wants. But this cannot settle the question of what he has chosen. A man who takes an apple rather than a pear when offered both may be expressing a preference for what is on his left rather than his right, what is red rather than yellow, what is seen first, or judged more expensive. Repeated tests may make some readings of his actions more plausible than others, but the problem will remain how to tell what he judges to be a repetition of the same alternative. Tests that involve uncertain events—choices between gambles—are even harder to present without using words. The psychologist, sceptical of his ability to be certain how a subject is interpreting his instructions, must add a theory of verbal interpretation to the theory to be tested. If we think of all choices as revealing a preference that one sentence rather than another be true, the resulting total theory should provide an interpretation of sentences, and at the same time assign beliefs and desires, both of the latter conceived as relating the agent to sentences or utterances. This composite theory would explain all behaviour, verbal and otherwise. (*TT*, pp. 162-3).

Davidson's claims in this passage raise important issues. To begin with, they seem to challenge the scientific methodology of a wide variety of psychological experiments. Concerning experiments involving human subjects, Davidson is certainly right in noting the extensive reliance on the use of verbal instructions. Does this mean that we must add a theory of verbal interpretation to each of the theories to be tested? In strictest terms, we could insist on such a theory, but exactly the same holistic problem arises in other sciences, such as physics. In the same spirit, we could insist on a theory of the actions of the physicist in performing an experiment. In this case, the actions the experimenter takes in preparing and using experimental apparatus correspond to the giving of verbal instructions to human subjects. It is part of the radical incompleteness of science that neither in physics nor in psychology do we ever satisfy the demands for the kind of composite theory including a full interpretation of instructions given to subjects or of actions taken with physical apparatus that Davidson seems to want. It is easy enough to agree with him that having such theories would be most desirable. But this will be a case of science made in heaven and not on earth.

Davidson also argues for the necessity of a theory able to interpret a subject's utterances about his preferences. He gives the example of a man who has taken an apple rather than a pear, but we cannot really tell, Davidson says, whether he is expressing a preference for what is on his left or what is on his right, what is red rather than yellow, or what. This problem is not in the least special to agency or psychological experiments. It is a standard problem of experimental design. If I have a hypothesis that a certain force is moving particles that are to be observed in a Wilson cloud chamber, I have exactly the same problem of eliminating other causes in order to give a univocal interpretation to the experimental results. I see nothing special about the case of preference. This is exactly what the subject of experimental design is about, and it is one of the marks of scientific progress in the twentieth century to recognize the need for and to have developed a theory of experimental design to disentangle the ambiguities of interpretation that Davidson poses, although I would not, of course, claim that we are always successful. We can bring the matter closer to psychology by examining the very extensive literature on preference in animals. If we took Davidson's arguments literally, we would not be able to make inferences of a definite kind about the preferences of animals (for example, for kinds of food, various solutions of sugar, etc.)

because we are not able to relate the agent or subject to utterances, potential or actual. I certainly agree with Davidson about the importance of speech and its central role in understanding many kinds of decisions. What I cannot accept and do not believe is correct is his insistence on the necessity of tying the theory of decision and the theory of interpretation so closely together. It may be that he wants to make the more reasonable claim that for a certain important class of decisions a theory of interpretation of speech is necessary. In the passage cited and in other places he does not put such qualifications, and in his discussion of the question of whether animals can have beliefs, he clearly moves in the other direction. I am puzzled by how he would therefore want to interpret the vast literature on learning and preference in animals.

Finally, there is another, quite different point I want to make. Even in the case of complex and highly significant decisions, I am sceptical of an individual's ability to verbalize the basis for his choices. It seems to me that decisions we make about a variety of important matters are marked just by our inability to give anything like adequate explanations of why we have made the choices that we have made. To hold otherwise is a fantasy of rationality. If I am at all near the mark on this point, it is another reason for separating the theory of decision and the theory of how we talk.

I have been critical of various arguments of Davidson's that seem to raise important issues and yet have not been given by him in sufficient detail to be considered conclusive. Indeed, in some cases it seems to me his arguments move in a direction that is philosophically or scientifically mistaken. On the other hand, I want to stress my agreement with much of what Davidson says. His focus on the need for a general theory of desires, beliefs, and actions, and for a general theory of how we talk, rightly emphasizes matters that should be central to psychology but do not yet have a proper scientific foundation.

REPLIES TO ESSAYS I–IX

DONALD DAVIDSON

REPLY TO MICHAEL BRATMAN

Bratman's thoughtful discussion and criticism of my views on intention go to the heart of an important problem, the relation between intention and belief. He is certainly right to stress the role of general strategies and plans in the formation of intentions and in action, and to emphasize the need to provide for the constant monitoring of the results as we act out our intentions. He is also right that I have said little about these matters. The question is whether what I did say concerning intentional action, and particularly intending to act, in some way 'distorts' or 'limits' the treatment of the subject, or even creates insoluble difficulties.

In 'Actions, Reasons, and Causes' I accepted a simple, rather standard, account of those aspects of practical reasoning that enter into explanations of actions in terms of the intentions with which they are performed. If someone turns over a new leaf with the intention of seeing what is on the next page, the reason must be that he wanted to see what was on the next page and believed that he could achieve that purpose by turning over a new leaf. This much is obvious; the problem is to specify propositional contents for the want and the belief in a way that makes clear how they rationalize the action from the point of view of the actor. I accepted the view that the propositional contents of the explanatory want and belief should provide premises from which the desirability of the action could be deduced. Not that I thought of the agent as first deducing the consequence and then acting. Instead, I embraced Aristotle's idea that drawing the conclusion could be identified with the action. This had the advantage (I thought) of eliminating the need for an intermediary between reasons and action that might be called an act of the will, or an independent state to correspond to a phrase like 'the intention of seeing what is on the next page'. I declared that 'The expression "the intention with which James went to church" has the outward form of a description, but in fact it is syncategorematic and cannot be taken to refer to an entity, state, disposition, or event.'

Anscombe had already pointed out in *Intention* the absurd consequences of the deductive picture of practical reasoning, but apparently I had not appreciated the point. The difficulty is, of course, that if one can deduce the desirability of an action from the fact that it satisfies some desire or other, then almost every action is desirable (and undesirable). In 'How is Weakness of the Will Possible?' I gave up the deductive model, and changed what I took to be the logical character of the propositional content of a want or desire. The premiss someone has who wants to see what is on the next page is not 'Any act of mine that has a good chance of letting me see what is on the next page is desirable' but something more like 'Any act of mine is desirable in so far as it has a good chance of letting me see what is on the next page.' This premiss does indeed combine with the contents of a belief to the effect that turning over a new leaf has the desirable characteristic, but what can be deduced is only 'Turning over a new leaf is desirable in so far as it has a good chance of letting me see what is on the next page.' Such a conclusion, I argued, could not correspond to or be identified with an action since it is compatible with the agent knowing that the action (because of other characteristics) is highly undesirable. Actions, I urged, correspond to 'all-out' judgements like 'Turning over the page is desirable', and such judgements do not follow by ordinary logic from the premisses provided by our desires and beliefs.

It still would be possible to identify the action with the all-out judgement, but this sounds less attractive once it is recognized that the all-out judgement has no simple relation to the reasons on which it is based. A further consideration seemed to me to settle the matter: the existence of intentions in the absence of the intended actions. The separation of intention and action may be only temporal, or it may be complete, as it is when we never do what we intended. In neither case can the action be identical with the judgement. Since a state of intending must exist independently in many cases, there seems little point in identifying it with an action in the remaining cases. We are stuck, it now seems to me, with states of intending which are independent of our reasons for intending and of our actions. I say this without, I hope, committing myself one way or another to an ontology of states. The independence of intentions is logical: it does not follow from the existence of reasons for an action and a corresponding action that there was an intention based on those reasons that explains the action (though if the action was performed for those reasons, the intention must have existed).

An all-out judgement that some action is desirable, or, better, an all-out judgement that some action is more desirable than any available alternative, is not distinct from the intention: it is identical with it. So I argued in 'Intending', and it is here that Bratman's objections begin.

Bratman's objections centre on the solution I offered to a difficulty I thought I saw in my analysis of intention. Just as I had rejected my original view of the propositional content of desires because it implied that any action was desirable if it had so much as one desirable feature, so it now seemed to me that the content I was assigning to all-out judgements gave them far too broad a scope. For an intention cannot specify all the characteristics of the intended act that are relevant to its desirability. No matter how elaborately detailed an intention is, there are certain to be endless ways in which it could be realized that are unwanted and unintended by the agent. How can an agent intend to perform *any* action with a certain characteristic while knowing that many such actions are ones he would never choose to perform? The answer I gave was that the intention was based on the belief that the disagreeable outcomes, though *possible*, would not in fact be realized.

This answer still strikes me as essentially correct, though reflecting on Bratman's criticisms has made me rethink the subject. It seems to me now that I made unnecessarily heavy weather of it when it came to explaining the relation between intention and belief, partly because of a number of confusions. It was wrong of me, for example, to think that ignorance of some of the desirable or undesirable characteristics of an action is a problem peculiar to intentions for the future. All actions, past, present, and future, have properties of which their agents are ignorant. Some of our past actions we now regret, for we have learned more about them; some past actions we still think were desirable but we would not now think so if we knew more. Some things that, thinking desirable, we are now intentionally doing we would not be doing if we were better informed. How could I have overlooked such an obvious point? For some reason I thought that it made sense to make an all-out judgement about a past or present action (even though the judgement might turn out to be wrong) because we could pick out a particular past or present action, whereas there are not yet any future actions to be picked out. This now seems to me simply wrong. Future actions, like any other entities, have unique descriptions, and so can be 'picked out' like other things. It is not even the case, as I apparently thought, that future actions can't be identified through the use of indexical devices. Of course they can: 'the next time I drink a Pernod in Paris' picks out, I hope, a unique future action, just as I believe 'my present typing of the word "word" ' does.

Putting these confusions aside, the question remains whether it is reasonable to identify an intention to perform an action with an all-out judgement that any such action is more desirable than any alternative. Bratman thinks not. He argues that two unacceptable results follow from my characterization of intention. The second of these is the more serious, so I take it first. According to Bratman, it can easily happen on my analysis that an agent separately intends each of two actions while believing them incompatible, and therefore not intending to perform both. This certainly would be an unwelcome result. Bratman thinks it nevertheless follows from my view, because he thinks I have inadvertently eliminated as alternatives to a course of action other actions that an adequate account would allow. Since a course of action is intended if judged most desirable among courses believed to be alternatives, reducing the number of alternatives would have the consequence Bratman rightly deplores.

But does this reduction in the number of alternatives really follow from anything I said? Bratman's reason for thinking it does is given by an example. He imagines that he covets two books, *The Fixer* and *The White Hotel*, believes only one will be in stock, and knows not which. In this situation, he claims, buying *The White Hotel* is not an alternative to buying *The Fixer* since according to my analysis 'the latter is not open to me in any future which is both consistent with my beliefs and in which I can buy *The Fixer*'. The trouble lies in the last phrase: on my analysis it would not be included. Since each purchase is consistent with his beliefs, each purchase is an alternative to the other.

The alternatives or options that matter to intention are those an agent believes available to him, not those actually available; since one can't intend what is inconsistent with one's beliefs, this means there are often if not always things an agent can do that he can't, given his beliefs, intend to do. If Bratman believes only one of the books he wants will be available, among the relevant options he can consider are: buy the available book, buy *The Fixer*, buy *The White Hotel*, buy *The Fixer* only, buy *The White Hotel* only, and buy neither. Under the circumstances, the first option is the one Bratman will rank highest, and it will determine his intention.

In several places Bratman expresses uncertainty as to what beliefs I have in mind that I say 'condition' the intentions an agent forms. (Other ways I put it in 'Intending': I form intentions 'given what I now know and believe', or 'in the light of what I believe'; my intentions are based on my 'best estimate of the situation'.) Of course, *all* of an agent's beliefs form the context in which he evaluates possible actions and forms his intentions; but some only of his beliefs enter directly into his practical reasoning. The problem seems to me not the scope of the relevant beliefs, which may be taken as the totality; the problem is how beliefs condition evaluations and intentions. What a person intends must, I have urged, be consistent with what the person believes, but this merely reduces the number of alternatives to be considered, it does not help select one. The conditioning I had in mind, and this I ought to have made more explicit, is the sort of conditioning the common calculus of decision under uncertainty describes. I do not mean that agents are rational or consistent in the idealized way that theories of decision demand, but that actual choices and decisions are governed by the sort of consideration that decision theories systematize. The idea is simple: the value an agent puts on a contemplated action depends on the values he places on the various ways he thinks the world may turn out to be given the action, and how probable he thinks the various outcomes are. This is what makes an all-out judgement of the desirability of an action plausible: it does not mean that all the ways the action may turn out are more desirable than any of the ways the alternatives might turn out, but that the weighted sum of the desirabilities of the outcomes of the chosen course of action is greater than the weighted sum of the desirabilities of the outcomes of any of the alternatives. The 'weights' are, of course, the probabilities the agent assigns to the outcomes; in other words, his beliefs.

It would be wrong to say that this process of weighting is usually conscious, or that people always base their all-out judgements (or intentions or actions) on a rational survey of the alternatives. All I wanted to show was that if an all-out judgement is rational in the sense described, it is reasonable to treat it as an intention. A rational judgement is one that takes account of all an agent's relevant beliefs: these will include beliefs about other intentions an agent has, as the first passage Bratman quotes from 'Intending' explicitly remarks. A rational judgement will also enlist all of the agent's relevant values, including his other intentions and plans (these being values of a special kind on my account). Bratman is wrong to think I have somehow placed restrictions on what may reasonably be considered in forming an intention. 'As time goes on we add to and adjust our plans' he says. I agree, and indeed said as much in defence of my rejection of the common view that an agent must believe he will do what he intends to do. 'A present intention with respect to the future [I wrote] is in itself like an interim report; given what I now know and believe, here is my judgement of what kind of action is desirable . . . My intention is based on my present view of the situation; there is no reason in general why I should act as I now intend if my present view turns out to be wrong.'[1]

Only if an agent values one line of action more highly than any alternative does he act intentionally in the present, or harbour intentions for the future. So the 'Buridan problem' which Bratman brings up in relation to my analysis of intentions for the future applies equally to my analysis of acting intentionally. And of course it is easy to describe the problem in such a way as to make it insoluble by anyone: how can you rationalize a preference when there are no grounds for preference? Bratman doesn't answer this question; no one could. He correctly points out that sometimes we have to decide even when we can find no obvious grounds for decision. But if there is reason to reach some decision, and there are no obvious or intrinsic grounds for decision, we find extrinsic grounds. Perhaps I flip a coin to decide. My need to choose has caused me to prefer the alternative indicated by the toss; a trivial ground for preference, but a good enough one in the absence of others. The reason for my preference in this case does not depend simply on the intrinsic merits of the alternatives (since this was part of the description of the problem) but on further plans, needs, and

---

[1] 'Intending', *EAE*, p. 100.

intentions. So far as I can see nothing in my analysis of practical reasoning and intention rules out such considerations.

Many philosophers including, we are told, Socrates could not see how it was possible for someone knowingly and intentionally to act contrary to his own best judgement. According to the story Socrates decided it really wasn't possible, so that only ignorance could explain wrong action. Others, though, have been certain there were cases of acting against one's best judgement; they have had a hard time reconciling such actions with the close connection they believed held between evaluative judgements and intentional action. I side with this second group.

In 'How is Weakness of the Will Possible?' I suggested a new way of resolving the problem by distinguishing between prima-facie or conditional evaluative judgements and 'all-out' or unconditional ones. Our 'best' judgements, I urged, could naturally be taken to be those conditioned on all the considerations deemed relevant by the agent; but action is geared to unconditional judgements. Since there is no principle of logic or psychological law that says we must trim our unconditional judgements of what is best to our best judgements, someone can judge, and act, contrary to his own best judgement.

If I have followed their subtle argument correctly, Grice and Baker do not reject my distinction between conditional and unconditional evaluative judgements. Their central difficulty lies with my use of the distinction to introduce conditional 'all things considered' judgements. They argue that there is no way to construe such judgements that is both consistent with what I say about conditional judgements generally and yields a satisfactory analysis of incontinence. In their view, if one accepts the best interpretation of 'all things considered' judgements, it will be seen to be far less plausible that someone should fail to reason from the 'all things considered' judgement to an unconditional judgement than that one should reason to the unconditional judgement and then fail to act on it. Grice and Baker do not argue for this 'naïve' view; in their paper they are content if they can show that it is better than mine. My discussion of Grice and Baker's paper will have two main parts. First I shall say how I think 'all things considered' judgements should be understood if they are to work as I claim; if I am right, my understanding of the logical situation does not correspond to any of the possibilities Grice and Baker consider (though I am by no means sure of this). Then I shall urge that there is every reason to suppose that there are cases of incontinence that satisfy my description.

What is the nature of an 'all things considered' judgement? So much depends on the answer that I shall first say a bit about conditional or 'pf' judgements generally. I take such judgements to constitute tastes, values, principles, inclinations, and other evaluative attitudes. I use the word 'judgement' here simply for convenience, since no one word is appropriate to all the cases. Perhaps a conviction that pornography is wrong is properly called a judgement, but it is surely odd to think of a distaste for salt cod, or a passing preference for a cherry soda over a watermelon, as a judgement. The point is that the 'logical form' of the propositional expressions of these inclinations, preferences, and attitudes is the same: in each case, the fact that an action or state of affairs is perceived or thought to have a certain property is the ground or cause of a conditional attitude of approval towards actions or states of affairs that have the property. To the extent that an agent knows his own mind, he will refer to these properties as his reasons for wanting, seeking, avoiding, promoting, liking, valuing the actions he performs or omits, or the states of affairs he values as he does. Someone might for instance think it a count in favour of buying a Porsche rather than a Cadillac that a Porsche corners faster than a Cadillac. He would then have a reason (not, of course, necessarily conclusive) for buying a Porsche rather than a Cadillac. It is this relation of reason to positive or negative attitude that I call a prima-facie judgement, in this case expressible in slightly abbreviated form by the sentence 'pf(my buying a Porsche is better than my buying a Cadillac, a Porsche corners faster than a Cadillac)'. Here 'pf' is a sentential connective with a meaning analogous to the words 'is supported by the evidence that' appearing between a sentence expressing a hypothesis and a sentence expressing evidence.

Several comments are in order. To speak of a reason or of evidence already suggests that someone who makes a prima-facie judgement accepts the reason-sentence or evidence-sentence as true. But this suggestion should be cancelled; a 'pf' judgement expresses a view of the relation between two propositions, and makes no commitment to the truth of either. So it is quite wrong to paraphrase a 'pf' judgement in such words as 'Given that so and so is the case . . .'. It would be more accurate to say 'if so and so is (or were) the case . . .'. I am to blame for confusion on this point. In 'How is Weakness of the Will Possible?' I gave examples of practical reasoning like the following:

(M) pf(x is better than y, x is my buying a Porsche and y is my buying a Cadillac)

(m) a is a purchase of a Porsche and b is a purchase of a Cadillac

(C) pf(a is better than b, (M) and (m))

This is, I think, a correct inference, but it misleadingly suggests, by putting the premises in as 'reasons', that the conclusion may be read 'Given that the premises are true...'. But this is wrong. (C) merely says that (M) and (m), whether true or false, would, if true, be reasons for judging that a is better than b. Someone who endorses (C) does not necessarily have any reason to purchase a Porsche—unless, of course, he also believes (m). The sensible conclusion to draw from the premises is:

pf (a is better than b, a is the purchase of a Porsche and b is the purchase of a Cadillac)

This follows without the help of (m). A related point is that we cannot interpret a 'pf' judgement as saying something like 'Prima facie, relative to such and such evidence...', since the relevant relation is *between* the propositions expressed, and so cannot be expressed by one of them. A final point: Grice and Baker think I should add to my repertoire of 'pf' judgements ones in which the supported evaluation is not a comparative judgement that one thing is better than another, but a judgement that some action, or kind of action, is best. I agree that there should be provision for such judgements, but I think they are directly definable in terms of comparative judgements: a course of action is best (in a given set of alternatives, and relative to a 'reason') provided it is better than any other course of action (in the set, etc.). One can judge this without having ranked, or even identified, every alternative.

I now return to the central issue, how we are to understand 'all things considered' judgements. Grice and Baker point out that it is not open to me to represent the judgement that all things considered a is better than b by the expression 'pf(a is better than b, all things)', nor would it help to substitute any other noun phrase, such as 'all available evidence' for 'all things'. For since 'pf' is a sentential connective, only sentences, open or closed, can occupy the relevant space. But, and this is the important point, nothing whatever can be put inside the parentheses to give the force of an 'all things considered' judgement. For as we noted in the last paragraph no 'pf' judgement in itself gives a reason for an evaluation: 'pf' judgements simply say what would count as a reason. To have a reason, one must add something to the 'pf' judgement. What should be added in the case of an 'all things considered' judgement?

In 'How is Weakness of the Will Possible?' I mentioned several possibilities, but made no choice among them. My reason, which still seems to me valid, was that I thought each of the variants had a claim to be called a form of irrationality, even a case of incontinence or weakness of the will, and that my analysis could be made to cover all of them.

The simplest case makes no use of the notion of an 'all things considered' judgement, but captures an important aspect of that idea. Incontinence is here characterized simply as intentionally doing one thing while judging that an available alternative is better. The agent has a reason, r, for doing what he does, but he has another reason, r', one conjunct of which is r, on the basis of which he judges an available alternative better. In each case his reason for acting in a certain way consists of a 'pf' judgement *plus*, of course, a belief that the justifying condition holds. Thus his reason for acting as he does consists in a 'pf' judgement of the form pf(a is better than b, r) plus the belief that r. He is incontinent because he does a although holding that pf(b is better than a, r') and believing that r'. Clearly enough, action b might also have been incontinent, since the agent might have had an even better reason for doing some third thing. But we might define one kind of continent action as an action such that there is no other action the agent has a better reason to perform.

We have not yet reached a notion of an 'all things considered' judgement. For someone might judge b better than c on the basis of a reason r and a better than b on the basis of an unrelated reason s. Then for all we have said it would not be incontinent of him to do b. The agent should have considered his ranking of the alternatives in the light of the conjunction of r and s. Rather than pursue the various ways in which we might construe the phrase 'all things considered', it seems best at this point (all things considered) to observe that there are many plausible construals, each of which defines a different form of irrationality. Included here are the considerations mentioned by Grice and Baker which suggest that sometimes there is relevant information the agent ought to obtain before he acts. The problem ramifies in well-known ways. But so far as I can see, my answer to the question how incontinence is possible given my principles (1)-(3) holds for all the conceptions of incontinence we have yet considered.

But is a man irrational in going against his own best judgement if he is not aware that this is what he is doing? I am inclined to say: he is irrational in one sense, but not in another. In any case, I certainly intended my analysis to apply to situations in which the agent is aware that he is not acting in accord with his own best judgement. Does my analysis run into trouble here?

There are several possible ways in which we might characterize what it is that the agent is aware of. One is this: although he intentionally does *b*, he believes he could do *a*, that pf(*a* is better than *b*, *r*), that *r*, and that *r* is all the reasons that are relevant. This introduces one more notion of what an 'all things considered' judgement is like, and so one more kind of irrationality. (We can get many variations on this theme by playing with the concept of relevant reasons.) But again there is no reason to say such actions are incompatible with the conditions that created my problem about incontinence, nor is there any obscurity about what is meant by an 'all things considered' judgement, or the sense in which such a judgement is conditional.

Here, however, is where Grice and Baker find their greatest difficulty with my analysis. Since my interpretation of an 'all things considered' judgement does not, I think, correspond to any of the options Grice and Baker offered me, I shall have to improvise some aspects of their difficulty to fit my interpretation. But unless I am mistaken, they would not think I have yet met the worst objection to my view of incontinence. For I have not yet mentioned what I called the *principle of continence*, the principle that says that if an agent believes all the relevant reasons support a certain course of action, then he should pursue that course of action. Grice and Baker are willing enough to suppose people don't always abide by this principle. What bothers them follows from my commitment to the thesis that intentional action always is accompanied by an 'all-out' or unconditional judgement that the intended action is better than (or at least as good as) any alternative believed to be available. For this means that I am committed to the view that an agent is incontinent only if he fails to reason from a conditional 'all things considered' judgement that a certain course of action is best to the unconditional conclusion that that course of action is best. I am indeed committed to this view: such a failure is just what I defined to be a case of incontinence, and what I argued was possible. I'm not sure whether Grice and Baker think such a failure in reasoning is impossible, or merely unlikely, or whether they think it does not deserve to be called a case of incontinence.

It seems to me clear that such a failure in reasoning is possible. Simple failures in deductive reasoning are fairly common, even among those who know some logic. However, I did not want to explain incontinence as like making a logical mistake. But the principle of continence is not a principle of logic. As Hempel says of the 'requirement of total evidence' on which the principle of continence was modelled: 'The requirement of total evidence is not a postulate nor a theorem of inductive logic; it is not concerned with the formal validity of inductive arguments. Rather, as Carnap has stressed, it is a maxim for the *application* of inductive logic; we might say it states a necessary condition of rationality of any such application in a given "knowledge situation".'[2] A failure to reason in accord with such a 'maxim' is possible even for someone who knows the maxim; even for someone who realizes that the maxim ought to be applied to the case in hand. Of course there is a strong sense in which 'knowing the maxim' could be taken to require uniformly applying it. Such a person would be inductively rational. Similarly, being continent is acting and intending in accord with the principle of continence. But one can know one ought to be continent and fail.

I find it strange, though, to think of an incontinent intention or action as an error in belief, since I think of evaluative judgements as conative propositional attitudes. So to fail to reason to the right 'conclusion' means, in practical reasoning, to fail to form attitudes in a rational, coherent way. Among those attitudes are intentions. Failure to form an intention in accord with the principle of continence is, I still think, all too possible.

---

[2] Carl Hempel, *Aspects of Scientific Explanation* (New York, 1965), p. 397.

REPLY TO CHRISTOPHER PEACOCKE

Peacocke has, I think, missed the point of the analogy I suggested between the way factual (and perhaps other) considerations can be held to support evaluations and evidence can be held to support a hypothesis. In both cases what is involved is a relation of support or confirmation that holds between propositions; it is expressed, therefore, by a two-place sentential connective. Possibly Peacocke was misled by the word 'probability', which has meant such different things to different people. The notion I had in mind is what Carnap called 'inductive probability', and is discussed by Hempel under this name.[3] But other words or phrases would probably have done less to invite misunderstanding, for example, I could have spoken of one statement providing a legitimate ground for another.

There are, of course, many versions of inductive probability, some of them making it a logical relation (or giving us a choice among many different logical relations), some of them basing it on relative frequencies, and so on. And there are the comparative notions ('*a* is more probable than *b* relative to the evidence *e*') and the numerical ones which substitute a functional expression for the connective ('$pr(H, E) = n$'). Nothing I said was connected with the differences among these treatments of this general notion of probability, so I chose the simplest, non-numerical, and non-comparative notation. Only a confusion between the concept of evaluation (which I used the comparative 'better than' to express) and the concept of support or ground can explain Peacocke's strange view that what I really intended was something like his 'btr' connective.

As I mentioned in the discussion of Grice and Baker's paper, the principle of continence, which counsels a move from an 'all things considered' judgement to an unconditional evaluation, is in analogy with Carnap's requirement of total evidence for inductive reasoning, and, like it, is not a principle of logic, just as Carnap's requirement is not a principle of inductive logic (assuming there is such a thing). Peacocke thinks the inductive principle I have in mind has (or should have) this form:

From '$pr\ (H, E)$ and E is the total available evidence' infer 'probably H.'

[3] Carl Hempel, *Aspects of Scientific Explanation*, (The Free Press, 1965), p. 58.

whereas my principle of continence incorrectly, or by a failure of analogy, says:

From 'pf(*A* is better than *B*, *R*) and *R* is the total available evidence' infer '*A* is better than *B*'.

Apparently Peacocke thinks I have it wrong because he believes that since the element of probability that emerges in the inferred 'conclusion' of the inductive argument comes from the 'pr' and not from the *H*, the evaluative element in the conclusion when the principle of continence is employed should be in the 'pf' and not in the first of the two related sentences. Here Peacocke has, in my opinion, made several mistakes. In the first place, there are many versions of the principle of acceptance; some counsel giving the degree of credence to the 'conclusion' that corresponds to the degree to which the total evidence supports the hypothesis, some counsel simple acceptance under certain conditions. So there is no failure of analogy in my treatment of the principle of continence; I was simply following a slightly different model than the one Peacocke likes.

A more important matter concerns Peacocke's idea that some concept of probability has been transferred from the 'pr' connective to the 'conclusion' in the inductive inference. For what concept can this be? Not the same one, clearly, since the former is a relational notion, a notion of support or confirmation, while the latter attaches meaningfully to single sentences. But the case is worse than this grammatical point suggests. For no one thinks that because all the evidence available supports a hypothesis to a certain degree, the hypothesis must have that probability. Nor is it reasonable to interpret the 'conclusion' as urging a person who accepts the 'premises' to believe that the hypothesis has that probability. What he or anyone else is in most cases bound to believe is that the hypothesis is simply true or false. The 'probably' is rather part of the advice to the rational man: if he accepts the premises, he should give some degree of credence to the hypothesis. The concept of probability involved here is the psychological concept of subjective probability or degree of belief. As such, it does not belong in the 'conclusion'; it is an aspect of the inference. To think that some single notion of probability is transferred from the connective to the 'conclusion' in this kind of inductive inference is like thinking that the certainty that relates premises and conclusion in a deductive inference somehow gets transferred to the conclusion.

Peacocke's attempt to find an analogy between the probability of a statement and its desirability or status as an object of intention is not without a point, but this point is only by confusion related to my (or Hempel's or Carnap's) notion of inductive support. The valid analogy is between subjective probability, or degree of belief, and intention or desire. These are various attitudes that can be taken to propositions. I do not see how the distinctions and relations among these attitudes can be directly combined with the notion of inductive support. Peacocke's 'fav' attempts the mingling of the concepts, but the result seems to be a bad pun: he wants to infer from 'fav(I ϕ, E) and E is the total available evidence' to 'I will ϕ'. The insertion of the 'will' here can hardly be the point: if it means 'intend to', the inference is faulty, since a reason for its being the case that I do something is not necessarily a reason for doing it intentionally. However, if the 'will' does not add anything, 'fav(I ϕ, E)' must be read 'E is in favour of my favouring ϕ-ing (or intending to ϕ).'

We must distinguish between what someone expresses by uttering a certain sentence and what the sentence expresses. Thus someone may express a belief that murder cannot be hid by saying 'Murder cannot be hid' or 'I believe that murder cannot be hid' or any of a dozen other things, just as someone may express an intention to break the ice by saying 'I'll break the ice' or 'I intend to break the ice' or any of a dozen other things. But the *sentence* 'I believe that murder cannot be hid' does not express the belief that murder cannot be hid; it expresses the proposition that the speaker believes that murder cannot be hid. Similarly the sentence 'I intend to break the ice' does not express an intention. But neither does the sentence 'I am going to break the ice': it expresses the propositional object of the intention to break the ice.

When we try to set out schematically the form of practical reasoning, we must settle on some way of representing in sentential form the difference between the sentences that express evaluations and those that express 'factual' matters. The point isn't that someone who used the sentences would necessarily be expressing any particular attitude; the point is that we cannot represent the nature of practical reasoning unless the forms of the sentences we use can be recognized as expressing different attitudes. As in any attempt at formalization, regimentation and stipulation must play a part: on the one hand we will probably find it convenient to assign to certain words meanings that they do not always bear, and on the other hand we will not count on the 'normal' readings of the words we have temporarily appropriated to lend those symbols an undeserved suggestiveness.

My own practice has been to let indicative sentences express the contents of beliefs and sentences with explicitly evaluative words express the contents (*not* the objects) of a host of pro and con attitudes. Thus I would symbolize my view that lying is wrong as 'pf(x is wrong, x is a lie)' while a Kantian might be taken as holding simply 'For all x, if x is a lie, then x is wrong.' In order to state the contrast, it is obviously necessary to use the same predicate ('is wrong') in both symbolizations: it would not do to use an unrelated predicate, such as 'prima-facie wrong', in one case and not the other. Similarly, if Kant or I believe a certain act a is a lie, then I want to be able to infer 'pf(a is wrong, a is a lie)', while Kant should infer 'a is wrong'. Kant has, I suppose, no use for my principle of continence. But I want to say that if I also believe that the premissed fact is the only consideration relevant to my doing a, then I also should accept 'a is wrong'. It is essential here that the same sentence appears in the 'conclusion' that appeared in the 'pf' sentence, since what is concluded is exactly what was supported by a reason.

So far, perhaps, the degree of regimentation is allowable. But now there is the following difficulty. Shoulds, oughts, goods, and evils compete for our final approval or choice of a course of action: therefore we need to be able to construct 'pf' sentences that combine considerations. This is the point at which I have pressed into general service words that are often used to make important distinctions: desirable, better, best, etc. Which word is used makes little difference, since none is right. Some people understandably conclude from the fact that no word already available is right that there is no general concept of the kind I imagine for which to find a word. But it is difficult to think of a way to represent the nature of practical reasoning without introducing a general-purpose evaluative word, for the following reason. Suppose we keep our rich array of evaluative words in our regimented notation. Then we will have 'pf' statements of many kinds, to express our reasons for holding some things to be obligatory, other things desirable, still further things good, and so forth. But now all these considerations are relevant to the question whether to perform a given action (or try to). We need a word or phrase to use in sentences that express an intention—a word or phrase that will distinguish such sentences from sentences that simply express a belief. Since intentions are propositional attitudes, let us construct an explicit phrase for the purpose: 'it is intention-worthy (for me) that', and here will follow a sentence such as 'I wash the dishes' or 'I tell the truth in this situation'. Now we will need a principle of inference corresponding to each evaluative word which says that if something is a reason for holding something to be obligatory, or good, or desirable, etc., then it is a reason for holding the thing (ultimately a proposition) to be intention-worthy. Perhaps such a scheme would be closer to some of the complexities of practical reasoning than the simplified schemes I have proposed. Still, if this scheme does capture the point of the objections to the portmanteau use of words like 'desirable', it also answers the objections. For if each of the evaluative words I have awkwardly pressed into general service plays a legitimate role in expressing one or another sort of reason for holding something to be intention-worthy, then there is something all those evaluative concepts do have in common after all.

In any case, I don't think anything important that I say about incontinence, intention, or practical reasoning depends on my choice of 'better than' as the workhorse in 'How is Weakness of the Will Possible?' Indeed, nothing crucial depends on my having put things in terms of a comparative concept; with a little work my position could have been using 'desirable' or 'optable' or 'intention-worthy'.

Aside from matters of terminology and questions of appropriate symbolism, how far apart are Peacocke and I on the nature of intention? Not very far, it seems to me. We agree that to intend to do something is to have an attitude towards a proposition. He calls this a disposition and I call it a judgement; but what I call a judgement is a disposition, and I am happy to give up the word 'judgement'. He doesn't like my use of the phrase 'better than' as an all-purpose evaluative term, and I don't mind giving it up. But it seems to me he needs *some* term to help express the particular attitude that consitutes intention; otherwise it is not easy to see how to represent the structure of practical reasoning.

REPLY TO DAVID PEARS

I think Pears is right in holding that there is a conceptual connection between intending to do something and a belief that one will do it, and he is also right that this connection explains, at least in large part, why it is that in saying one intends to do something an agent entitles a hearer to believe the agent has some degree of confidence that he will do what he intends. This is an interesting and important point much of the subtlety of which I missed in 'Intending'. But it seems to me Pears does not show that I was wrong in rejecting what he calls 'the traditional theory'; on the contrary, he supports that rejection by substituting for the 'traditional theory' another theory he believes is more defensible. I think his substitute theory makes a real addition to what I wrote. But I cannot see that anything I said is in contradiction to his more detailed, and therefore superior, view.

What Pears calls the 'traditional theory' was never, in my mind, a 'rival' to my conception of intention. The rivals to my theory, as I thought of them, were theories that identified intentions with actions of some sort, and those that identified intentions with beliefs. I opted for a third view, which identified intentions with certain 'all-out' or unconditional evaluative attitudes. Pears's 'traditional theory' does not identify intention with belief, and so is not a rival to mine; his 'traditional theory' merely maintains that there is an entailment between statements that say someone intends to do something and statements that say he believes he will do it. I did, however, argue against this view, and Pears accepts my arguments.

In his first paragraph, Pears takes me as claiming not only that there is no such *entailment*, but that there is no logical *connection* between the concepts of intention and belief. This misstates my view, for I repeatedly insisted that an agent cannot intend to do something unless he believes he can do it. This 'connection' is a logical implication, and so cannot be cancelled by a verbal performance. Pears is wrong, then, when he says that in my view no connection with belief is 'built into the essence of intending' and that the connection is 'only a feature of communicating intentions'.

It seems fairly easy to track down one source of this misunderstanding. Pears writes:

when someone intends to perform [an] action, he must have a positive belief about his future . . . action, but the precise content of his positive belief may vary from minimal upwards. The reason why he must have a positive belief has nothing to do with his announcing his intention to anyone else. It is simply that it is an essential part of the intention itself.

There is nothing here with which I ever disagreed, though in place of saying the minimal belief is 'part of' the intention I would say the existence of the intention entails the existence of a minimal belief. But it is easy to get confused as to what a 'positive' belief might be. If it means a belief with a subjective probability greater than zero, then the 'positive' belief may be just what I insisted on: a belief in the possibility of doing what one intends. But in this sense, there are no negative beliefs. Indeed, in this sense, a 'positive' belief in a proposition p can be what would normally be taken as a belief in the negation of p. For to say simply that someone believes something surely means that his subjective probability is greater than $1/2$. The same difficulty seems to infect another passage, in which Pears says that the agent must believe that his intention to perform an action makes it 'probable' that he will perform it, but this probability 'may be very low'. If it is probable, then at least it must be more probable than not; but a very low probability must mean the reverse. In any case, the view against which I argued was stated far more strongly than this: according to Grice, a man who intends to do something is 'sure' that he will do it, which implies a subjective probability close to 1.[4]

It may be said, however, that the belief I insisted that an intending agent must have, namely the belief that what he intends to do it is possible for him to do, is not the same as a belief that it is possible that he will do it. For there are many things a person is sure he could do that he is equally sure he will not do (at least intentionally). This intuitively correct observation flies in the face of what we are taught about possibility, but never mind; there is a valid point to the distinction. For the kind and degree of the belief one has that one will do what one intends does not spring from the idle observation that one could do it if one wished.

I agree with Pears that an intention does imply a 'minimal' belief that one will do what one intends, provided this does not mean, in the ordinary sense, that he believes he will do it, but only that his subjective probability is greater than zero. What explains this connection between intention and belief? I think the answer should go something like this. The reasons an agent has for intending to do something are basically of the same sort as the reasons an agent has for acting intentionally: they consist of both desires (and other pro-attitudes) and beliefs. If someone intends to polish his right shoe, it

[4] H. P. Grice, *Intention and Uncertainty*, British Academy Lecture (Oxford, 1971).

Donald Davidson

must be because there is some value he wants to promote by polishing his right shoe (perhaps he has already shined his left shoe and wants the two to match), and he believes that by shining his right shoe he has a chance of promoting what he wants. This shows, of course, that there is a perfectly general conceptual connection between beliefs and intentions; and it explains why an intention entails that the agent must believe that he has some chance of achieving what he intends.

The intentions involved in a single action or intended action can be arranged in a sequence by the 'in order to' relation: the agent intends to move his hand in order to smooth the polish in order to shine the shoe in order to make his shoes match. Each 'in order to' represents a conditional subjective probability. As the sequence is collapsed, the associated probability declines: there is less chance that the hand motion will result in a shined shoe than that it will result in smoothing the polish. And given some probability that the hand will be moved, each subsequent step in the sequence has a lower probability (or at least no higher a probability). Decision theory invites us to think of the situation as quantifiable: the value an agent assigns to his action is determined by the value he assigns to the desired outcome multiplied by (that is, diminished by, since probabilities are between zero and one) the subjective probability that the action will produce the desired outcome. If, as I think, intentions are 'all-out' positive evaluations of a way of acting, it is now clear why an intention requires some degree of belief in success; for if an agent believes his action has no chance of success, the value he assigns to his action will be the value of the desired outcome multiplied by zero.

Although we have traced a number of essential connections between intention and belief, we have not yet explained why the intending agent must believe there is some probability that he will take the first step. The answer has, I think, two parts. First, there is a conceptual connection between pro-attitudes and action. If someone likes to play squash, he will be disposed to perform actions he believes will make his playing squash more likely. The reason for this is, I have suggested, that he will have prima-facie reasons for performing such actions, and so in those cases when such reasons win out over others, he will act. The connection between an unconditional evaluative attitude, such as intention, and action is stronger. If someone forms an intention to act immediately, and nothing stops him, then he acts. And since the intention requires the belief that there is some chance he can act as he intends, if the agent intends to act this instant, he must believe there is some chance he will act as he intends.

But the concept of acting 'this instant' is not really clear; all actions take some time to perform. Why should the agent believe he will continue? As long as his relevant beliefs and desires and intentions do not alter, and nothing stops him, he will continue in his course of action. Knowing this, he must believe he will continue to act as he intends if his relevant beliefs and desires and intentions do not change. But (and this is the last step in the argument) his intention was formed in the first place in the light of his beliefs, and these beliefs necessarily included beliefs about his own future beliefs, desires, and intentions. (I discussed this issue in a different context in my reply to Bratman.)

Take an example. I intend to take three aspirin at noon tomorrow, since I will have just had a painful session with the dentist. Of course I realize that the dentist may not turn up, that I may forget the appointment, that I may forget to provide myself with aspirin, or that the session may not be painful; under any of these circumstances I will not do as I now intend. But my intention was formed in the light of my expectations. I would not have the intention if I did not believe I will go to the dentist's office, he will turn up, I will provide myself with the aspirin, and the session will be painful. So I believe I will have the relevant beliefs, desires, and intentions when the time comes to execute my present intention. This gives me reason in this case to believe I will do what I now intend. In other cases, the probability may be thought to be very low, but it can never be zero.

Pears is certainly right, then, that there is a conceptual connection between intention and belief, and this connection does explain, as he insists, the various and subtle implications of our remarks about what we intend. Others, as he says, often have a good idea how likely a course of action is to produce a given result, as well as some conception of the reasons an agent is apt to have for acting, and the possibility that he will change his mind. By shading his remarks about his intentions, an agent can modify these assumptions and expectations, thus giving his hearers a fairer idea of how he sees the situation and a better estimate of the probability that he will act as he intends.

On my view, a specification of the propositional objects of the belief and desire that cause an action or a 'propositional passion' allows us to say what the intention was with which the action was performed or to give the content of the passion. Conversely, we can infer from the intentional contents of action or passion the nature and contents of the belief and attitude that caused it. (In the case of action, there is some loss of specificity in the converse inference.) Thus the causes of an action or emotion that give its propositional content 'rationalize' it in the sense that someone who knows the propositional causes sees what the agent saw in his action or why he feels as he does. I think this pattern of rational causes pervades our picture of the mind, and forms the necessary background against which we explain deviations from the norm.

Dan Bennett suggests that the causal relation may run the other way. Perhaps the pattern of 'rational causes' does pervade our *picture* of the mind, but our mind does not work that way. The reasons we give for our actions and feelings, the motives and values we ascribe to ourselves, are in reality caused by the actions and emotions they are supposed to explain. What we call the reasons are not the causes but mere rationalizations. Bennett's idea is not, incidentally, the idea made popular by Wittgenstein that the relation between the mental states that are called on to explain actions and certain emotions and those actions and emotions is not causal at all; Bennett thinks it is causal, but that the direction of causality is the reverse of the supposed order of explanation.

There can be no doubt that we do often afterwards imagine that our actions were due to values, thoughts, or motives that were in truth brought into existence by those very actions. The heavy smoker may now believe that the casual and imitative first puffs that brought on his present passion for smoking were the result of that passion. People constrained to perform pointless or disagreeable tasks go to greater lengths to find reasons for their behaviour than those who clearly are better motivated.[5] Means, as Aristotle and Dewey among others have pointed out, become ends, thus creating their own *ex post facto* justification. And as Hume remarked, since everyone likes to think well of himself, we tend to discover

[5] For a systematic account, and experimental confirmation, of this phenomenon, see Leon Festinger, *A Theory of Cognitive Dissonance* (Stanford, 1957).

laudable characteristics in ourselves, or to decide that the characteristics we have are, after all, laudable. Thus our pride, as Bennett
would put it, creates its own rationale.

The inclusion of Aristotle and Hume as proponents of Bennett's
view should make us suspicious, for they both held to what I think
of as the 'standard' view, that our reasons for acting or feeling as
we do both cause and explain our behaviour and emotions. They
were not being inconsistent; our actions and emotions are both
caused by and cause our likes and dislikes. Loving someone, oneself or another, makes us find characteristics of that person pleasant. (Again, Hume would be the first to agree.) But the sort of
love that Hume sought to explain, and that he believed to have a
structure much like pride, was love of a person *for having a certain
quality*. It seems clear that it is a causal condition of such love that
one believes the person loved has that quality, and that the quality
is found pleasing. No doubt love in a more general and usual sense
sustains the belief in the quality and the pleasure one takes in the
quality; they in turn sustain the pleasure one takes in the loved
one's possession of the quality. The smoker's desire to smoke is
reinforced by his smoking, and his smoking may be the sole cause
of his desire. This does not prevent his present smoking from being
caused by the desire.

It is difficult to see how it can be true that 'there is nothing
causally prior' to our actions. A hungry man eats; while it can happen that he discovers, on eating, how hungry he was, this cannot be
the usual case. All too often one is hungry first; this stirs an unmis-
takable desire to eat; one seeks the means, and acts on what one
believes or hopes will lead to food. It cannot be that the desire and
the beliefs that precede the eating are causally irrelevant to it.

REPLY TO BRUCE VERMAZEN

We often seem to count among the things an agent does things that
he does *not* do: his refrainings, omissions, and avoidances. How
can we explain away the apparent contradiction? Vermazen is right
that one of the things I have done is fail to discuss the problem.
Fortunately he offers a solution that is persuasive and, as far as
I can see, consistent with what I have written.

Suppose that although I love persimmons I believe they are
harmful to my health; I resolve to abstain from eating persimmons,

and this afternoon I remain true to my resolve though a persimmon is available. Then not only is it the case that I did not eat a persimmon, but not eating a persimmon is something I did. This is what Vermazen calls a negative act.

A problem arises when we try to fix the logical form of a sentence saying a negative act was performed. If 'I ate a persimmon' says something like 'There was an eating of a persimmon by me', how should we represent the fact of my not eating a persimmon? Not by 'There was an action that was not an eating of a persimmon by me', since this would be true even if I had never been tempted and no persimmon had been in sight. But neither do we get the right sense if we try 'There was no eating of a persimmon by me', though this is true, and is entailed by my not eating a persimmon. The trouble is finding a reasonable place to insert the sign for negation.

Let us put the ontological puzzle aside for a moment and ask what makes it natural to attribute a negative action to an agent. One good answer, as Vermazen observes, is that we say not doing something is something a person did if the not-doing is intentional. This is promising, since we expect non-existent entities to figure as objects of intention. Still, if someone acts intentionally, how can the action itself be non-existent? 'I intentionally abstained from eating a persimmon' doesn't mean merely that I didn't intentionally eat a persimmon, and 'I intentionally did not eat a persimmon' again fails to assign a standard role to negation.

The style of the problem is familiar from the study of sentences about propositional attitudes. Consider Quine's sentence 'I want a sloop'.[6] If there is some particular sloop I want, it may seem that the logical form of this sentence is obvious: there exists a sloop such that I want it. But suppose the sentence just means (as Quine puts it) that I want relief from slooplessness? The only course is to recognize the embedded sentence 'I have a sloop', that is, 'There is a sloop I have.' Then 'I want a sloop' becomes 'I want that there is a sloop I have.' This can be true without there being a sloop in the world. (Having come this far, it is clear that when 'I want a sloop' means there is a particular sloop I want, the analysis is 'There is a sloop such that I want it.')

'I want a sloop' is deceptive because it suppresses what would be a redundant reference to the subject, and for good measure also

---

[6] W. V. Quine, *The Ways of Paradox* (New York, 1966), p. 183.

suppresses the verb specifying the relation the subject wants to have to the wanted object. If I wanted Ann to have a sloop, I would express my desire by saying 'I want Ann to have a sloop.' Here all the elements of the embedded sentence are manifest. Sentences about what is done intentionally are uniformly deceptive; since the doing and the intention always attach to the same person, the second reference to the agent is always suppressed. Worse still, 'intentionally' comes out an adverb, and so seems to modify the verb. Under the surface, however, 'intentionally', like 'wants', helps form a non-truth functional sentential operator. This aspect of 'I intentionally did not eat a persimmon' could be made perspicuous by saying 'It was intentional on my part that I did not eat a persimmon.' Or, to get back to the ontological point, 'It was intentional on my part that it was not the case that there existed an action of mine that was an eating of a persimmon.' Here there is a natural function for negation, but no suggestion that the non-eating somehow existed.

This does not quite dispose of the problem, for usually when an agent does something intentionally, there is an action, often an actual movement, that does exist. If it is intentional of an agent that there is no action of his of a certain sort, must there not be something he does to make this the case? Sometimes there is, and in some of the cases where there is the negative action can, as Vermazen proposes, be identified with the positive action, so that the negative action does exist. Thus if it is my intention to avoid causing a draught, and I accomplish this by rapidly closing the door behind me, then my not causing a draught just *is* my rapidly closing the door behind me. What the example makes clear is that even when a negative act exists, being negative is not a characteristic of the act but of the *characterization* of the act.

Mistakes and failures can also exist, and invite us to describe acts in negative terms. So if someone intends to climb the Matterhorn but climbs the Eiger by mistake, his climbing of the Eiger is his not climbing the Matterhorn. Or if I hope to ski down the headwall in Tuckerman's Ravine in one piece and fail, my not skiing down the headwall in one piece is my actual attempt. Here again intention plays an essential role in our willingness to say that not doing something is something an agent did, but in the case of mistakes and failures what is done is not intentional under the negative description.

I think it is likely that every action can plausibly be described as not doing various things. But do all negative acts exist? We have seen that sentences about negative acts can be construed in such a way that they do not entail the existence of negative acts. But of course it still might be the case that when such sentences are true, there is an existing act we can identify with the negative act. If, for example, all negative acts depend on the formation of an intention, and the forming of an intention is an act, then there will always be an existing act with which to identify the negative act.

Vermazen laudably resists this line. His picture of the situation is this: for the sake of discussion anyway, he accepts my view that an action exists only when it is caused 'in the right way' by a belief and a desire that rationalize the action in the agent's eyes. But in some cases a relevant belief and desire rationalize an agent's not doing something, and the belief and desire cause it ('in the right way') to be the case that he does not do it. Then he has intentionally not done something, and we may say that his not doing it is something he has done. But this way of speaking only makes clear that the non-existence of an act of a certain sort was intentional: there need be no action at all.

I embrace Vermazen's solution. It remains to say why I think the account of practical reasoning and intention that I gave in 'Intending' does not interfere with his solution. Already in 'How is Weakness of the Will Possible?' I had given up the deductive model of practical reasoning which I espoused in 'Actions, Reasons, and Causes'. After distinguishing prima-facie evaluations from unconditional or 'all-out' evaluations, I identified the former with the desires that constitute reasons for acting (or not acting), and claimed that actions corresponded to unconditional evaluations (or 'judgements' as I unfortunately called them). I also suggested that sometimes the action might be identified with the 'all-out' judgement. In 'Intending' I gave up this last idea. I gave it up because I had come to realize that the state of intending, which I identified with an unconditional evaluative attitude (under certain conditions not here relevant), can easily exist without a corresponding action, and so should not be identified with an action even when the formation of the intention coincides with the initiation of the action. Thus I gave up what I had thought of as a version of Aristotle's dictum that the conclusion of a piece of practical reasoning is the action, and with it the idea that in intentional action nothing corresponds to the state of intending. Vermazen points out I should have given up the identification of the action with a judgement anyway, since an action is an event, while a judgement, as I described it, was an attitude.

But does my present view stand in the way of Vermazen's solution to the problem of negative acts? I think not; but first I must clear away the obscurities he finds in it. One obscurity I just touched on; he isn't clear whether the 'all-out' judgement which I identify with an intention is an event or a state. The answer is that in 'Intending' I gave up anything that would suggest that it might be an event. The second obscurity concerns the causal relation between the reasons an agent has for acting and his intention. The answer is that the reasons cause the intention 'in the right way'. Of course events must play a part in explaining how states cause states, but I assume that this is not the issue here (for example, coming to believe there is a persimmon at hand may cause me to form the intention not to eat it). This leaves the question what the relation between the intention and the action is. In some cases there is no relation because the intention is not acted on. If the intention exists first, and is followed by the action, the intention, along with further events (like noticing that the time has come), causes the action 'in the right way'. If the action is initiated at the moment the intention comes into existence, then the initiation of the action and the coming into existence of the intention are both caused by the reasons, but the intention remains a causal factor in the development of the action. (This continuing role of the intention is one reason I decided the intention could not be eliminated from the account of intentional action.)

I think this picture of the relations among actions, reasons, and intentions, while rather absurdly mechanical given the complex messiness of the facts it tries to cut and dry, is consistent in itself and with Vermazen's analysis of negative acts. I hope so, since I like his analysis, and I have no picture of the nature of intentional action that I like better than the one I have just sketched.

REPLY TO RODERICK CHISHOLM

Chisholm holds that events are abstract eternal objects, a variety of what he calls 'states of affairs', while I think there must be events that are dated and particular. The difference between us is not as extreme as this may make it seem, however, since both of us are happy to admit that we are talking about very different things—if, of course, those things exist. Not that our basic disagreement is about what entities exist. Chisholm has, it is true, declared that there are no particular events in addition to states of affairs, but his argument for this claim is only that particular events are supernumerary. Thus he has not, I think, argued that particular events don't exist; and I am sure I have not said a word against the existence of his states of affairs. What we disagree about is the usefulness of one sort of entity or another in interpreting sentences that seem to be about events. Chisholm has pointed to a kind of sentence he holds cannot be understood to be about, or solely about, particular events, while he urges that the sentences I interpret as being about particular events can be 'reduced' to sentences about states of affairs. I have denied that the 'reduction' works. But the results are, as Chisholm says, 'inconclusive', largely because we seem to be engaged in rather different enterprises. So, at least, it looks to me.

This is not the place to pursue the details of our debate, since Chisholm's present paper says nothing more about events, but I will mention the main points on which we differed. Chisholm attached a good deal of importance to what he called 'the fact of *recurrence* . . . the fact that there are some things that recur, or happen more than once'.[7] He provided no clear case of a sentence that implies recurrence, but perhaps this will serve: 'Last Saturday Floyd fell in the lake; tonight he did the same thing.' Chisholm points out that this sentence cannot be taken to say that some dated particular event is identical with itself. His view is that there is a single eternally existing event which occurred and then recurred. I think the sentence means no more than that Floyd fell in the lake last Saturday and fell in the lake again tonight, in other words, that the predicate 'x is a falling in the lake by Floyd' is true of two particular events.

On the question whether all sentences that seem to be about events can be 'reduced' to sentences about states of affairs, I was able to show, I think, that systematic application of Chisholm's principles of reduction leads to a semantics that fails to support the validity of many intuitively valid inferences, some of them infer-

---

[7] The four articles, two by Chisholm and two by me, were first published in *Noûs* 4 and 5 (1970 and 1971). My two articles constitute Essays 9 and 10 in *EAE*.

ences that are supported by the usual applications of first-order quantification theory to natural languages. On the other hand, a semantics that appeals to an ontology of particular events supports these inferences as well as further intuitively valid inferences.

Chisholm's present paper makes two claims about states of affairs that I find puzzling. These points bear on the nature of events only in that events are a species of states of affairs according to Chisholm, but it is possible that what I find puzzling here is related to the troubles I had with his earlier papers. The first point concerns what Chisholm calls negative states of affairs. A negative state of affairs is one that 'explicitly denies something'. But when we look to the definition of explicit denial, it turns out that p explicitly denies q if and only if q explicitly denies p; thus the negation of any negative state of affairs is also negative. It also seems to be the case that every state of affairs has an explicit denial. If so, all states of affairs are negative. This cannot be a satisfactory answer to Frege's challenge (quoted by Chisholm) that 'it is by no means easy to state what is a negative judgement (thought)'. My second difficulty is with Chisholm's suggestion that we identify possible worlds with his states of affairs. The trouble is that states of affairs are abstract and eternal, and so the actual world, being itself one of the possible worlds, must be abstract and eternal. It seems to me the actual world surely does not have the first of these properties, and probably does not have the second.

I realize that these puzzlements may be due to my not having understood Chisholm's views. But in any case, I suspect that Chisholm is less interested than I am in reconciling ontological and metaphysical views with a semantics of ordinary language; he has intuitions about the general subject-matter of sentences, and thinks of the task of attaching these intuited entities to particular words and phrases in such a way as to implement the right entailments as a matter for semantic engineering. In the case of recurrence, he may not much care whether the semantics of certain sentences can be worked out by supposing there are only particular events; he is sure that the recurrence of states of affairs is an important metaphysical fact, not unlike the fact (if it is one) that different people can entertain the same proposition. I am dissatisfied with the semantic theories with which I am familiar that try to make systematic use of states of affairs to interpret sentences about propositional attitudes or events; Chisholm on the other hand is sure these sentences are about states of affairs, and so believes the semantics can be worked out.

These differing approaches to, or emphases in, the study of metaphysics are familiar, and I see no reason why we have to choose between them. We should, of course, try to decide whether or not there are particular events; but no one method, interest, or preconception is uniquely guaranteed to promote the search for an answer.

REPLY TO P. F. STRAWSON

I am gratified by the extent to which Strawson's and my views on events, causality, and causal explanation now seem to agree. Starting with 'Actions, Reasons, and Causes' I have emphasized the distinction between reason-explanations, which are one kind of causal explanation, and are expressed by intensional sentences, and the causal relations between events or states and other events which they imply exist, but which are not in any direct sense language-dependent. The causal relations themselves are reported by extensional sentences the truth of which is not affected by how the related events happen to be described. It was this that led me to reject the then widely accepted doctrine, which many believed they had learned from Hume, that causal relations are contingent and therefore not logical. For it is sentences (or statements or propositions), or the relations between them, that are properly classified as contingent or logical; if causal relations are 'in nature', it makes no sense to classify them as logical or contingent. In 'Causal Relations' I again emphasized the distinction between the extensional causal idioms that express relations between events and the intensional explanatory idioms that must be treated as non-truthfunctional sentential connectives.

If I now mention what I have rather boringly insisted on in a number of articles, it is because despite Strawson's flattering remark that my views are so well known that he does not need to say where we agree and where we disagree, I find I am uncertain where he thinks we disagree (and therefore, of course, where we agree). He may believe our areas of disagreement are larger than they are; the preceding paragraph was intended to make clear important matters on which it seems to me we agree. These are certainly not matters on which there is general agreement, as a glance at

Mackie's fine book, *The Cement of the Universe*, makes obvious.

I now come to some issues where there may be a nit or more to pick. Strawson writes:

Once we are clear about the distinction I am drawing, we can avoid certain tangled ways of speaking which seem to have gained currency in recent philosophical writing. Thus we sometimes read of an event *under such-and-such a description* being the cause—or being the explanation—of some other event or state-of-affairs. But both these ways of talking, whether of cause or explanation, must be thoroughly confused if there is in truth such a distinction as I have drawn.

Since I have often spoken of an event or action 'under a description', I must suppose that this complaint is aimed at me among others. What is strange, though, is that I have used this phrase in just the places where I was insisting on the distinction that Strawson has in mind. It would, I agree, be confused to say that an event caused another under a description, and I do not believe I have used this idiom. But I do not think it is 'thoroughly confused' to talk this way about causal explanations when the talk is accompanied by a careful account of what is intended. Chisholm once asked me to explain what I meant when I spoke of an action or event 'under a description'; he correctly called this a 'technical locution', and thought it was up to me to explain it. I did, at some length. After allowing that without an explanation the expression is 'misleading', I went on to suggest that used with caution the locution is appropriate for discussing events and actions as they are mentioned in certain kinds of intensional sentence. I said, among other things:

It was intentional of Oedipus that there was an event that was his striking the old man at the crossroads. But though that event was identical with his striking his father, it was not intentional of Oedipus that there was an event identical with his striking his father. We may harmlessly compress the point by saying: the striking of the old man was intentional under one description but not under another. This does not mean the event did and did not have a certain property, but that the event, Oedipus, and a certain description, have a relation that does not obtain between the same event, Oedipus, and a different description.[8]

What makes the locution suitable is the point made in the last sentence; certain intensional sentences, among them sentences like

[8] *EAE*, p. 195.

'Oedipus intentionally struck the old man at the crossroads' and 'The storm explains the flood', imply the existence of the events mentioned, even though such sentences can change in truth value when the same events are differently described.

One might think that the distinction between causal relations and the events they relate on the one hand and explanatory relations and the facts or propositions they relate on the other would be so salient that no philosopher interested in causality could miss it (whether or not we decide in the end that the best way of putting this requires an ontology of facts or propositions). But as Strawson points out, 'the two levels of relationship are often and easily confused or conflated in philosophical thought'. He thinks the reason for this is partly that the distinction is not made clearly in everyday thought, since most of the time making the distinction 'would serve no practical purpose'. I agree that *making* the distinction is of interest mainly to philosophers, but I think that in 'ordinary thought' the distinction is *used* all the time. So I am inclined to question Strawson's claim that the 'ordinary language-speaker . . . often . . . does not distinguish the levels'. It may be, however, that all that Strawson means is that we cannot tell, simply from the words he uses, how a speaker is using the distinction. This is certainly right. But it would be a mistake to conclude from this that there must be something vague, indeterminate, or ambiguous about the sentences we use. Strawson says there is much evidence that 'the distinction is not clearly marked in ordinary speech'. Yet the distinction is marked in language by one of the relatively definite lines we know how to draw, that between sentences that show intensionality and those that do not.

This distinction is not, of course, to be drawn in terms of the sorts of referring expressions or predicates that turn up in sentences, but in terms of the substitutivity *salva veritate* in whole sentences of singular terms for co-referring singular terms, predicates for coextensive predicates, or embedded sentences for equivalent sentences. It is therefore confused to suppose that just because a sentence shows intensionality it cannot be supposed to refer to the usual referents of its singular terms. Let us suppose that 'His death caused the breakdown of the negotiations' is extensional and 'The fact that his death came when it did causally explains the breakdown of the negotiations' is intensional. Since the second sentence implies the first, it is concerned with both the explaining relation and its relata *and* the 'natural' relation and its relata. This does not show that these sentences are ambiguous or 'mix' the levels.

There is, I think, a deeper source of confusion, not *in*, but *about* what the 'ordinary language-speaker' means when he talks of causes. The source is a failure to attend to the difference between what a speaker conveys, or intends to convey, by what he says, and what the sentences he uses mean; or the difference between the entities a speaker refers to and what the words he uses refer to. These can, as we all recognize in many situations, be distinct without either being ambiguous, uncertain, or 'mixed'. When one irate parent says to the other 'It was your child, not mine, that spilled the glue', there is no confusion either about what the speaker means or what his words mean. Everyone knows that if one of his 'sentences' is true the other is false; this does not obscure what he means. The point of much talk of causality is explanation; this fact does not have to be, and very often is not, shown by the use of explicitly intensional sentences. Thus the use of one extensional sentence may convey an explanation which an equivalent sentence fails to convey. I suggest that the sentences 'His death caused the breakdown of the negotiations' and 'His death, coming when it did, caused the breakdown of the negotiations' are both extensional, and one is true if the other is. But someone might make clear use of the distinction between causal relations and explanatory relations by electing to use one of the sentences and declining to use the other. (I do not want to suggest, of course, that no sentences are semantically ambiguous, or that there are no problems about how to interpret particular sentences.)

Strawson is right in holding that to identify an object as a physical object of a certain kind is already to have endowed it with certain causal dispositions; we cannot first classify an object and then discover that it has those causal properties. Thus the ground floor connection of causality with regularity is not made by experience, but is built into the idea of objects whose changes are causally tied to other changes. As this reference to changes suggests, events are as much caught up in this highly general net of concepts as objects.

REPLY TO IRVING THALBERG

I welcome Thalberg's defence of an ontology that includes particular events, and I like his answers to a number of questions that have been raised in the literature. Here I add a few general remarks to his more detailed study of cases, and then append a brief more or less self-contained treatment of some of the issues Thalberg considers. When it comes to certain subjects, especially the analysis of transitive 'causal' verbs, it will be seen that I have augmented or altered my own earlier doctrines considerably. In a few cases I have not taken exactly the same line that Thalberg does.

Many of the criticisms of my event-laden ontology and semantics fall into one of two broad categories. In the first category I would put criticisms that mention a real difficulty, but a difficulty that arises equally with respect to an ontology and semantics of objects. Thus three of Thalberg's critics (Aune, Trenholme, and Ziff) mention troubles with 'slowly'. Perhaps the popularity of the example is due to my having emphasized the difficulty with this adverb (and similar ones) in my first article on the semantics of sentences about actions and other events. But it seems to me that anyone who thinks this difficulty shows we should give up supposing there are events ought also to argue against an ontology of ordinary objects, since a familiar and entirely analogous problem arises in connection with adjectives like 'tall'. Indeed, the problems are identical if one nominalizes verbs as I do, since on such a treatment most adverbs become adjectives. Those who think they know the right way to treat the semantics of 'tall' will have no trouble with 'slowly'. Similar remarks go for the adverb 'allegedly' and its companion in distress, the adjective 'alleged'. Horgan's challenge to produce an interpretation of 'Sebastian almost strolled' in terms of events that will validate the inference to 'Sebastian didn't stroll' has nothing special to do with events, since exactly the same problem turns up when we try to give a semantics that validates the inference from 'There are almost five letters in "five", to 'There are not five letters in "five".' The fact that 'almost', which is a quantifier with unique features, has an application in sentences like 'Sebastian almost strolled' as well as where quantification over objects is clearly in sight, seems to me an argument for, not against, an ontology of events.

There is a second category of criticisms that argue that events are not needed to implement the entailments that intuitively hold between sentences. And of course it is true that one can set down formal rules of inference, which are purely syntactic in nature, without touching on matters of ontology at all. It is only when one interprets sentences by systematically relating expressions to entities that one can raise the question whether the rules of inference are valid. Many of those who have urged the dispensability of events have not shown in a satisfactory way, or in some cases even attempted to show, that without events the inferences they accept are valid.[9]

[9] There is more on this theme in *EAE*, pp. 137-46.

ADVERBS OF ACTION[1]

DONALD DAVIDSON

Actions are events, and most of the linguistic devices we have for talking of actions are in use for events generally. This may seem strange at first since actions invite such special modes of description and explanation. But what is special turns out to be neither a matter of ontology nor, primarily at least, of grammar.

Adverbial modification provides a lead for understanding what actions and events are, and how they are individuated. Adverbs modify verbs: so etymology and our teachers tell us. As a way of identifying adverbs, this is no great help, but it does contain a hint. Modifiers are attendants, not first movers. Sentences can get along without them; remove them from a sentence and you get a sentence. Thus 'intentionally', 'gracefully', 'in the water', and 'on Fridays only' usually leave a sentence behind when dropped from a sentence. Equally impressive is the fact that in very many cases the truncated sentence is entailed by the sentence from which the adverbial phrase was pruned. Aside from some adjectives, no other part of speech has the self-effacing character of the adverb. Hence often there are gains in brevity, style, and truth when adjectives and adverbs are deleted, as Gertrude Stein counselled Ernest Hemingway.

The parallel between adjectives and adverbs is incomplete. Adjectives have a standard predicative use ('He was young and bold') which does not allow deletion. What this brings to our attention is that adjectives can easily be converted to complete predicates (by the addition of an 'is' or 'was', etc.), and once converted are no more self-effacing than verbs, names, or common nouns.

Seeing adjectives, common nouns, and verbs as alike in forming predicates works wonders for our ability to analyze logical form in

[1] This paper is to appear in Spanish in a volume containing the Proceedings of the Second International Conference of Philosophy held in Oaxaca, Mexico in August 1981.

a way that gives inference a semantic base. For while in '*x* is a woollen hat', 'woollen' mysteriously modifies 'hat', in '*x* is woollen and *x* is a hat', 'is woollen' openly attaches to whatever the subject names. The rule of inference that leads from 'This is a woollen hat' to 'This is a hat' and to 'This is woollen' is just the rule that says that if a conjunction of predicates applies to an entity, each of the predicates does.

The same line does not work for adverbs. For though the predicate '*x* flew swiftly' does imply '*x* flew', there is no obvious way to convert 'swiftly' into a free-standing predicate we can apply to *x* whenever we can apply '*x* flew swiftly.' This may not seem quite true. For we can infer from '*x* flew swiftly' that there is something *x* did that was done swiftly. Here, however, 'swiftly' is not predicated of *x*, but of something done by *x*; in short, an action.

So it is that adverbs prompt us to recognize actions and other events as entities required to make sense of our ordinary talk. Once recognized, events solve other semantic problems. The relation between a sentence like 'Eleanore of Aquitaine married Louis VII in 1137' and the noun phrase 'the marriage of Eleanore of Aquitaine to Louis VII in 1137' becomes clear. (If the phrase refers, the sentence is true, but the sentence entails that the phrase refers only if there was exactly one such marriage.) Sentences like 'He ran to her side' do not *refer* to events, but they imply the existence of an event of a certain sort: in this case a running of which he was the agent, and which was to her side. Existential quantification over events is the underlying logical form of such simple sentences; universal quantification comes in naturally in sentences like 'A game of tennis is a pleasure', which is rendered, 'For all events *e*, if *e* is a game of tennis, then *e* is a pleasure.'

Adverbs and adverbial clauses indicating times, and a variety of expressions and constructions concerning causal or temporal relations, also fall in line. Treating 'in 1137' as a predicate of events validates the inference from 'Eleanore of Aquitaine married Louis VII in 1137' to 'Eleanore of Aquitaine married Louis VII', while taking such sentences to be about events yields a natural treatment of 'Eleanore of Aquitaine married Louis VII before she married Henry II' and 'Her marriage to Henry II caused the Hundred Years' War.' (In the second sentence 'caused' stands between descriptions of events and so is clearly about particular events; the first sentence says there were two marriages, one of which came before the other, but it does not impute uniqueness.) It seems clear that phrases that locate where something happened, or specify the instrument or other means by which an event was effected, fall into the same category.

There are more inferences that surely ought to be justified as matters of logical form. Thus 'Chloe boiled the lobster' entails 'The lobster boiled', but 'The lobster boiled' does not entail 'Someone or something boiled the lobster.' If we want to preserve the former entailment while blocking the latter, we must treat the underlying predicate of events as having two places, one for events that are boilings, and the second for things boiled. Then from 'There was a boiling' we can infer that something was boiled, but not that something did the boiling. 'Gregory sang a song', or 'Peter ran to Canterbury' seem, on the other hand, always to require an agent, but not to require an object. One may run without running anywhere, and sing without singing anything. But there is no singing without a singer. If this is right, we must think of singing as always represented by a predicate of an agent and an event; the event may then be characterized at will as having an object, or not.

Finally, there appear to be events, like apologies, that require both an agent and a receiver; these will be symbolized by predicates relating apologizers, and those apologized to.

I do not wish to be dogmatic about particular predicates; it is the principle that matters. So, for example, if Sam flew his glider to Reno, should we infer both that his glider flew and that he flew? I incline (now) to think not: the glider did fly, but in the sense in which the glider flew, Sam did not have to, for he may have been sitting on the ground with remote radio controls. Birds can fly as the glider did, through the air; so the glider required an extraneous source of control no more than the bird. If Sam flew the glider, that was in addition. Flying is basically a relation between an event of flying and an object that flies; there may or may not be a controlling agent. It is irrelevant that the bird may, in addition to being something that flies, also be in control of its flight. For stones may fly through the air without being agents.

The lesson of these brief remarks may be summarized: to determine the logical form of a verbal expression, reduce the number of places of the underlying verbal predicate to the smallest number that will yield, with appropriate singular terms, a complete sentence. But do not think you have a complete sentence until you have uncovered enough structure to validate all inferences you consider due to logical form. If 'There was a breaking' logically implies 'Something broke', give the first sentence the form 'There was a breaking *e* and an object *x* such that *e* was a breaking of *x*', not 'There was an *e* such that *e* was a breaking.'

If we think of predicates in the usual way as having a fixed number of places, there are no simple predicates that are both transitive and intransitive. 'Shem kicked Shaun' contains an intransitive verb provided it entails 'Shem kicked' and provided 'Shem kicked' does not entail 'Shem kicked something.' 'Shem apologized' contains a transitive verb if it entails 'There is someone to whom Shem apologized.' (In these examples I omit the necessary quantification over events.)

The discussion up to here has not so much urged final decisions about the logical form of sentences with particular verbs and adverbs as promoted principles to guide such decisions. Now we must consider some of the difficulties in applying the principles. Many of the difficulties are connected with the individuation of actions and events.

If adverbial clauses are correctly perceived as predicates of events, it follows that by adding adverbial clauses to characterize events we can at most be reducing the stock of events characterized. Suppose some egg hatched on 15 July in Antibes, that is, there is a hatching of an egg that took place on 15 July and in Antibes. Then at least one hatching of an egg is identical with a hatching of an egg on 15 July and with a hatching of an egg on 15 July in Antibes and with a hatching of an egg in Antibes. And if by chance there was only one hatching of an egg in all of space and time, and it was on 15 July in Antibes, then *the* one hatching of an egg would be identical with the hatching of an egg on 15 July in Antibes. (Is all this too obvious to bear mention? No, for there are many philosophers who think that events picked out by different properties are not identical.)

Consequences for individuation of another kind follow from the present analysis. If a predicate contains a singular term, then that predicate will have the same extension if a co-referring singular term is substituted for the original. So, if Eleanore of Aquitaine married Henri Plantagenet, and Henri Plantagenet was the man about to become King Henry II of England, then Eleanore of Aquitaine married the man about to become King Henry II of England. The relevant underlying predicates of events are '*e* is a marrying of

Eleanore of Aquitaine to Henri Plantagenet' and 'x is a marrying of Eleanore of Aquitaine to the man about to become King Henry II of England.' Given that Henri Plantagenet was the man about to become King Henry II of England, the two predicates must apply to exactly the same events. If there was just one event falling under the first predicate, that same event would exhaust the extension of the second: there is just one marriage picked out by the two descriptions 'the marriage of Eleanore of Aquitaine to Henri Plantagenet' and 'the marriage of Eleanore of Aquitaine to the man about to become King Henry II of England'.

Here is the trouble. Eleanore of Aquitaine intended (we may suppose) to marry Henri Plantagenet; she may not have intended to marry the man about to become King Henry II of England. If being intentional is a property of actions, we have an inference from true premisses to a false conclusion. The tragedy of Oedipus was that he insisted on such invalid inferences: because he intentionally struck an old man and married Jocasta, he felt as guilty as if he had intentionally married his mother and killed his father.

It had seemed that adverbs and adverbial phrases were predicates of events and actions alike, but now actions take on a character of their own. Earthquakes and quarrels may be similar in starting suddenly, being in the mountains, enduring a decade, or causing a death, but actions alone are intentional, deliberate, purposeful, or inadvertent. Unfortunately the very devices that validate the desired inference from 'He killed the goose' to 'He killed the goose that laid the golden egg' when combined with the premiss 'The goose = the goose that laid the golden egg' also carry us invalidly from 'He intentionally killed the goose' to 'He intentionally killed the goose that laid the golden egg.'

The solution that recommends itself is to take such words and phrases as 'intentionally', 'inadvertently', and 'on purpose' as creating semantically opaque contexts, on a par with 'possibly' and 'probably'. If this is right, then such adverbs are not to be treated as predicates of events or actions at all. If they are predicates, then they are predicates of propositions, sentences, or utterances—whatever, that is, predicates like 'Smith said that x' or 'Jones hopes that y' are predicates of. To say someone did something intentionally is not to speak of a manner of doing but of a way an agent viewed his action. It is not surprising that the light in which an action recommended itself to an agent should not provide the only way of describing the action.

There is a cost to treating 'intentionally' like 'necessarily', which is that the inference from 'Jason did it intentionally' to 'Jason did it' does not follow from the logical form of the sentences, unless, of course, we treat 'intentionally', as some would treat 'necessarily', as a logical constant. Otherwise, the implication is just a matter of the analysis of the particular concept. In any case, there is a parallel between the pairs necessarily—possibly, intentionally—intending to (with appropriate change in grammar), and knowing—believing. In each case the first concept has an implication the other lacks. These are areas where we probably ought not to ask logical form to do the work of validating the implications.

Similar considerations encourage a similar treatment of 'allegedly'. Alleged acts, like intended acts, may or may not exist; so they are not, of course, a kind of action. And while Oedipus may have been alleged to have married his mother, he may not have been alleged to have married Jocasta. It comes to this: either we give up simple inferences like the one that takes us from 'Oedipus married Jocasta and Jocasta was his mother' to 'Oedipus married his mother', or we recognize that being intended, alleged, or inadvertent are not properties of actions, and so cannot serve to individuate them.

It should not, by the way, be thought that actions alone invite misleading adverbs like 'intentional' and 'inadvertent'. Eclipses can be alleged to have occurred just as elopements can, and the dawn, like the tax collecter, can arrive unexpectedly, surprisingly, or inexplicably.

The analysis of sentences containing verbs of action and adverbs has some obvious ontological consequences. Not only must there be particular actions and events if many ordinary sentences are to have a truth value, but we also can draw conclusions about the individuation of actions. So far, the main conclusions are two: an action- or event-sentence (without a negated main verb) cannot be turned from true to false by dropping an ordinary adverbial modifier; and the truth value of an action- or event-sentence can't be changed by replacing a qualifying predicate by a coextensive predicate. From the first of these principles, it follows that if, for example, there is just one event that satisfies the predicate 'e is a flight of a *Libelle* and *x* is piloted by Karl and *x* resulted in the award of an Altitude Diamond' and exactly one event satisfies the predicate '*e* is a flight of a *Libelle* and *e* is piloted by Karl', then the two events must be identical. From the second principle it follows, as we have seen, that Oedipus' marriage to Jocasta was identical to his marriage to his mother. We have seen why adverbs like 'intentionally' and 'surprisingly' do not require a multiplication in the number of events: they do not represent properties of events.

These elementary reflections on the individuation of actions and events do not settle a number of curious questions concerning identity. I return to a puzzle I first raised a number of years ago. Suppose Arthur places a time bomb in a suitcase, and puts the suitcase on an aeroplane. The aeroplane is subequently destroyed by the explosion. When did Arthur destroy the plane? Let us imagine Arthur placed his time bomb just once, that the aeroplane was destroyed just once, and Arthur destroyed the aeroplane just once. We have, then, three events:

(1) Arthur's placing the bomb
(2) The destruction of the aeroplane
(3) Arthur's destroying the aeroplane.

Clearly enough, (1) caused (2); and clearly enough, that is why there was such an event as (3). Arthur's act of placing the bomb caused the destruction of the aeroplane, and that is why it is true that Arthur destroyed the aeroplane. But what is the relation between events (1) and (3), Arthur's placing the bomb and Arthur's destroying the aeroplane? Since Arthur did nothing more than place the bomb, it is natural to say the two acts are one: his placing the bomb *was* his destroying the aeroplane. But against this conclusion is the fact that the destruction of the aeroplane came long after the placing of the bomb. How can we allow that Arthur had already destroyed the aeroplane long before it was destroyed?

The right answer to the central question is, I think, that actions (1) and (3) are identical, and therefore took place at the same time. Part of the difficulty in accepting this answer is due to the complications of tense. There is a period during which it is true to say 'Arthur has placed the bomb' but not clearly true to say 'Arthur has destroyed the aeroplane.' But it does not follow that he performed two actions. His one action had a consequence. We cannot speak of the action as an action that has that consequence until the time of the consequence arrives. But the arrival of the consequence does not change the cause. It merely changes what we can, in the present tense, say of it. The situation does not seem different from one in which we can say of a man that he is president, or a grandfather at some times and not at others; yet he remains the same man. This 'remains' is not temporal: it is the concept of timeless identity that is required. A is not the grandfather of B until B is born. Yet A may be dead by the time he is a grandfather. So Arthur may be quite finished with his deed—in fact, *he* may be dead—when the consequence of his deed makes it a destroying of an aeroplane.

There is more to the story than this. When the question is how many actions Arthur performed, whether his placing the bomb and his destroying the aeroplane were one or two, then I think the answer is clear. There was just one action. But we ask a different question when we ask when Arthur destroyed the aeroplane. For this demands that we analyse the sentence 'Arthur destroyed the aeroplane', and this sentence contains no singular term purporting to refer to an event. 'Arthur destroyed the aeroplane' entails 'The aeroplane was destroyed', while 'The aeroplane was destroyed' does not entail 'Someone destroyed the aeroplane'. We therefore must treat the underlying predicate of events as '*e* is a destruction of an aeroplane.' So 'Arthur destroyed the aeroplane' must have a form something like 'Arthur caused a destruction of the aeroplane.' But agents cause things to happen by *doing* something—perhaps by placing a bomb. (Of course they may do this in turn by doing something else.) So 'Arthur destroyed the aeroplane' necessarily involves *two* events: something Arthur did, and a destruction of the aeroplane'. A fuller analysis of 'Arthur destroyed the aeroplane' then takes us to:

> There exist two events such that Arthur is the agent of the first, the second is a destruction of the aeroplane, and the first caused the second.

Given the form of this sentence, it is clear why the question 'When did Arthur destroy the aeroplane?' is hard to answer, for the original sentence says there are two events which may have happened at quite different times. A full answer should specify the time at which Arthur performed the act that caused the destruction and the time of the destruction.

No ambiguity attaches to the question 'When did Arthur's action of destroying the aeroplane occur?' for the description of this action is 'the action of which Arthur was agent which caused a destruction of the aeroplane', and this has a definite date. If this is the right way to describe his action, then on a further natural assumption, we can prove that Arthur's placing of the bomb was identical with his destroying of the aeroplane. The assumption is that in the framework of the story, only one action of Arthur's caused the destruction of the aeroplane. This was the placing of the bomb, which, on our analysis, was his destroying of the aeroplane, for this was the action of which Arthur was agent and which caused a destruction of the aeroplane.

A parallel problem arises with respect to place. Consider the case of The People v. Robert J. Thomas. Thomas and a man named Humphries were on an Irish ship sailing from Liverpool to Dublin. 'They had both been drinking, when, some fifteen miles out from the Welsh coast, about midnight, there was a fight in which Humphries went overboard and was lost.' Thomas was convicted of manslaughter, but appealed on the ground that since the death did not occur on the ship, the Irish court that tried him did not have jurisdiction. Thomas' counsel argued that 'jurisdiction was confined to the trial of persons committing offences on board an Irish ship on the high seas where such offences were committed and completed on the ship'. He went on to contend that manslaughter is a 'complex crime consisting of two essential ingredients. The first is some unlawful act . . . which causes the death, and the second is the fact of death itself.' The court correctly held that the appeal failed, though the court deserved only a pass for its reasoning. The appeals court ought to have noted that the crime was both committed and completed on board the ship. The *definition* of manslaughter is indeed complex, in requiring an unlawful act which causes a death, but the unlawful act does not include the consequence that makes it unlawful. Thomas' counsel confused a conceptual ingredient of the crime with a material ingredient. 'Thomas killed Humphries' means 'There were two events such that Thomas was agent of the first, the second was a death of Humphries, and the first caused the second.' If we ask 'Where did it happen?' the response should be that the first event occurred on board the ship and the second in the sea; and the response might be accompanied by a complaint that the 'it' of the question is, under the circumstances, ambiguous.

It should be remarked again that puzzles about the time and place of actions are not peculiar to actions; impersonal events are equally infected. 'The sun melted the snow' means, nearly enough, 'The sun did something that caused a melting of the snow.' Two times and two places are obviously involved, so there can be no single right answers to the questions 'Where and when did the sun melt the snow?'

A number of closely related problems are met in related ways. In an excellent article Terence Parsons objects to my view (which I took from G. E. M. Anscombe) that if I inadvertently alert a burglar by advertently turning on the light, then (supposing I do each only once) my alerting of the burglar is identical with my turning on of the light. I have already urged that we should not let the fact that one of these actions is inadvertent and the other advertent make us think the actions are discrete. This is just a misleading way of saying that I viewed the action as a turning on of the light, but did not know it was at the same time an alerting of the burglar. But Parsons has a simpler objection. If there is just one event, it must have all these properties: I am its agent, it is a turning on, it is of the light, it is an alerting, it is of the burglar. Then we can infer, among many other things, that I turned on the burglar and alerted the light.[2]

I am inclined to avoid these particular troubles by being selective about how many places each predicate has. Turning on, in its meaning here (no jokes, please), is always transitive: there must be an agent and there must be something turned on. Alerting, on the other hand, does not require an agent, but does require an alertee. My single action therefore had these properties: it was a turning on of the light by me, and it was an act of mine that caused the burglar to be alerted. In other words, my alerting of the burglar was my doing something that caused the burglar to be alerted, and this was, as it happened, my turning on of the light.

Parsons takes the following case from John Wallace:

if I hit the eight-ball into the corner pocket, and, in one and the same action hit the seven-ball into the side pocket, then, if there is really only one action involved, we can infer (from Davidson's symbolization) that I hit the eight-ball into the side pocket and the seven-ball into the corner pocket . . . I . . . suggest . . . that we keep the analysis while giving up the view that the two hittings are identical.[3]

[2] Terence Parsons, 'Modifiers and Quantifiers in Natural Language', in F. J. Pelletier and C. G. Normore (eds.), *New Essays in Philosophy of Language* (*Canadian Journal of Philosophy*, Supplementary Volume VI), 1980.

[3] Ibid., p. 36. The objection is from an unpublished paper by John Wallace, 'On What's Happening'.

There are, I think, a number of events involved here, but only one action. 'Hit' may be irreducibly transitive (I'm not sure about this), but the hitter need not be an agent—one ball may hit another. So 'I hit the eight-ball into the corner' should be analysed 'There were two events such that I was agent of one, another was a hitting of the eight-ball into the corner pocket, and the first event caused the second.' Even if '*e* was an into-the-corner-pocket event' is an independent predicate of events, it is not a predicate of the action, but of an event that was caused by the action.

I have a large catapult which is armed by stressing a wooden arm, using a system of gears and levers. I arm the catapult by turning a crank. I turn the crank rapidly, but the catapult is armed slowly. Yet my turning of the crank is identical with my arming of the catapult. How can one and the same action be both rapid and slow? Once again there are two (or more) events, but only one action. My arming the catapult is my doing something that causes the catapult to be armed. The cause is rapid, the effect slow.

Here we have come to a new class of adverbs, such as 'slowly' and 'rapidly', that do not in general yield to the methods so far advanced. Although the case of the catapult goes smoothly, other cases do not. Suppose I swim the Channel in record time. Then my swimming of the Channel is fast. But my swimming is also a crossing of the Channel, and as a crossing it is slow. There are, to be sure, events we can distinguish: it is by moving my limbs as I do that I cause my body to cross from England to France. And no doubt the movement of my limbs may be agitated or rapid while the crossing of my body from England to France may be calm and slow. But this does not solve the problem, for the problem springs from the fact that one and the same event is slow for a crossing, and fast for a swimming, of the Channel.

The difficulty is familiar from the case of adjectives like 'large' and 'tall'. Indeed, since I have treated adverbs as adjectives (having nominalized verbs in specifying logical form), it is no wonder that some adverbs show the traits of attributive adjectives. I confess that I know no really satisfactory way to deal with attributive adjectives and what we may as well call attributive adverbs. I resist the idea that in saying someone is a tall man, or that someone swam the Channel swiftly, we must be referring to the class of men, or of swimmings, or the property of being a man or of being a swimming. I resist for a number of reasons. If 'tall' is a functional expression mapping classes or properties on to properties or classes, then the idea that 'Jones is a tall man' entails by its form 'Jones is a man' goes by the board. Far worse, if 'man' here refers to a class or property, there can be no good reason to deny that any common noun (or verbal predicate) refers to a class or property. Although some such semantic theory is popular these days, it seems to me an unattractive way of interpreting the simplest predicates (as apart, perhaps, from *describing* their logical features) because we must use in an explained way the very predicates whose semantics we want to understand.

These are deep matters that go beyond my present concern. We can say this: adverbs like 'slowly' raise just the same difficulties for my analysis of action and event sentences as adjectives like 'tall' raise for the usual analysis of sentences about men or giraffes. So much the worse for both analyses. But I find some comfort in the thought that events once more seem on a par, ontologically, with familiar objects like men and giraffes.

REPLIES TO ESSAYS X-XII

DONALD DAVIDSON

REPLY TO HARRY LEWIS

I am counting sheep as they jump one by one over the fence. I describe each sheep: 'sheep one', 'sheep two', 'sheep three'. Now comes a goat. Not knowing what may be next, I start using a new vocabulary: 'animal one', 'animal one', 'animal two', 'animal three'. My old vocabulary is *supervenient* on the new in this sense: if two items can be distinguished in the first vocabulary, they can be distinguished in the new (and this would remain true if 'goat' were added to the old vocabulary). One might say that the question whether an animal is a sheep or a goat is described, determined, or fixed by its place in the sequence of animals. Yet nothing in the animal vocabulary means 'sheep'; if the number of sheep is infinite, there may be no finite expression in the animal vocabulary that applies to all and only the sheep; there may be no lawlike sentence of the form 'x is a sheep if and only if x is an animal with a number satisfying the (numerical) formula f.' The animal vocabulary can pick out each individual sheep and goat, but it cannot in general tell the sheep from the goats.

The notion of supervenience, as I have used it, is best thought of as a relation between a predicate and a set of predicates in a language: a predicate p is supervenient on a set of predicates S if for every pair of objects such that p is true of one and not of the other there is a predicate of S that is true of one and not of the other. All the individual entities that can be distinguished using the supervenient predicate can be distinguished using the subvenient predicates; supervenience guarantees that the ontology of the subvenient predicates suffices for the supervenient predicate. Supervenience characterizes a very general, and so very weak, concept of reduction, what might well be called ontological reduction. It is trivially obvious that ontological reduction does not entail definitional reduction, though it is entailed by it, nor does it entail nomological reduction. Semantic predicates are provably not definable on the basis of syntactic predicates, though supervenient on them, and if naturalism is the mistake Moore believed it to be, evaluative predicates are supervenient on though not otherwise reducible to descriptive predicates. The sheep and the goats provide another example.

These simple matters would not be interesting if the 'nothing but' fallacy were not so common in philosophy. But I suspect that this fallacy accounts for the plausibility of most important reductionistic programmes: phenomenalistic reductionism, naturalism in ethics, and definitional behaviourism in the philosophy of mind. The fallacy is to reason from ontological to a stronger form of reductionism, or simply to conflate the two; for example, to reason from 'For each animal that is picked out by the predicate "sheep" there is a predicate in the animal-number vocabulary that is uniquely true of it' to 'There is a predicate in the animal-number vocabulary that is true of each animal picked out by the predicate "sheep".' Obviously the fallacy can be used to discredit a view as easily as to promote it: if mental events are physical events, the properties of mental events are 'nothing but' physical properties. *Non sequitur.*

I do not mean to suggest that Harry Lewis has committed the 'nothing but' fallacy. He is after a concept of supervenience more subtle and, as he demonstrates, more elusive than the one I have just characterized. Taking the relation between moral properties and descriptive properties (as conceived by Moore?) as the model for supervenience, he explores attempts to define this relation. He concludes that no definition he has found seems both clear and correct, and that whatever the relation between moral and descriptive properties may be, it is not the same as the relation between psychological and physical properties. So far as I understand these matters, I think he is right on both counts.

Supervenience of the sort that Lewis and others have sought to characterize is, I assume, a special case of my broad rude version, which is why I counted the moral-descriptive relation as a familiar example of the (perhaps not so familiar) relation I had in mind. In any case, supervenience as I have defined it here is clearly all I needed for the argument in 'Mental Events', since what I was arguing for there was only the identity of mental events with physical events. I wanted to emphasize that such ontological reduction does not imply that mental properties are physical properties, nor that there are causal or bridging laws relating events classed by mental properties with events classed by physical properties. By emphasizing the failure of these implications I hoped to defuse some of the stronger objections to monism. At the same time I tried to show how someone who, like me, thought that psychophysical generalizations could never have the same strong nomological character as purely physical laws, could use this fact, if it is one, as part of an argument for monism.

Lewis says that 'it is a truism that there cannot be two events alike in all physical respects but differing in some mental respect, because it is a truism that there cannot be two events alike in all physical respects'. To hold that there cannot be two events alike in all physical respects is to hold that there is a physical predicate uniquely true of every event (assuming there is a predicate for each 'respect'). Such an event is, however, what I would call a physical event (since it is *the* event that has such-and-such physical characteristics). So if Lewis is right that it is a truism that there cannot be two events alike in all physical respects, the truth of monism is a truism.

REPLY TO J. J. C. SMART

Smart, who has done so much to promote contemporary interest in physicalist monism, is more sympathetic to the monism in my anomalous monism than to the anomaly. One can hardly blame him. It is one thing to hold, as we both do, that mental events are identical with physical events; it is another to argue, as I did in 'Mental Events', that psychophysical correlations can never aspire to as high a level on the scale of nomologicality as the laws of physics. Smart understandably worries that though I may be right about this, my reasons are not compelling. Before turning to the issue of psychophysical laws, however, I want to say a word about a word or two. Terminology, once one's position is clear, ought not to matter; but it often seems to. I have resisted calling my position either materialism or physicalism because, unlike most materialists or physicalists, I do not think mental properties (or predicates) are reducible to physical properties (or predicates), nor that we could, conceptually or otherwise, get along without mental concepts.[1]

---

[1] I discuss this aspect of anomalous monism in *EAE*, pp. 243-4.

Monistic my view is, since it holds that mental events are physical events, but a form of materialist chauvinism it is not, since it holds that being mental is not an eliminable or derivative property.

The basic reason the mental concepts connected with propositional attitudes cannot be incorporated in a system of exceptionless laws is the normative character of these mental concepts. Beliefs, intentions, and desires are identified by their objects, and these are identified by their logical and semantic properties. If attitudes can be identified at all, then, they must be found to be largely consistent with one another (because of their logical properties), and in tune with the real world (because of their semantic properties). Smart asks 'whether people might not actually *be* approximately rational and consistent in their patterns of belief and desire'. In my view this cannot be a factual question: if a creature has propositional attitudes then that creature is approximately rational.[2] Rationality is, however, a normative notion which by its nature resists regimentation in accord with a single public standard. Even the individual interpreter has trouble deciding on the best way to understand another person when he finds what seem serious deviations from his own norms of internal coherence and outward correspondence with the truth.

It is at this point that indeterminacy is relevant. Indeterminacy as such does not necessarily militate against the formulation of strict laws; the inscrutability of reference, for example, makes no more trouble for a science of psychology than is made for the physical sciences by the arbitrary nature of the numerical measure of distance (until an arbitrary unit is chosen). What does matter is the indeterminacy that results from the absence of a clear line between the analytic and the synthetic. A theory to explain a person's verbal and other behaviour requires the assignment of propositional contents to his sentences and attitudes. But where theory constrains us to draw a sharp line, only a shaded area is indicated by the evidence. Within this area there is, as Quine has insisted, no fact of the matter. We draw the line as best we can, tailoring our theory to the multiple demands of 'charity'. The application of the principle of charity is an application of normative considerations (among others).

The unsuitability of certain psychological concepts for incorporation in strict laws is shown in another way. Strict laws do not

---

[2] I try to show this in 'Rational Animals', *Dialectica* 36 (1982), 317-27.

deploy disposition terms nor do they use causal concepts. It is just when the relevant mechanisms are unknown that diseases are defined by their causes or their symptoms. Everyday explanations of non-mental phenomena are conveniently if not necessarily often couched in terms that bypass serious science and its laws; there is no need to search for the cause of sunburn, nor can medicine set out to discover the most obvious symptom of jaundice. But in these cases there is no clear obstacle save ignorance to substituting non-causal ways of describing the phenomena we are interested in. The same cannot be said of intentional actions and the propositional states and events that explain them. An intentional action is an action caused by states and events that rationalize it; it is a basic aspect of a belief or desire that it will cause certain sorts of action under appropriate conditions. These are, I think, irreducible aspects of reason-explanations; a science that tries to eliminate the causal element from these concepts will succeed only by changing the subject, for here causality is connected with the normative demands of rationality.

Smart raises the question whether my argument for the identity of mental events with physical events, which applies directly only to events that are clearly related to propositional attitudes, can be made to apply also to 'occurrent experiences' like pains and itches. I think it can, though to make a convincing case is far more than I can hope to do here. But there are several suggestive leads that can be drawn from the sketchy remarks of the last few paragraphs. Pain, to pick what seems to be the philosopher's favourite sensation, is attributed on the basis of its causes, its consequences for behaviour, and verbal claims. To the extent that pain is inseparable from these connected phenomena, it is irreducibly causal in much the same way that beliefs, desires, and intentions are. Like them, it plays a basic role in explaining, and hence rationalizing, intentional behaviour. Finally, though pain is not typically a propositional attitude nor defined in terms of one, honest claims to be in pain share with self-attributions of attitudes a presumption in favour of truth. It is hard to see how this presumption could be reconciled with the existence of precise correlations of pain states with objectively identifiable physical states.

According to Smart, many philosophers who may agree with me that there are no strict psychophysical laws may disagree with my claim that causal relations have strict laws to back them (whether we know those laws or not), and so will not have to accept my monistic conclusion. Of course I agree, and stressed the point in 'Mental Events'. But this does not, in any ordinary sense, make my argument circular, since monism does not follow from this premiss, but only when this premiss is combined with premisses with which it is not usually combined. All the same, one would like to be given a reason for supposing there is a close connection between laws and causal connections. I think there is such a connection, and I plan to argue for it in print one of these days. But I am certain, with Smart, that neither these nor any other considerations in its favour will turn the argument for anomalous monism into a knock-down argument.

REPLY TO PATRICK SUPPES

In this chapter Flippant Philosophy meets Serious Science. Philosophy survives, if that is the correct interpretation of the outcome, only because of the godlike restraint shown by Science. Nobly, though nearly not, controlling his exasperation, Suppes spares my feelings by merely glancing at the libraries groaning with the fully mastered tons of data from skilfully controlled experiments which I have never read and could not understand, the profound and subtle mathematically sharp theories of learning, language acquisition, and concept formation which it is for ever beyond me to grasp, and the remarkable way in which physicists have brought the intensional and humanistic into spooky contact with the quarks and quantum jumps. Suppes delicately declines to discuss my actual arguments, hinting that since they lack the rigor of Tarski's proof that no consistent language with much expressive power can contain its own truth predicate, it is premature at best to take my arguments seriously.

Not that I am not grateful for the tutorial by the master. Much of the little I know about science and its methods I learned from Suppes. He is a superb and patient teacher, and his work on measurement, probability, and the nature of theories and models has greatly influenced my thinking. In my opinion this work is not sufficiently appreciated by philosophers. It comes as no surprise to me to learn that I am one of the philosophers who has not learned his lesson.

In two of the articles that Suppes discusses, 'The Material Mind' and 'Psychology as Philosophy', I was mainly concerned to argue for the irreducibility to physics of those divisions of psychology that deal with intentional matters. This is a thesis accepted by a great many psychologists, of course, and Suppes says he also agrees with it, though he does not say why. Where he thinks I go wrong is in my description of the differences between psychology and physics; he says physics is far more like psychology than I realize, and psychology more like physics. I am sure that he is right in insisting that 'it is common in physics as well as in psychology to study systems that are not closed, that are not deterministic, and that are holistic in character'. The question I would like to examine is how my main argument for the irreducibility of the intentional is affected when account is taken of Suppes' remarks.

Holism cannot be an issue, since I never suggested that this was a distinguishing feature of the psychological; I pointed to a holistic feature of the propositional attitudes in an attempt to strengthen my irreducibility thesis (more on this presently).

I was aware that present-day physics is not deterministic, but claimed that this was irrelevant to my position. Suppes wants me to explain this; I will try. If physics is not deterministic, neither is any fully worked out science; so this cannot be a point of difference. I may have made a mistake in suggesting that the laws of psychology operate on a level so far from that of microphysics that there is no point in their taking account of quantum phenomena. Suppes reminds us that the human eye can register the impact of a single photon, and while this is a fact from a discipline I was not discussing, it is clearly conceivable that the indeterminism of microphysics is important to the study of mental events. But my central claim is unaffected. I was urging that laws that connect events described in mental terms with events described in physical terms differ not just in degree but in kind from purely physical laws. Let us agree that psychophysical laws incorporate the indeterminism of quantum physics. If I am right, there will be a further indeterminism over and above the ubiquitous physical indeterminism, an indeterminism due to the nature of the propositional attitudes. I did not (as Suppes may have thought) argue from the indeterminism of psychological laws to the irreducibility of psychology, but from the irreducibility to an indeterminism *in addition to* the indeterminism of physics.

Again, it was careless of me to speak of quantum mechanics as a closed system. Suppes has said what I ought to have said: 'there may well be closed systems in physics but we shall never be able to observe them'. There *couldn't* be a closed system of the mental, observed or unobserved, because of the endless ways in which the mental interacts with the physical. My reason for wanting to make this point was not so much to draw a distinction between physics and psychology as to insist that anything like a complete science of the mental would have to include psychophysical laws.

I conclude at this point, somewhat tentatively, I admit, that even though physics may be incurably non-deterministic and not deal with closed systems, yet something much like the crude differences I found between any possible physics and any possible science of the propositional attitudes remain. That is, the crude differences exist *if* I am right about the propositional attitudes. And here the essence of the matter is, as I remarked in my answers to Lewis and Smart, the way in which normative considerations enter. (Perhaps I should mention that the fullest statement of my views on this matter is in 'Mental Events', which Suppes does not discuss.) Here again, though, Suppes takes me to task, this time for not appreciating the extent to which intensionality enters into physics.

Suppes has two interesting arguments for intensionality in physics. The first is that the concept of probability enters essentially into physics and probability statements create intensional contexts. Let us suppose this is true. My claims about the nature of psychology depend on the propositional attitudes, not intensionality as such. Suppes may rejoin that if we adopt a 'thoroughly subjective view toward probability, the same concept would apply to belief that applies to the expression of probability in physics'. Once upon a time I would have been completely sympathetic with this reply; now I find I don't understand it. Of course I understand the way decision theory measures degrees of belief: such a theory, when interpreted, can be said to give a meaning to a three-place predicate like '*x* holds *p* to be at least as probable as *q*.' Sentences using such a predicate are certainly about propositional attitudes. But are there sentences of physics that use *this* concept? Whose name is to be put for '*x*'? Is there a separate physics for each physicist? I agree with Suppes when he says 'I can see little difference between the theoretical status of trying to infer something about the probabilistic structure of beliefs of an individual and the probabilistic structure of the decay in radioactive atoms.' The concept of probability must be the same in both cases; but of course in one case the subject-matter is atoms and in the other a propositional attitude.

Suppes has a second argument for intensionality in physics, which is that reports of experiments are necessarily intensional. I suspect that not all physicists would agree; but let us suppose it is so. Again, if this is true of physics, it must be true of all fully worked-out sciences. What is special about psychology is not the fact that the subjective states of the observer intrude, but that the object of study is subjective states.

In trying to take account of Suppes' educated comments on my potted physics I have not repeated what I take to be my arguments against the reducibility of psychology to physics, nor my reasons for thinking that psychophysical laws are not as sturdily lawlike as the laws of physics: I have not repeated them because Suppes does not discuss them. But I am certain that my arguments would not satisfy Suppes; a number of critics have found what I say on the subject in 'Mental Events' obscure or unconvincing or both. Suppes says he wishes I would state my position with the clarity of Tarski's 'Wahrheitsbegriff'. I wish I could. But on one small matter, I do want to defend myself. Suppes hints that I trade on Tarski's proof of the irreducibility of semantics to syntax as if this gave weight to my claim that the mental can't be reduced to the physical. That was not my idea. In 'Mental Events' I pointed out at some length that 'nothing I can say about the irreducibility of the mental deserves to be called a proof.'[3] I called on Tarski only because I wanted an incontestable example of a phenomenon that philosophers often seem to forget about; a language rich enough to distinguish each of the members of a class but not equipped to pick out the class.

The last point about which Suppes scolds me concerns the relation between language and the other propositional attitudes. A sizable number of philosophers have held that thought in any moderately sophisticated sense depends on language: the view has been held by many analytically minded thinkers, and also by most of the American pragmatists, Dewey, Peirce, Mead, and Wilfrid Sellars among them. Curiously, though, none that I know of has tried to give an argument. In 'Thought and Talk' I tried. Few have found my reasoning compelling, and Suppes joins them, though he does

---

[3] *EAE*, p. 215. In this passage I emphasized how little my case for the irreducibility of mental concepts to physical was like Tarski's rigorous proof of the indefinability of semantic concepts in a language to which they apply.

not say exactly where my argument fails. I confess that though I think the conclusion true, 'Thought and Talk' is not as persuasive as I think it should be. Recently I have attacked the subject again.[4] I will not repeat its argument here, but I will comment on some of Suppes' reasons for rejecting the conclusion.

First there is the question whether decision theory should be coupled with a theory of language interpretation. The point of the suggestion is not practical but theoretical. Suppes is right that all experiments that assume successful verbal communication between experimenter and subject raise the issue, but experiments in decision theory raise it in an especially important way because they are designed to test a kind of rationality. When rationality is at stake, it is bound to be a pressing question whether what the experimenter takes to be irrationality is not better understood as a failure of communication. There are, as Suppes notes, endless experiments designed to sort such matters out. Yet a recent issue of *The Behavioral and Brain Sciences* contained an article questioning whether it makes sense to try to test for irrationality experimentally, and commentators from many related fields failed to agree on the issue.[5] I do not take Cohen's extreme view myself; but neither do I think it is being naïve to think it is not just a matter of good experimental design to get around the problem of interpretation in the case of decision theory. Let me quote one of the most clever and careful psychologists working in this area: 'The question of whether utility theory is compatible with the data or not . . . depends critically on the interpretation of the consequences . . . The key issue, therefore, is not the adequacy of the axioms, but rather the appropriateness of the interpretation of the consequences . . . In the absence of any constraints, the consequences can always be interpreted so as to satisfy the axioms.'[6] The appropriate constraints are, I suggest, to be given by a theory of verbal interpretation.

Finally I come to the claim, so annoying to animal-lovers, that animals don't have propositional attitudes—unless, that is, they have language. Here I do think it is possible to sharpen the issue usefully, along lines that I hope Suppes will find congenial. He

[4] In 'Rational Animals', *Dialectica* 36 (1982), 317-27.

[5] *The Behavioral and Brain Sciences*, 4 (1981), 317-17. The 'target' article, 'Can Human Irrationality be Experimentally Demonstrated', is by Jonathan Cohen.

[6] Amos Tversky, 'A Critique of Expected Utility Theory: Descriptive and Normative Considerations', *Erkenntnis*, 9 (1975), 171. This quotation also appears on p. 272 of *EAE*.

raises the question how, if I am right about the interdependence of language, belief, desire, and the other propositional attitudes, a child can ever get started. I do not really think I must produce 'the details of an actual theory of language acquisition and cognitive development' in order to answer this question for there is no reason a child cannot slowly master a complex system without it ever being accurate to say he has mastered part of it first. The trouble with this answer is that it leaves us not knowing how to describe the early stages, just as the general thesis that animals don't have beliefs leaves us without our usual useful way of explaining and describing their behaviour. A better and less contentious way of putting my view is this. We identify and discriminate between beliefs, desires, and the meanings of sentences by attaching propositions to them (or sentences of our own which we understand). In trying to understand you, I match up my own sentences or propositions with your utterances and attitudes. My sentences are related to one another by logic, inductive and deductive, and are hooked to the world in various ways. I cannot ignore these properties of my propositions in interpreting you, since these are the properties that individuate and identify propositions. But given the multitude of considerations, and the richness of the field of propositions, there will not be one best way for me to interpret you. Some choices among alternatives systems of interpretation have no empirical significance; these choices are like the choice between metres and miles to measure distance (this point can be made sharp in the case of alternative definitions of satisfaction). Now let us say small children and animals have beliefs and the rudiments of speech up to some system of transformations of ways of assigning propositions to their utterances or intentions. The fewer acceptable transformations, the more thought. With animals, for example, it is unclear that we can change true attributions to false by substituting coextensive terms; if so, that marks a big distinction, since failure of such substitutability is often taken to be the mark of the intensional. Or to take another example, it is only when the machinery of quantification is present that questions of ontology have a clear application. My suggestion comes to this: we will in any case continue to talk as if animals have propositional attitudes. We can do so with a good conscience if we keep track as best we can of the level of significance of such talk.

POSTSCRIPT TO REPLIES

DONALD DAVIDSON

Over a period of years I corresponded with Gilbert Ryle. From time to time we did some successful drinking together and even talked philosophy. Once he ended a letter to me saying (something like) 'Let's not stand on ceremony any longer. Don't call me Professor Ryle, just call me Ryle.' In these Replies I have not stood on ceremony but have democratically deleted all titles such as 'The Hildegard Z. Crush Memorial Distinguished Professor of Comparative Adjectives' or 'Academician Third Class'. It was easy to leave these lofty titles out. But I have found it a strain to address so many old friends by anything other than their first names. I hope that when they read the names I have given them they will pronounce them according to the phonetic rules of friendship.

Before one starts to write one thinks one knows what one is going to say. But in my case at least it is only as I write that I discover what I think, and this is almost never what I thought when I began. Writing these replies has been even more of an eye-opener in this respect than I expected. I suppose it is natural when reading comments and criticisms of one's own work to suppose one knows how to respond; on this supposition I have generally avoided public answers to my critics. This volume has changed my attitude. I enjoyed and learned from the essays included here when I read them, but it was only in putting my thoughts on paper that I realized how often someone had skilfully located a real confusion or a plain mistake, or simply had a better idea than I did how to approach some problem. There is not one essay in this book to which I found it easy to reply.

It is not surprising that the contributors to this volume have noticed many errors, obscurities, and omissions in my work, or that they have better things to say than I do on topics on which I have written. But it is remarkably kind of them to have taken the trouble to write out their thoughts for the present volume. I am complimented above all that they have felt free to tell me where they think I went wrong and have tried to set me straight. I have done my best to return the compliment.

Special thanks are due the editors. It was Merrill Hintikka who first suggested a book like this one. Bruce Vermazen not only has composed the Introduction, edited the manuscript, improved my Replies, read the proofs and made the index; he has also written a fine essay.

INDEX OF NAMES